DISSERTATIONS SR

Volume 2

Literature as Pulpit
The Christian Social Activism of Nellie L. McClung

Randi R. Warne

Published for the Canadian Corporation for Studies in
Religion/Corporation Canadienne des Sciences Religieuses
by Wilfrid Laurier University Press

1993

Canadian Cataloguing in Publication Data

Warne, R. R. (Randi Ruth), 1952-
   Literature as pulpit : the Christian social
activism of Nellie L. McClung

(Dissertations SR ; v. 2)
Includes bibliographical references.
ISBN 0-88920-235-4

1. McClung, Nellie L., 1873-1951 — Criticism and
interpretation. 2. McClung, Nellie L., 1873-1951 —
Political and social views. 3. McClung, Nellie L.,
1873-1951 — Religion. I. Canadian Corporation for
Studies in Religion. II. Title. III. Series.

PS8525.C52Z97 1993   C813'.52   C93-094873-4
PR(199.2.M33Z97 1993
          76 760
© 1993 Canadian Corporation for Studies in Religion/
          Corporation Canadienne des Sciences Religieuses

Cover design by Jose Martucci, Design Communications,
using a photograph supplied by the Glenbow Archives, Calgary, Alberta

Printed in Canada

Literature as Pulpit: The Christian Social Activism of Nellie L. McClung has
been produced from a manuscript supplied in electronic form by the author.

Order from:
WILFRID LAURIER UNIVERSITY PRESS
Waterloo, Ontario, Canada N2L 3C5

For my grandmothers,
Anna Kaluzniak Bobowski
and Ruth Dahl Warne

Contents

This book was published with the
support of the Dissertation Series prize
of the Canadian Corporation for
Studies in Religion.

Acknowledgements

No work such as this is completed through the efforts of solely one person. I would like to acknowledge here some of those whose support has been essential in reaching this point. Professor Paul Gooch, Chairman of the Graduate Centre for Religious Studies, welcomed me "back into the fold" with cheerful confidence, an inestimable boon. Ms. Muna Salloum, the Centre's Administrative Assistant, was there from the beginning, and was an unfailing source of enthusiastic support. My colleagues in Women's Studies, at the University of Toronto and elsewhere, showed continued interest in my work, and spurred me on through their dedication to excellence. Of these, I owe a special debt of gratitude to Drs. Ruth Pierson and Thelma McCormack, whose practical support in the last stages of this work allowed its completion. Instrumental, too, was Ms. Rea Wilmshurst, who painstakingly edited and transcribed the manuscript, and who, delightfully, is a true "kindred spirit." During the long journey through graduate school, part-time teaching, and the general chaos of life I have been privileged to enjoy the friendship of Dr. Maureen Muldoon. Her counsels have been many, and wise. Finally, I owe my deepest obligation to my supervisor, Roger Hutchinson, who has helped me in more ways than it is possible to name. My heartfelt thanks to him for always treating me like the scholar I hope one day to become.

Introduction

> In Canada we are developing a pattern of life and I
> know something about one block of that pattern. I
> know it for I helped to make it, and I can say that now
> without any pretence of modesty, for I know that we
> who make the patterns are not important, but the pat-
> tern is.[1]
>
> ... still I cannot look back without regret. I can see
> too many places where I could have been more obedi-
> ent to the heavenly vision, for a vision I surely had for
> the creation of a better world.
>
> But I hope I am leaving at least some small legacy
> of truth. (SRF, xiii)

Nellie L. McClung is an important figure in Canadian religious history, and in Canadian history in general. Yet while lip service is paid
to this stature, what has actually been written about her does not meet
what might seem to be reasonable expectations regarding a person of
such national — indeed, in her lifetime, international — renown. Some
of the reasons for the *lacunae* will be suggested below. The purpose of
this work, however, is not to provide addenda to existing scholarship,
or to "fill in the gaps" with historical minutiae, for this would merely
perpetuate the problems generated in the past. What I wish to do
instead is to provide an alternative reading of McClung's life and
work. I shall weave together various strands uncovered by prior
scholarship with those emerging out of McClung's narratives in such

---

Notes to the Introduction are on pages 7-9.

1

a way that the larger pattern of her work becomes plain, and the fullness of her no "small legacy" is restored.

The title of the thesis indicates the focus of the work to be undertaken to this end. While there is little doubt in either the popular or the scholarly mind that Nellie McClung was a crusader, what is less often recognized is the extent to which her literature, and the moral and religious impetus which gave it birth, provided a significant forum for her social and political activism. As I shall show, McClung's major narratives provide an essential resource for understanding the entirety of her vision, and stand as important correctives to the interpretation of McClung which emerges from a single-minded attention to her famous "feminist polemic," *In Times Like These*. As Chapter I illustrates, McClung believed literature had a crucial role to play in the creation of a better Canada, and her own writing was geared specifically to that end. Denied ordination by virtue of her sex,[2] McClung wrote novels, short stories, essays and newspaper columns in order to preach spiritual renewal alongside social transformation. Moreover, she wrote with clear feminist intent, to challenge and change those elements of the social world which were unjust to women and, in being so, were opposed to the "Fair Deal" for everyone which she was convinced was intrinsic to God's plan for Creation.

Even a partial recounting of McClung's many accomplishments supports the contention that she is an important figure deserving of renewed investigation. To begin with, she was a prolific writer. In a literary career which spanned four decades she produced four novels, two novellas, seven volumes of collected speeches, stories and essays, a ghost-written World War I soldier's story, and a two-volume autobiography (see Primary Bibliography). In addition, there are over four hundred articles, stories and essays, published and unpublished, in the McClung Papers held in the Provincial Archives of British Columbia in Victoria.[3] She wrote for Sunday School publications, *Maclean's*, *The War Cry*, *The White Banner Bulletin*, and the *Grain Growers' Guide*, among others, and in the 1930s and '40s she continued her contribution to Canadian political life through her syndicated newspaper column, "Nellie McClung Says."[4]

Her international reputation as a writer was further enhanced by her involvement in the temperance and suffrage battles of the 'teens, both in Canada and the United States. She served as a Liberal Member of the Alberta Legislative Assembly from 1921 to 1926, and in 1929 became one of the "Famous Five" who were successful in their fight to have women declared legally "persons" in the matters of rights and privileges, not solely in the matters of "pains and penalties," as had been previously the case.[5] McClung was also a member of the Women's International League for Peace and Freedom, and in the 1930s she served as a Canadian delegate to the League of Nations. Her wide and varied experience, combined with her stature as a Canadian national figure, led to her being named to the first Board of Governors of the Canadian Broadcasting Corporation. She was the only woman appointed thereto.

Nellie McClung was also a religious activist. She supported the work of J.S. Woodsworth's All People's Mission in Winnipeg, and spoke in at least one lecture series with Social Gospel leader Salem Bland.[6] A staunch critic of the church in the service of women's rights, she lobbied for over two decades for women's ordination, first in the Methodist, and then in The United Church of Canada. Her presentation to the Fifth Ecumenical Methodist Conference held in London, England, in 1921, to which she was the only female Canadian delegate, still stands as a succinct and witty, but firmly argued statement of her intertwined vision of religion, feminism and social activism.[7]

Moreover, an important part of the Canadian story is told through McClung's life. She was born in a little stone house on 20 October 1873, "a mile from Chatsworth, on the Garafraxa road, in a stony part of the county of Grey" near Owen Sound, Ontario.[8] Her father, John Mooney, had come from Ireland to Bytown (Ottawa) in 1830, spending several years there as a logger before moving westward to Georgian Bay to try his hand at farming. There he met and married the former Letitia McCurdy, who had emigrated from Scotland with her mother following her father's death from cholera in 1856. McClung was the youngest of their six children. Heeding the advice of their eldest son, Will, the family left Ontario for the West in 1880, travelling by boat and train to St. Boniface, Manitoba, and thereafter by foot and oxcart until they reached Millford, Manitoba, a small town southwest of Brandon near the Tiger Hills.

The experience of carving out a new life in a fresh frontier marked McClung's imagination deeply, and she became dedicated to the task of conveying to the public the experiences of common labouring people like her parents, whose efforts contributed to the building of the Canadian West. As it happened, McClung began writing at a time when the Canadian literary market was rapidly expanding,[9] and much of her original popularity may be attributed to her skill in telling this particular story precisely at "a time of talk and writing about the need of a native literature to body forth a new nation."[10] In meeting this demand, McClung believed she was making her own small contribution to the work of nation-building.

Too, McClung's pioneer experience made her acutely sensitive to the actual worth and extent of women's labour, and how the full recognition and power which ought to have attended it were often denied.[11] Her skill as a storyteller became a potent weapon in her struggle to have women's work recognized and rewarded, as she attempted to infuse her readers with a feminist and religious vision which would empower them to the work of social change. That she was able to do so in a humorous and witty way stands as further testimony to her art.[12]

While existing materials on McClung touch upon various of these elements, what has been lacking is an accurate treatment of her which is both integrated and scholarly. The two biographies of McClung currently in print reflect this problem. Candace Savage's *Our Nell: A Scrapbook Biography of Nellie L. McClung*, is indeed a "scrapbook," filled with snippets from the McClung Papers and publications and tied together by Savage's accurate but brief historical introductions. Carol Hancock's *No Small Legacy* is similarly popular in tone[13] and is geared as a study guide for United Church women wanting to learn more about their own heritage. The full-length biography of McClung promised by historian Mary Hallett remains unfinished after the author's untimely death.

Where McClung appears in other works, her depiction depends much upon the agendas of the scholars producing the work. I have been able to identify four broad categories of material in which McClung appears. The first is that of mainstream history, which limits McClung's significance to those issues seen as most important by traditional historians, i.e., events in the political and legislative spheres. McClung's involvement in temperance and suffrage campaigns is therefore acknowledged, as is her participation in the "Persons" case of 1929. What is omitted is any fuller exploration of the character of her feminism, nor are her religious and literary activities subject to scrutiny. Even a "woman-oriented" text like Catherine Cleverdon's *The Woman Suffrage Movement in Canada* suffers from the limits of this perspective.[14]

A second category emerges out of feminist attempts to reevaluate the traditional historians' accounts of first-wave feminism. As I shall show through a discussion of Carol Bacchi and Veronica Strong-Boag in Chapter IV, such feminist reappropriations have often been heavily driven by current political agendas, and have tended to judge McClung somewhat harshly by those standards. In particular, McClung's religion is subject to rather heavy-handed treatment, with religion understood as male-defined, institutional, and limiting to women, by definition. Moreover, in its search for theoretical adequacy, this scholarship tends to focus almost exclusively upon *In Times Like These*, and ignores McClung's literature entirely.

A more complex set of problems is presented by the third body of scholarship, which deals with Canadian religious history and with the Social Gospel movement in particular. The concern for institutions and their activities characteristic of mainstream history has likewise tended to dominate the scene in Church History, so that if McClung appears at all, it is in her connection with the battle for women's ordination.[15] Unfortunately, this emphasis upon the clergy, and upon other religious men and their ideas, has been extended to scholarship on the Social Gospel Movement in Canada as well.[16] As I suggest in Chapter IV, whether or not McClung ought to be included as a Social Gospel figure is open to further discussion, depending upon how the Social Gospel itself is defined. What is clear is that available materials in Canadian religious history do not provide an adequate basis for evaluating McClung's integrated feminist religious social activism.[17]

Finally, there is the category of literary history, in which McClung appears as a rather quaint example of a by-gone era.[18] I make some attempt in Chapter I to demonstrate McClung's own understanding of the purpose of writing, and to suggest reasons for her fall from literary favour. In particular, the increasing dominance of a school of literary criticism which emphasized form over content virtually guaranteed that intentionally didactic fiction like McClung's would be discounted. However, renewed interest in feminist literary traditions is beginning to challenge these negative evaluations of her work.[19]

While each of these scholarly perspectives is important and valuable in its own way, overall the picture of McClung which emerges from these literatures is truncated and static. The full dimension of her involvement is lost, as is the wit and passion which constituted so much of her popular appeal. This dissertation takes the position that it is in McClung's narratives that an integrating vision which discloses these elements may be found. Further, in demonstrating this point, I hope also to illustrate the worthiness of an approach which shifts attention from theory to cultural systems, and from abstract "ideas" to narratives, in order that the full complexity of the cultural realities of religion and gender be allowed to appear.[20]

In preparation for this study, the entire McClung corpus, including the McClung Papers, was read and re-read until a sense of "the world behind the text" began to develop. Particularly helpful in this regard were contemporaneous reviews of McClung's writing, as these provided a fascinating chronicle of McClung's transformation into "Our Nell," the Canadian cultural heroine.[21] No attempt was made to impose theory upon the material examined, although a number of operative assumptions helped steer the course of the study. The first was that there was indeed a story yet to be told about McClung. The labels "maternal feminist," "Methodist evangelical," "temperance advocate" and so forth, while useful as general reference points, ultimately limited exploration of an exciting Canadian figure for whom conventionality for its own sake was anathema. Secondly, as evidenced by McClung's narratives, religion was a central unifying category for her life and work. However, drawing upon insights gleaned from the study of women in religious systems, the adequacy of mainstream categories for the assessment of McClung's religion could not simply be assumed. Rather than look for McClung's "theology," understood as an abstract system of beliefs, an attempt was made to convey McClung's religion accurately, as depicted in her novels and expressed in her life.[22] Finally, a pluralistic understanding of religion, feminism, and social activism was maintained throughout. Rather than adopt the normative stance characteristic of some treatments of McClung, a more descriptive route was taken. It was assumed that, consonant with the complexities of cultural systems in general, a variety of strategies might legitimately be employed in effecting social change, a pragmatic approach in keeping with McClung's own famous dictum: "Never retract, never explain, just get the thing done and let them howl."

The study is limited to McClung's four novels and to the text and context of *In Times Like These*. While the entire McClung corpus merits further scholarly attention, her four novels provide the most sustained expression of her world view. Too, the novels neatly bracket the text which has become the pivotal point for McClung scholarship, *In Times Like These*.[23] A thorough examination of the context of that work revealed a number of crucial factors which more theory-driven examinations of the text had obscured, most particularly the extent to which the anti-feminist context of the day determined the shape of many of McClung's political arguments. By locating *In Times Like These* within the larger context of McClung's work as a whole, and comparing the vision embodied in her novels with that expressed in the collection of speeches from which *In Times Like These* was compiled, distinctions could begin to be drawn between long-standing convictions and what were merely rhetorical flourishes employed to a particular political end. Throughout, religion emerged as a consistent and harmonizing theme integrating McClung's feminism and social activism in the service of building a better world.

Chapter I of this dissertation addresses briefly the question of the nature and purpose of McClung's writing. It then turns to a close examination of her most coherent fictional construct, the Pearlie Watson trilogy. Chapter II continues the focus on narrative in its analysis of McClung's most complex novel, *Painted Fires*, and suggests a growing loss of resonance between McClung's fictional vision, conveyed through the genre of melodrama, and the rapidly changing world of the 1920s. Chapter III attempts to illuminate some of the possible causes of that disruption through an examination of the anti-feminist context of *In Times Like These*, setting the stage for a reinvestigation and reinterpretation of the text itself. Chapter IV addresses current analyses of McClung based on *In Times Like These*, then offers an alternative perspective based on insights derived from the novels and the anti-feminist context explored in Chapters I-III. The thesis concludes with a brief consideration of McClung's loss of cultural "voice" and suggestions for its recovery. In sum, it is hoped that this thesis will provide a fuller, more vibrant and more accurate understanding of this important Canadian figure and that it will establish the centrality of religion for her feminist social activism.

Notes

1 Nellie L. McClung, *The Stream Runs Fast* (Toronto: Thomas Allen, 1945), x. Subsequent references will be given parenthetically in the text.

2 Asked whether his mother would have wanted to be a minister herself, McClung's youngest son, Mark, replied, "Absolutely. There's no question about it. She would have been a minister if the Methodist Church at the time had permitted it. . . . She would have been a humdinger of a clergyman. She would have filled the churches." Mark McClung, interviewed by Florence Bird, "The Incredible Nellie McClung," broadcast on CBC Radio's "Between Ourselves," 6 June 1975, quoted in Candace Savage, *Our Nell: A Scrapbook Biography of Nellie L. McClung* (Saskatoon: Western Producer Prairie Books, 1979), 181.

3 For a full listing of the holdings of the McClung Papers, see Appendix A.

4 McClung was one of the few Canadians to speak out for Jewish immigration to Canada in the early years of World War II. See, for example, "What of Jews in Canada?" 27 April 1940, and "The Old Year Passes," 30 December 1939. She also spoke out against the internment of the Japanese: "What Did We Learn in 1941?" 3 January 1942. McClung Papers, Add. MSS 10, n.v.

5 Other participants in the so-called "Persons Case" were Henrietta Muir Edwards, Irene Marryat Parlby, Louise Crummy McKinney and McClung's longtime friend, Emily Murphy.

6 See "Rev. Dr. Bland Refers to It in Address to Saskatchewan Grain Growers," McClung Papers, Add. MSS 10, Vol. 33.

7 Nellie L. McClung, "The Awakening of Women," address to the Fifth Ecumenical Methodist Conference, in *Proceedings, Fifth Ecumenical Methodist Conference, London, England, September 6-16, 1921* (Toronto: Methodist Book and Publishing House, n.d.), 257-60.

8 Nellie L. McClung, *Clearing in the West* (Toronto: Thomas Allen, 1935), 7. Subsequent references will be given parenthetically in the text.

9 For a full discussion of the Canadian literary climate which McClung was entering, see Gordon Roper, "New Forces: New Fiction (1880-1920)," in *Literary History of Canada*, ed. Carl Klinck (Toronto: University of Toronto Press, 1965), 260-83.

10 Ibid., 263.

11 McClung used every available forum to get her point across, even the advertisements which she wrote for her husband's pharmacy. For example, one advertisement for "Beef, Iron and Wine Tonic" begins: "Her hours are from 4 a.m. to 4 a.m. and she is tired of baking bread and washing dishes. Her back aches and her nerves are shattered and she has no comfort in the eight thousand bushels of wheat she helped raise . . .": see Appendix B.

12 See Appendix C for representative examples of McClung's personal correspondence which confirm her skill as a storyteller and demonstrate the deep affection with which she was regarded.

13 Carol L. Hancock, *No Small Legacy* (Winfield, B.C.: Wood Lake Books, 1986).

14 Catherine L. Cleverdon, *The Woman Suffrage Movement in Canada* (1950; rpt. Toronto: University of Toronto Press, 1975).

15 Interestingly, the only detailed treatment of this issue I have been able to locate was undertaken by a feminist historian. See Mary E. Hallett, "Nellie McClung and the Fight for the Ordination of Women in the United Church of Canada," *Atlantis*, 4, no. 2 (Spring 1979), 2-16.

16 The two main texts consulted in this regard are Richard Allen, *The Social Passion: Religion and Reform in Canada, 1914-28* (Toronto: University of Toronto Press, 1973), and Ramsay Cook, *The Regenerators: Social Criticism in Late Victorian English Canada* (Toronto: University of Toronto Press, 1985).

17 Nor do the two Masters theses on McClung's religion of which I am aware offset this lack. Lloyd Clifton's "Nellie McClung: A Representative of the Canadian Social Gospel Movement" (unpub. M.Th. thesis, Toronto, 1979) is a superficial treatment of McClung's activism which focuses primarily upon her "piety." He does, however, provide a useful bibliography of McClung's many articles. Carol L. Penner's "The Theology of Nellie L. McClung" (unpub. M.A. thesis, Toronto, 1986) likewise locates McClung within the Social Gospel movement. While Penner's work is superior to Clifton's, it suffers from the same tendency simply to assume what needs to be demonstrated. Moreover, her focus upon McClung's "theology" distorts the character of McClung's activism, which was pragmatic, not theoretically driven.

18 Note that the small measure of praise granted McClung by poet Earle Birney in his overview of Canadian literature, *Spreading Time*, is modified by the shared ethic

which made McClung a favourite with his mother: "Mrs. McClung could scarcely lose with my mother in any case: Nellie was a Methodist (the next best thing in my mother's eyes to a Presbyterian), a crusader for 'temperance' (i.e., no liquor at all, except brandy for heart attacks), also for female suffrage and for the international peace which women's votes would bring." Even so, he is compelled to record: "Still, it was McClung's sharp eye for the small realities of the prairie experience and her sympathetic understanding of farmers' families which brought most pleasure to my mother and to many like her in their generation": Earle Birney, *Spreading Time* (Montreal: Vehicle Press, 1980), 4.

19 See, for example, Elsa Schieder, "She Came to the Rescue: The Life and Writings of Nellie L. McClung, Feminist," unpub. M.A. thesis, Concordia (Montreal), 1982, and Patricia Louise Verkruysse, "Small Legacy of Truth: The Novels of Nellie McClung," unpub. M.A. thesis, New Brunswick, 1975. Schieder's work is particularly valuable for its feminist insights, although she unfortunately reproduces the anti-religious bias characteristic of the feminist historical approach cited above.

20 The understanding of religion employed in this dissertation derives primarily from that presented in Clifford Geertz' important article, "Religion as a Cultural System." Geertz defines religion as follows "(1) a system of symbols which acts to (2) establish powerful, pervasive, and long-lasting moods and motivations in men [sic] by (3) formulating conceptions of a general order of existence and (4) clothing these conceptions with such an aura of factuality that (5) the moods and motivations seem uniquely realistic": Clifford Geertz, "Religion as a Cultural System," in his *The Interpretation of Cultures* (New York: Basic Books, 1973), 90.

21 See the McClung Papers, Add. MSS 10, particularly Vols. 22, 28, 29 and 36.

22 McClung explicitly disavows any interest in theology in a later article. She states unequivocally, "I have never been much of a theologian. Doctrinal discussions have a mouldy taste and are dusty to the palate. I believe we all know enough to live by. It is not so much spiritual food we need as spiritual exercise . . .": Nellie L. McClung, "My Religion," *Be Good to Yourself* (Toronto: Thomas Allen, 1930), 130.

23 The texts, in order of publication, are: *Sowing Seeds in Danny* (1908), *The Second Chance* (1910), *In Times Like These* (1915), *Purple Springs* (1921), and *Painted Fires* (1925). For full references, see the Primary Bibliography.

I

A Religion of Active Care:
The Pearlie Watson Trilogy

The best of all compliments, the people who were actually living the life described instantly recognized the kindly fidelity of the picture and were not slow to say, "nothing truer of the west has ever been written."[1]

Its wholesome, fresh vitality, its dramatic quality, and the extremely charming heroine make this novel, in spite of its excess of sentimentality in the first chapters, a very readable and admirable tale of modern Canada, a story that all intelligent Canadians will be proud to claim as representative of their Northwestern life.[2]

1. On Writing

Writing in 1975, McClung's youngest son Mark recalled a powerful debate on the ordination of women in Central United Church, Calgary, which pitted his mother against an important Calgary judge. He describes her:

sweep[ing] up and down the platform . . . she'd move here and then she'd walk away from the podium and she'd go over to this side and then she'd go over to this side and every now and again she'd round on this innocent judge, and point an accusing finger at him.

You know, judges are not accustomed to being verbally assaulted. . . . And this man would sort of rear back from this tiny creature giving him absolute billyo for being such an old fuddy duddy and a Tory.[3]

Notes to Chapter I are on pages 51-53.

McClung's skill as an orator and debater is the stuff of legend. She regularly demolished her opponents with a telling combination of irreverent wit and stern logic, combined with a complete lack of the "humourless self-righteousness" with which moral reformers are sometimes attributed.[4] For example, consider McClung's reply to a rather caustic critic in the *Vegreville Observer*:

> I like your candid statement that you think I am an overestimated person. I have thought so, too, for a long time. Indeed it was that sentence in your editorial which has inspired this letter. I had a fellow feeling for you when I read it.
> With all kind wishes . . .[5]

It was this gift of self-effacing humour, grounded in an absolute conviction of the rightness of her cause, which made McClung a speaker of international repute.[6]

Yet the vitality and power which underscored McClung's personal appearances were not the only reasons for her popularity. McClung was an established novelist of international stature before she battled on the hustings for temperance and suffrage, or in the churches for "fair dealing" and women's ordination. Her first speaking engagement, readings from *Sowing Seeds in Danny*, was occasioned by her mother-in-law's involvement in a fund-raising venture for the W.C.T.U. Home for Friendless Girls in Winnipeg.[7] Throughout McClung's life, literature and public speaking were two sides of the same coin; novels became speeches, just as speeches, such as those collected in *In Times Like These*, became so well known as books that their original context is largely forgotten. These speeches, many of which were given in churches and church halls, reinforce the notion of literature as pulpit; both the content of the lectures and the purpose of their occasion reflected McClung's religious commitment.

Given the widespread popularity of McClung's writing in her day,[8] it is ironic that only *In Times Like These* and the first volume of her autobiography, *Clearing in the West*, are currently in print. We shall now briefly consider McClung's fall from literary favour, and her own response to the changing values this reflected.

As Elsa Schieder has amply shown,[9] by the time McClung commented on the proper role of writing in the second volume of her autobiography, *The Stream Runs Fast*, the literary genre of melodrama which McClung typically employed had fallen out of critical favour. "Realism" had become the order of the day. In his famous 1945 essay, "The Novel in Canada,"[10] Desmond Pacey graphically calls for "a realistic and critical spirit. We need to see the festering sores in our social body, as well as its areas of healthy tissue."[11] Pacey criticizes the Canadian novel of the past as being "superficial" and "regional," lacking a "critical awareness of the contemporary scene, and a sustaining philosophy" which are the hallmarks of great fiction.[12] The bleak human landscapes of Frederick Philip Grove alone merit his approval.

In this, Pacey broke no new ground. The despair and disillusionment characteristic of Grove and others was lauded by the New Criticism which emerged in the late thirties and throughout the forties, and which continued to dominate literary criticism until very recently. Schieder's observations that McClung's work can be critically rehabilitated from a feminist perspective which values content as well as form, provides an important counterbalance to this view. So, too, does Joanne Hedenstrom's article, "Puzzled Patriarchs and Free Women: Patterns in the Canadian Novel."[13] Hedenstrom argues that a close examination of the Canadian novel reveals a "dramatic divergence between the novels of men and those of women in English speaking Canada,"[14] such that we are really dealing with "two novel traditions."[15] Naming some of the stereotypical female/male differences ("inclusive" vs. "exclusive," "empathetic with nature" vs. "patriarchal imposition of order on the land"), she goes on to note:

> somehow, Canadian women wrote novels that express the possibilities of growth, the achieving of a happier personal world, while male authors seem unable to break out of a set pattern of grim alternation between hope and defeat . . . the escape — survival — escape — survival cycle.[16]

Hedenstom's article treats contemporary novelists such as Margaret Laurence and Margaret Atwood. However, if one accepts her distinctions of the "two traditions" it is possible to see how McClung's colloquial stories of trial and triumph could fit congenially within the "women's tradition" of the Canadian novel, just as Pacey's negativistic approach could be seen as relating primarily to the "men's tradition." Given the critical dominance of this latter approach, it is easier to understand the discrediting of McClung's literary worth. The "realism" of Pacey and others focused on the world "as is." To paraphrase Marx's comment about the philosophers, McClung's intent was not only to describe the world, but to change it.[17]

Seven chapters in *The Stream Runs Fast* directly address the question of the power of words and the purpose of writing. Here McClung makes plain her position: "no one should put pen to paper unless he or she had something to say that would amuse, entertain, instruct, inform, comfort, or guide the reader."[18] Writers are properly prophets, whose true purpose is to "write words that will strengthen the weak, convict [sic] the stubborn, and shed light where darkness reigns."[19] This heavy moral responsibility has been shirked, to the peril of the nation. McClung implies that writers who fear they would be "caught preaching" are unwittingly sharing the same attitude of amorality which allowed the coming into existence of Nazi Germany. The writer thus shares a responsibility for the moral fabric of the nation.

The intensity of this charge reflects the degree of alienation from her literary colleagues that McClung was beginning to feel, a tension which is made palpable in her summary of the "Writer's Creed" below:

1st. We believe in the profession of writing. We gladly give our lives to it, counting it all joy. We will rise early and work late. We will "scorn delights, and live laborious days."

2nd. We believe that writers, who are capable of performing a public service, should not be hampered by poverty. A grateful Nation should provide for them, leaving them free to serve, without thought of rent, clothing or food.

3rd. We believe in the power of words and are ready to mine for them as miners dig for gold, to sift, and compare, and analyze. We promise not to run any word off its feet, or overload it, until it breaks at the knees, with a whole dictionary full of words at our service!

4th. We believe writers must have a vision of a better world before their eyes. Through the rain we must see the rainbow, after the storm, the sunshine. We must hear the church-bells ringing, above the noise of the street. We promise not to be quitters, deserters, or neutrals, cynics or mere observers. We have signed on for the duration and after.

4th [sic]. We believe in human beings, ever looking for the image of God in every human face. We believe that neither concentration camp or hell-fire or luxury kill the invincible spirit of man. We believe that when God said he would make man in His own image, he was not merely "making conversation." To that end we will listen to children, old people, the poor and the humbel [sic], and people of other color and creeds than our own.

5th. We believe God has not lost control of the world, and still speaks to men if they will listen.

6th. We believe in God, we believe in our country, we believe in each other and we believe in ourselves.

7th. We believe![20]

The religious fervour with which McClung delivered this speech was not well received by her erstwhile colleagues. In *The Stream Runs Fast* she notes that after she finished speaking, she "was assailed with particular vehemence by one of [her] fellow members who [was] a writer of novels — she cried out in disgust: 'Who wants to write books for Sunday Schools? I certainly do not'" (SRF, 70). (Rather bitterly, McClung "was able to assure her that her books were safe": SRF, 70.)

McClung's linking of the purpose of writing and religious faith, and the affirmation of the social function of literature, marked her as a member of an earlier literary generation for whom content was more important than form. As the fourth point of her creed suggests, regarding "quitters, deserters or neutrals, cynics or mere observers," she considered any other approach a fundamental betrayal of the purpose of writing, akin to selling out one's country in time of war. Given this mutual antipathy, the apparent ease with which McClung's writings fell into obscurity becomes more understandable. McClung set herself firmly against the prevailing literary paradigm, and paid the price.

Too, the world in which literature was expected to have a high moral purpose was fading away; even McClung's more sympathetic assessors felt compelled to note that "didactic enthusiasm . . . marred her art" (SRF, 69). McClung's reply confirms that, indeed, literature intentionally became her pulpit. She states:

> I hope I have been a crusader, and I would be very proud to think that I had even remotely approached the grandeur of a Sunday School hymn. I have never worried about my art. I have written as clearly as I could, never idly or dishonestly, and if some of my stories are sermons in disguise, my earnest hope is that the disguise did not obscure the sermon. (SRF, 69)

2. The Pearlie Watson Trilogy

Sowing Seeds in Danny (1908), *The Second Chance* (1910), and *Purple Springs* (1921) are set in and around Nellie McClung's childhood home of Millford, Manitoba, near the Tiger Hills. They tell the story of young Pearlie Watson, the uneducated eldest daughter of poor Irish pioneers who eventually goes on to bring down the corrupt Conservative government through her impassioned speeches for temperance and women's suffrage. These are not merely pious tales of noble service, however. In many ways, they reflect the experiences of McClung herself, as comparison with her autobiography, *Clearing in the West*, bears out. Pearl Watson's rise is no more incredible than McClung's own, although as author McClung has been able to see her enemies much more justly served than perhaps was the case in real life. For example, McClung's arch-enemy in the temperance and suffrage struggles was Conservative Premier Sir Rodmond Roblin. In *Purple Springs* he becomes "Premier Graham," a pompous, powerful man whose strangle-hold on the province is broken through Pearl's eloquent influence. After seeing himself lampooned by Pearl in the Women's Parliament—just as McClung lampooned Roblin—"Graham" thoroughly repents, and begs forgiveness of all the women he has wronged. He leaves politics, a better and more humble man.

Purple Springs was written in 1921, and reflects McClung's evolution from the Millford pharmacist's "authoress" wife to a political figure of national renown. *Sowing Seeds in Danny* and *The Second Chance*, in contrast, reflect the homey country life of Millford and environs, and the little interpersonal intricacies of this "simple" life. In *The Stream Runs Fast* McClung tells of the magazine salesman who drew her into this enterprise:

> What Dickens did for London, and Scott for Scotland, he believed I could do for southern Manitoba. "We want you to hold a mirror up to this country; or perhaps a microscope . . . and you must feel free to write as you please. No one wants bare facts . . . we want to light candles of imagination in the minds of our people." (SRF, 7-8)

The Pearlie Watson stories try to do precisely that. They are "inspirational," but they likewise express the realities of prairie life in such a way that McClung's readership could be genuinely empowered by following Pearlie's example—as, indeed, was McClung's express intention.

Sowing Seeds in Danny opens with the following quotation:

> So many faiths — so many creeds, —
> So many paths that wind and wind
> While just the art of being kind, —
> Is what the old world needs![21]

Active consideration of the needs of others is a central element of McClung's religion. *Sowing Seeds in Danny* is an extended, though humorous, sermon on the role of kindness in cementing the human community, and the disruption and dissension brought by selfishness and greed.

The story opens in the sitting room of one Mrs. J. Burton Francis, "a dreamy woman, who has beautiful theories" (SSD, ix). Mrs. Burton

Francis is a kind woman, but her lack of experience of the harsher realities of life ill-befits her for the role of social transformer she aspires to. Childless, she holds forth on "The Beauty of Motherhood" to her washerwoman, Mrs. Watson, the mother of nine; she lectures Pearl on "proper diet and aids to digestion" (SSD, 121) though none of the Watsons ever has enough to eat. It is completely in character that Mrs. Burton Francis records these incidents in a diary in aid of preparing a report to present at the "Annual Convention of the Society for the Propagation of Lofty Ideals" (SSD, 8).

McClung treats Mrs. Burton Francis kindly, and allows her to come to the realization that good comes through specific small acts of practical kindness rather than through the propagation of theory. The agent for this change is Mrs. Burton Francis' housekeeper, Camilla Rose, who is Pearl's friend and confidante, although she is considerably older than Pearl. When Mrs. Burton Francis fixes upon the importance of developing the "musical sense," it is Camilla who suggests that Pearlie and Danny (the youngest Watson, and the "Danny" of the title) are taken to a piano concert—with the added benefits of appropriate new clothes and a good supper beforehand (SSD, 63). A former bookkeeper now willingly working as a domestic, Camilla is truly a "new woman"—competent, practical and independent, and capable of making real changes in how others (in this case, Mrs. Burton Francis) see the world. Through Camilla, McClung shows that everyone can make a contribution to the betterment of human life, regardless of occupation or social status.[22]

Alcohol, however, can seriously undercut that contribution. Dr. Barner, the town physician, was "brilliant, witty and skilful"; he was also a drunkard (SSD, 31). Despite certain melodramatic touches (for example, Mrs. Barner sinks into invalidism and dies as she sees "honor and manhood slowly but surely dying" in her husband as a result of drink [SSD, 31]), McClung paints a balanced portrait of Dr. Barner himself, and accurately presents the effects of his alcoholism on his daughter Mary. The tragedy of Dr. Barner is not that he "took drink." McClung's concern was not that the "temple of the Spirit" was being defiled, but rather that alcohol abuse prevents Dr. Barner from living up to his true promise, in violation of God's gift to him. At the outset, Dr. Barner was extremely competent:

> Even in his worst moments, if he could be induced to come to the sick bed, he would sober up wonderfully, and many a sufferer was relieved from pain and saved from death by his gentle and skilful,

though trembling, hands. He might not be able to walk across the room, but he could diagnose correctly and prescribe successfully. (SSD, 31)

Years of abuse take their toll, however. Eventually all his skill leaves him, except for his "wonderful presence in the sick-room."

He could still inspire the greatest confidence and hope. Still at his coming a sick man's fears fell away from him, and in their stead came hope and good cheer. This was the old man's gift that even his years of sinning could not wholly destroy. God had marked him for a great physician. (SSD, 37)

For McClung, then, alcohol abuse is not simply a sin against oneself, or against God. It violates the whole community by preventing the afflicted person from giving active care in the full measure required.

Given that alcohol abuse affects the whole community, it is the whole community's responsibility to see that alcohol abuse does not occur. McClung considered alcohol a response to despair and loneliness. Rather than "blaming the victim" (the alcohol abuser), or demonizing the drinker, McClung lays the responsibility for this problem at the feet of those who ought to show active kindness, but do not: "When the church of God is cold and dark and silent, and the homes of Christ's followers are closed except to the chosen few, the bar-room throws out its evil welcome to the young man on the street" (SSD, 228).

This emphasis on social responsibility — not just of the individual to society, but of the society to the individual — is ongoing throughout McClung's work. McClung is not dealing in abstractions here. As individuals, we are all contributors to, and participants in society. It follows, therefore, that each one of us, as society, has an obligation to help and support all the others. Attributions of "bourgeois" self-seeking to McClung do not accurately reflect either her own heritage or the concerns with which her novels deal. The Watson family is both poverty-stricken and "lower-class," a reality which Pearl fiercely defends in *Purple Springs*.[23] It is the hard-working, but parsimonious Motherwells, whose desperate son Tom is driven to the bar-room through his parents' lack of charity, who receive McClung's censure. In McClung's world, it is not what you have, or who your "people" are that count — it is what you are, and what you do with your life. Hence her main protagonist, a little 12-year-old girl, whose imagination and practical good humour keep her family together, and inspire the whole community. McClung describes her ideal:

> Pearl Watson was like the rugged little anemone, the wind flower
> that lifts its head from the cheerless prairie. No kind hand softens the
> heat or the cold, nor tempers the wind, and yet the very winds that
> blow upon it and the hot sun that beats upon it bring to it a grace, a
> hardiness, a fragrance of good cheer, that gladdens the hearts of all
> who pass that way. (SSD, 40)

While Dr. Barner and Mrs. Burton, Camilla, Rev. Grantley and others provide the subtext of *Sowing Seeds in Danny*, its main action revolves around Pearlie Watson and the result of her efforts to pay off the Watson family debt. The father, John Watson, had been involved in a serious accident while working as a section hand, and Mr. Motherwell had donated an old caboose in which the family could live, on the assumption that John Watson would die. He failed to fulfil Motherwell's expectations, however, and the stingy Motherwell thereafter expected repayment for his "gift." To "wipe out the stain" of the $10 debt, Pearlie agrees to work for three months on the Motherwell farm. In the process, she saves a life, restores a doctor's faith, and effects several conversions; however, these are treated as by-products of Pearlie's attitude to life, not as glorious triumphs or self-righteous accomplishments. In *Sowing Seeds in Danny*, Pearlie is really just a little girl, albeit one with a rather weird and delightful sense of perspective, as this excerpt from her diary reveals:

> I made verses one day, there not very nice, but there true — I saw it:
>
>> The little lams are beautiful,
>>   There cotes are soft and nice,
>> The little calves have ringworm,
>>   And the 2-year olds have lice!
>
> Now I'm going' to make more; it seems to bad to leve it like that.
>
>> It must be very nasty,
>>   But to worrie, what's the use;
>> Better be cam and cheerfull,
>>   And appli tobaka jooce. (SSD, 221)

Pearlie, the prototypical McClung, accurately reads the world, and responds to problems with specific, practical solutions, in this case, "tobaka jooce"!

The Motherwells are influenced by Pearlie's arrival, but not immediately. Two elements are involved in their ultimate conversion. The first is the illness and imminent death of their former farm help, the immigrant English girl Polly Bragg. The second is Mr. Motherwell's lack of charity towards the Church. Both the Motherwells' selfishness and "petty meanness" alienate their son, potentially endanger the life of one of their tenant farmers, Arthur Wemyss, and generally make life harder rather than easier for those around them. The Motherwells are the other side of the human coin—just as Pearlie's generosity brings increasing joy, so their self-centred stinginess, in both spiritual and material matters, depletes those with whom they come into contact. It is McClung's justice to have one of Pearlie's ingenuous acts of kindness to one of their "victims" be the catalyst for their repentance.

At the time of Pearl's arrival, Polly Bragg is in a Brandon hospital dying of fever and homesickness, exacerbated by the Motherwells' refusal to believe in the reality of either. Polly had planted poppies from England outside her window which Pearl, upon learning of the severity of Polly's illness, cuts and sends to her in hospital. They arrive just before Polly's death, providing her with comfort in her last moments on earth. The nurse who attended her later wrote a note to the Motherwells, thanking them for their kindness. Mrs. Motherwell's conscience is troubled. She remembers her meanness to Polly, particularly in regard to Polly's homesickness, and she goes through Polly's belongings and reads her letters from home. She is shocked to find that Polly's mother is threatened with the poorhouse, and that Polly's earnings are all that have saved her thus far. Reading in these letters of a "poverty bitter and grinding, but redeemed from utter misery by a love and a faith that shone from every line" (SSD, 237), Mrs. Motherwell is shaken, and the seeds of her repentance are sown.

Meanwhile, Mr. Motherwell has quarrelled with the Church. To a worker asking for a donation, he complains that he gave $25 the preceding year, and asks, "Ain't that blamed thing paying yet? I've a good notion to pull my money out of it and be done with it" (SSD, 73-4). On his next visit to Millford he is stopped by the Rev. Hugh Grantley, who puts $25 into the shocked Motherwell's hands. When Motherwell protests, Grantley excoriates him at length. He chastises Motherwell for considering the Church as an "investment" which should give material returns, then uses Motherwell's own metaphor to indict him: "The Lord sends you seed-time and harvest . . . has given you health of body and mind, sends you rain from heaven, makes his sun to shine upon you, increases your riches from year to year. You have given Him twenty-five dollars in return and you regret it. Is that so?" (SD, 75). To Motherwell's sputtered response that "It isn't them as goes to church most that is the best" (SSD, 75), Grantley coldly suggests he might rather give his money for relief of the poor, or hospitals, or children's homes, but Motherwell's parsimoniousness is thoroughgoing. In a thundering sermon worthy of a revival meeting, McClung has Rev. Grantley damning Motherwell utterly:

> If you could see what a contemptible, good-for-nothing creature you are in God's sight, you would call on the hills to fall on you. Why, man, I'd rather take my chances with the gambler, the felon, the drunkard, than with you. They may have fallen in a moment of strong temptation; but you are a respectable man simply because it costs money to be otherwise. . . . The world will not be one bit better because you have passed through it. (SSD, 76-7)[24]

Motherwell stalks away, but for once his money gives him no pleasure. He shoves it in an old overcoat, where it turns up to tempt his son in the bar-room. In McClung's fictional world, sins have an ironic way of coming home to roost.

Pearl comes to live with the Motherwells some time after the encounter with Rev. Grantley. In a chapter appropriately entitled "Faith Moveth Mountains," McClung has Pearlie act as catalyst for the Motherwell's repentance. The room in which Pearl is staying belonged to Polly, and Pearl is terrified of catching a fever from the "gurms" there. Mrs. Motherwell refuses to allow her to open the window for ventilation, so Pearl prays to God for help. A freak hailstorm ensues, breaking Pearl's window and letting in the air. The cookhouse roof is also blown off, falling over Polly's poppies and protecting them from the storm. Exactly $25 worth of damage was done to the Motherwell crop, a fact which does not escape Mr. Motherwell's increasingly uncomfortable attention.

The nurse's letter to the Motherwells after Polly's death is the final element in their conversion. Reading its final lines — "Inasmuch as ye have done it unto the least of these, ye have done it unto Me" — Mr. Motherwell softens to his wife's pleas that they do something to make amends for their behaviour, and they send Polly's mother $100 to save her from the poorhouse. Pearl's prayer for ventilation, and her act of kindness to Polly in sending her the poppies sets up a chain reaction by which the Motherwells' conversion is achieved. Simply by being herself and thinking of others, Pearl becomes the instrument through which God's work is done.

However, Pearlie is not merely a bystander, innocently doing little acts of kindness without knowing their import. She can act decisively to achieve her ends: in *Sowing Seeds in Danny*, saving Arthur Wemyss' life. Wemyss was a tenant farmer on Motherwell's land, determined to make a "go" of it in the "new Country." He and Pearl become close friends, and she is distressed one day to find him writhing in pain. He denies his difficulty, but Pearl observes him secretly, and discerns his symptoms as appendicitis. Pearl tries to convince Mrs. Motherwell of the severity of the situation, but despite her recent change of heart, Mrs. Motherwell is still a "careful" woman, taking care of her own, although her concern here is not that it would cost money, but that her son Tom might go to the bar should he go to Millford for a physician.

Pearl is determined Arthur should have a physician, and Mrs. Motherwell finally agrees, but only if it is old Dr. Barner. When she dispatches Tom for that purpose, Pearlie's distress is palpable: "'Arthur's as good as dead,' she said as she went to the granary, crying softly to herself. 'Dr. Clay is the only one who could save him, and they won't have him'" (SSD, 255). Hearing Dr. Clay's cart on the road, she remembers that he is treating a quinsy patient down the road, and resolves to catch him as he returns to town. She succeeds, but Dr. Clay has lost his nerve. His patient has died, because, Dr. Clay is sure, of an error on his part, and he is paralysed by the fear of killing Arthur too:

> "I can't do it, Pearl," he cried. "I can't. He'll die, I tell you, like that other poor fellow. I can't send another man to meet his Maker."
> "Oh, he's ready!" Pearl interrupted him. "Don't hold back on Arthur's account." (SSD, 269)

(Pearl had already prayed with Arthur as he made his peace with God. This interjection of Pearl's common sense is typical of McClung's down-to-earth humour, and saves Pearl from being insufferably "holy.")

The doctor is sobbing and Arthur worsening by the minute, when Pearl drops on her knees:

> "O God, dear God," she prayed, beating her hard little brown hands together, "don't go back on us, dear God. Put the gimp into Doc again; he's not scared to do it, Lord, he's just lost his grip for a minute; it looks like it, but he isn't. You can bank on Doc, Lord, he's not scared. Bear with him, dear Lord, just a minute — just a minute — he'll do it, and he'll do it right, Amen." (SSD, 269-70)

When she looks up, Dr. Clay's equilibrium has returned, and he performs the operation successfully, with Pearlie acting as nurse. Tom returns considerably later with old Dr. Barner, after spending his father's cursed $25 in the bar-room and ending up for several hours in a drunken stupor.

There had been considerable resentment on Dr. Barner's part to the young new doctor in Millford, but this incident overcomes it. Barner praises Dr. Clay's work, and Clay replies, "I thank you for your good words, but I wasn't alone when I did it. The bravest little girl in all the world was here and shamed me out of my weakness and . . . I think God Himself steadied my hand" (SSD, 278). McClung allows this limited interpretation of divine intervention, which often characterizes religious melodrama. However, it is interesting to note that it is Pearl, and her influence, which receive first attention. In McClung's universe, God helps those who help others. Human partners are absolutely indispensable for God's work to be done.

It is likewise interesting to note the extent to which God works through Pearlie in particular and through women in general. Women are always "granting absolution" in McClung's novels.[25] They are the peacemakers, judges and nurturers whose responsibilities as agents of God transcend institutional boundaries. Pearl is the epitome of what female spirituality ought to be. Indeed, McClung's father-in-law, the Rev. J.W. McClung, remarked, "Pearlie is the finest in modern fiction and it is because of her Christlikeness — her evangelical character . . . I am more than delighted that the reading public delight to have one who is not ashamed to avow her love for the teachings of our great Master."[26] Pearlie's "Christlikeness" gathers increasing significance for this study as she grows up and becomes a feminist political activist whose experiences are barely fictionalized accounts of McClung's own. Through the character of Pearl Watson, the religious bases of McClung's feminism and political and social activism are made flesh.

Sowing Seeds in Danny concludes with the grateful Wemyss family sending Pearl a large gift of money for saving the life of their son. McClung is not arguing here for a kind of Christian "karma" wherein good deeds bring immediate rewards. She has the Wemyss' assure Pearl:

> We do not mean to offer money as a payment for what you have
> done, dear child, . . . for such a service of love can only be paid in
> love; but we ask you to accept from us this little gift as our own

daughter would accept it if we had one, and we will be glad to think that it has been a help to you in the securing of an education.... (SSD, 304)

Rather, good deeds are empowering, both to the actor, and to those around her. Good begets itself, as does evil. In acting unselfishly and out of love, Pearl has not only saved a life, she has saved Dr. Clay from his failure of nerve, a physician's worst sin. The people in *Sowing Seeds in Danny* do not become saints, nor are their lives perfect and without pain. More realistically, their lives have been enriched through Pearl's active care. There are many sermons in *Sowing Seeds in Danny*, but the most central is the partnership of God and humanity in the manifestation of God's active love.

The Second Chance is a tale of bad starts and new beginnings, and the power of people to change their lives for the better. Once again, Pearlie is a prime catalyst for these changes, both spiritual and mate-rial, and once again the positive repercussions of generous self-giving love set up a kind of chain reaction which affects the whole commu-nity. In this novel, McClung introduces a new theme, the importance of education. She had Pearlie say of the Wemyss' gift: "It seems as if the Lord sent us the money Himself, for He can't bear to have people ignorant if there's any way out of it at all, at all, and there's nearly always a way if people'll only take it."[27] In fact, education changes Pearlie's life, and acts as a spiritual catalyst, for it is when she attends Normal School in Winnipeg that she becomes an activist for women's rights.

Familiar themes from *Sowing Seeds in Danny* are also addressed, such as the relation between financial meanness and spiritual mean-ness. Here the Motherwells are replaced by two families, the Perkins and the Steadmans. Like the Motherwells, the Perkins alienate their son, whose rebellion serves as a partial trigger for his parents' repent-ance. (In the Motherwells' case, Mr. Motherwell realized his money meanness had driven Tom to the bar, and that the $25 Tom spent there was "devil's money" anyway.) However, the Perkins also have a daughter, and in *The Second Chance*, McClung's attentions are directed much more to her experience. Tom Motherwell found tempo-rary relief in the bar-room, but for Martha Perkins there was no such solace for her misery.

The Steadmans are worse than the Perkins family or the Moth-erwells, for their meanness extends even to their own kin. Mr. Perkins recounts:

> When old Mrs. Steadman, George's mother, was there sick, Mrs.
> Steadman followed the Doctor out one day and asked him how long
> the old lady would last . . . for she was wantin' to send word to the
> paperhangers; and then she told him that they was goin' to have the
> house all done as soon as Granny was out of the way, "but," says
> she, "just now we're kinda at a standstill." (SC, 317-18)

Given this family's self-serving inhumanity, it is no accident that
McClung makes George Steadman Dr. Clay's Conservative opponent
in the politically polemical *Purple Springs*. The Conservatives, like the
Steadmans, fail to realize one of the central tenets of McClung's faith,
that God's love is expressed through the active care of others, not of
conserving what one has for oneself.

The Second Chance is a rich creation, and it would be possible to
devote several pages apiece to even the minor characters and events.
Having established her audience with *Sowing Seeds in Danny*,
McClung can be far more "preachy" in *The Second Chance*, although
witty observations on human foibles still abound. Pearlie's ingenuous
verbatim account of the Ladies Aid meeting, for example, devastat-
ingly reproduces the chattering pandemonium which can characterize
these events. However, for the purposes of clarity, we will focus primarily on the two issues which form the foundation of Pearl's activism in *Purple Springs*, temperance and the question of the condition of
women. The temperance issue is addressed through the story of Bill
Cavers' family and the bar-keeper Sandy Braden, while the "Woman
Question" is treated primarily through the rehabilitation of Martha
Perkins. In both cases, Pearl directly intervenes and changes the situation for the better. In so doing, she is also given several opportunities
to expound her religion, which she does at some length. Where *Sowing Seeds in Danny* focuses upon humour, and *Purple Springs* focuses
upon inspiring feminist social activism, *The Second Chance* has the flavour of a revival meeting, albeit one with wit and a social conscience.

McClung had expressed her concern for the plight of the farm wife
even in her early ads for her husband's pharmacy (see Appendix B).
Martha Perkins is a farm daughter, not only economically exploited,
but also denied even a miserable life of her own. Her father, Tom Perkins, grew wealthy on her unpaid efforts, yet begrudges her a $2 mag-
azine subscription, which would have also helped Mrs. Cavers, the
alcoholic's wife, to earn enough money to go back to Ontario to visit
her mother. Economic dependence upon men not only destroys personal autonomy here, but it prevents women from helping other
women. McClung's central tenet of active care is hence impeded by

economic inequality between the sexes. However, it is not simply poverty which is the problem — if it were, Pearlie Watson would be helpless — but rather the grinding sense of defeat which having no control over one's own life produces. A "slave mentality" is created, wherein women become miserably resigned to the very situations which God calls them to transform.

As *The Second Chance* opens, Martha Perkins is one such woman, cowed into silence by her father's control. She has followed the path of traditional womanhood — she obeys her father, works hard and unquestioningly for her family, she is an excellent cook, and her handi-work wins prizes at the Agricultural Fair (SSD, 119). Martha is so used to constant work that she does not know how to have fun, and when at a party at the neighbouring Slaters, wishes she had brought her knitting so as to have something to do (SSD, 199). Indeed, she does not even know she is unhappy. It is only when she gets a glimmer of the sense of wanting something for herself, and Mrs. Cavers, that she begins to experience "a great loneliness, vague and indefinite, a longing for some-thing she had never known" (SC, 6). Through Martha, McClung accu-rately portrays the dangers of total self-effacement in women, a theme to which she returns in *In Times Like These* and elsewhere. Martha knows how to do "things" but she lacks the ability to care for others actively, because she does not know how to care about herself.

Through Pearl's influence, Martha learns to value herself, and by the end of the story patient Martha has won the heart of Arthur Wemyss, although not without the requisite complications of Arthur's fickle English fiancée Thursa, and his ensuing depression and tempo-rary return to England. The metaphor for Martha's inner transforma-tion is her outer appearance. One of McClung's constant themes is "the leaven of good clothes" (SC, 178). If one is well-dressed and happy with how one looks, one will be more confident and outgoing; good grooming is a sign of self-care. Too, the world puts a high value upon appearance, particularly for women. When Pearl is teaching, she has to break the news to the neighbourhood that she is going to board with the notorious woman from Purple Springs. She realizes this is going to cause a scandal, as the woman is allegedly an unwed mother, and she comments to herself: " 'There will be a row — there will be a large row — unless I can make the people understand, and in a row there is nothing so sustaining as good clothes — next to the conscious-ness of being right, of course,' she added after a pause" (PS, 239). McClung continues:

An hour later, Pearl Watson, in her best dress of brown silk, with her high brown boots well polished, and her small brown hat, made by herself, with a band of crushed burnt orange poppies around the crown, safely anchored and softened by a messaline drape; with hair drawn over the tops of her ears, and a smart fawn summer coat, with buttons which showed a spot of red like a pigeon-blood ruby. Pearl looked at herself critically in the glass:

"These things should not count," she said, as she fastened a thin veil over her face and made it very neat at the back with a hairpin, "but they do." (PS, 240)

Just as Pearl's conviction is reflected in her appearance, so too is Martha's lack of it, although McClung indicates her potential for development:

Martha was twenty-five years old, and looked older. Her shoulders were slightly bent, and would suggest to an accurate observer that they had become so by carrying heavy burdens. Her hair was hay-coloured and broken. Her forehead and her eyes were her best features, and her mouth, too, was well formed and firm, giving her the look of a person who could endure. (SC, 7-8)

Pearl, whose family has moved from Millford to a neighbouring farm (the Watsons' "second chance"), begins to visit Martha frequently to effect her transformation. She soon realizes Martha has been trained to see only usefulness, not beauty, and in this she has been the unwitting victim of her parents' sin of spiritual meanness. Martha's good points, both physical and personal, have been obscured, her light hid under a bushel, and it is Pearlie's intention to let it shine out. Pearl does a "rapid summing-up of Martha's chances for beauty" (SC, 137) and concludes that while Martha will never be pretty, she can be made much more attractive: " 'She's got hair, too,' Pearl was thinking, 'but she rolls it into such a hard little nub you'd never know. It needs to be all fluffed out. That nub of hair is just like Martha herself. It's all there, good stuff in it, but it needs to be fluffed out' " (SC, 138).

Encouraging self-regard through good grooming is not McClung's only point here. What is at stake is what constitutes a "good woman." For McClung, a good woman is like Pearlie — strong, independent, caring, full of humour, resilient, faithful, and not afraid to fight for what she knows to be right. Martha, however, has been brought up to value herself only insofar as she is some material use to others. By being treated like a machine, Martha has become one, and she has missed out on the joy of living which McClung considered one of God's greatest gifts.

Parsimonious parents like the Motherwells might consider their son's marriage to Martha a good "investment" (SSD, 198), but Martha herself knows this to be insufficient: "no man would ever fancy me — why should he? A man wants his wife to be pretty and smart and bright, and what am I? . . . I am old and wrinkled and weather-beaten" (SC, 141). Pearl protests vigorously, and starts Martha on a health programme highly reminiscent of that recommended by the W.C.T.U. In this connection, McClung is reaffirming the importance of women's physical well-being for spiritual health. A woman who thinks too little of herself, who hunches over in her shoulders and bows her head when she speaks, is in no shape to transform the world, which is precisely what McClung's religion requires.

Martha begins a programme of calisthenics, and learns how to "treat her hair" (the metaphor for Martha herself) "to make it lose its hard, stringy look" (SC, 162). Her increased self-regard is evident in her using her butter money for the magazine subscription rather than for some more "practical" purpose. This chapter, significantly entitled "Spiritual Advisors," ends with McClung's observation of Martha: "Pearl had inspired in her a belief in herself, and it was wonderful to see how soon she began to make the best of herself" (SC, 162).

For all who read her, McClung's writing was intended to do the same. McClung expounds on the plight of the farm woman in *In Times Like These* to influence voters and politicians. Novels such as *The Second Chance* were intended to convert women themselves, and to empower them to take responsibility for transforming the conditions of their lives. On the surface, Martha's "beauty make-over" could be read as trivial, or "bourgeois." In fact, McClung is being quite radical. In demanding that women take care of themselves instead of totally sacrificing themselves for others, in showing that women can and ought to depend upon and help each other, and in insisting that these things have a fundamentally spiritual dimension, McClung is preaching a Christian feminism so subversive that her readers may not even have noticed its political import.

The political issue to which McClung explicitly applies this perspective is that of temperance. *The Second Chance* tells a sad, but realistic story of the effect of alcoholism on families, and reasserts McClung's contention that resolution of this problem is a social responsibility. Bill Cavers is a poor farmer whose intermittent problems with the bottle have left his wife and daughter tense and troubled, and made saloon-keeper Sandy Braden a wealthy man. Cavers is portrayed as a good man with a fatal weakness over which he has little control. He does not beat his wife, nor abuse his child, nor disrupt the community in any direct way. Rather, his sins are those of omission, a failure to be responsible. When his son is ill with the croup, he is sent to get the doctor, but he meets a group of threshers, goes drinking, and forgets to come home (SC, 94). He returns in the morning, dead drunk, without the doctor, too far gone to realize that in the meantime his child has died. Even so, his wife's love for her husband is so constant that she makes excuses for him, and never mentions his drinking to other members of the community.

If recent research on families of alcoholics is to be trusted, McClung is accurately describing a common phenomenon in alcoholic families.[28] Her aim is not to depict Caver's wife as a long-suffering angel, but rather to show how alcohol can cut one off from the deepest dimension of human community. Bill Cavers has a problem which he cannot control. McClung's response is to urge the community to help keep the Cavers of this world out of harm's way. She has Pearl approach Sandy Braden at the Pioneers' Picnic where the Cavers are going to have a picture taken to send back to Mrs. Cavers' mother in Ontario, in lieu of the trip which Bill's drinking has made unaffordable:

> what I want to ask you, Mr. Braden, as a real favour, is not to fill Bill up until they get the photo taken, anyway. You know how his lip hangs when he's drunk—he wouldn't look nice in a photo to send home. Mrs. Cavers went all white and twitchy that day you took him away from church. I was right behind her, and I guess that's how she'd look in a photo if he got drunk, and she wouldn't look nice, either; and even Libby Anne wouldn't be lookin' her best, because she gets mad when her father is drunk, and says she's like to kill you, and burn up all your whiskey, and lots of things like that that ain't real Christian. So you see, it would spoil the whole picture if you let him get drunk. (SC, 171)

Pearl does not condemn Braden; rather, she assumes that "maybe you don't know what a bad time Mrs. Cavers and Libby Anne have when Bill drinks" (SC, 172). By informing him, and trusting in his good will, Pearl expresses McClung's attitude to many of those persons who condone liquor use. It is less a question of "demon rum" defiling the spiritual body of the drinker than of the destructive social consequences of its use. The argument that "every man has a perfect right to drink as much as he wants" (SC, 173), made by Braden's partner, fails to acknowledge the interdependence of the human family, and the unjust social structures which support men's rights at the expense of women's lives.

Braden's partner sells Cavers liquor at the picnic, encouraging him to drink and extending credit to allow him to do so. This malevolent act results in Cavers' death: he wanders off to the riverbank and spends several hours insensible in the blazing sun. By the time he is found, he is dying, and McClung renders his passing with appropriate melodramatic flourish, as he lies surrounded by his grieving wife and daughter, the helpless doctor, Pearlie, and the now-repentant Sandy Braden, who resolves to sell his saloon immediately.

Braden spends the rest of the story attempting to make reparations for his part in Bill Cavers' death. It is worth noting that Bob, the partner who urged liquor on Cavers in the first place, felt absolutely no responsibility for his actions. As an individual he chose to sell to Cavers, and as an individual Cavers chose to buy. Bob thus maintains the fiction of free choice in support of individual liberty, when in fact it is his most unscrupulous prompting which overcomes Cavers' prior resolve to stay sober. The addict has no "free choice," nor do his family. And as we shall see in *Purple Springs*, McClung reserves her deepest scorn for the government which gets fat at the price of these people's pain, and all in the name of liberty.

In contrast, Sandy Braden recognizes his responsibility, and attempts to make reparations to the remaining Cavers family by providing medical care anonymously when Libby Anne falls seriously ill. "Crisis conversions" are all very well, in McClung's view, but constructive action is necessary to prove their reality. It is likewise appropriate that Mrs. Cavers does not forgive Sandy Braden at first. She utterly rejects the gifts to Libby Anne in her illness, once she determines their origin:

> Restitution! Does anyone speak to me of restitution? Can anything bring back my poor Will from the grave? Can anything give him back his chance in this world and the next? Can anything make me forget the cold black loneliness of it all? I don't want Sandy Braden's money. Let it perish with him! Can I take the price of my husband's soul? (SC, 325)

There is no "cheap grace" here. Braden must suffer with the reality which he helped to create.

Sandy Braden's punishment for his part in Bill Cavers' death is to be cut off from the community, to be denied forgiveness. He now wants to help, but his help is refused. He is being told, in fact, that there can be no restitution, that the damage has been done. It is only once Braden suffers, and accepts that this is necessary, when he acts to help not out of guilt, but out of concern for Libby Anne herself that McClung allows Mrs. Cavers to forgive him.

The main action occurs in the chapter, "Another Neighbour." Libby Anne's condition is worsening, and an operation appears to be necessary. However, the specialist, Dr. McTavish, refuses to travel to see her in the face of the gathering blizzard, despite Sandy Braden's persuasion and offers of money. Finally Braden physically forces the doctor into his cutter, and risks both their lives to drive through the blizzard to save Libby Anne. After they arrive, Braden waits unobtrusively in the barn until he is sure Libby Anne is out of danger. He realizes he has no claim on Mrs. Cavers' gratitude, and disappears without thanks. Yet it is precisely this "loving service freely given" which softens Mrs. Cavers' formerly (and justifiably) hardened heart. The chapter concludes with Mrs. Cavers says: "Dr. Clay . . . tell Sandy Braden I have only *one* word for him . . . only one word, and that is, May God bless him — always" (SC, 336).

McClung describes Braden's final reconciliation in "The Contrite Heart." Libby Anne and Mrs. Cavers have finally made their pilgrimage back to visit Mrs. Cavers' mother in Ontario, and Mrs. Cavers is contemplating her future. Just then, Sandy Braden appears at the gate, and begs her to accept the gift of a half-section of land near Brandon, a new farm for the old one bankrupt by Bill Cavers' drinking. This gift is the "second chance" for both Braden and Mrs. Cavers, and her initial refusal is overcome by Braden's desperate plea:

> Mrs. Cavers, I've been a guilty man, careless and hard, but that day — on the river-bank — I saw things as I never saw them before, and I'm trying to be square. My mother . . . has been in heaven twenty years. She always told me about God's mercy to — the very worst — that He turned no one down who came to Him. My mother was that kind herself, and knowing her — made it easier to believe . . . (SC, 358-9)

He implores Mrs. Cavers once again to take his gift, and she finally accedes.

Thus Sandy Braden makes his peace with humanity; he has yet to make his peace with God. It is instructive that McClung does not send Braden to church, or to a minister, but to a woman to be shriven of his sins. In the following passage, McClung makes most plain that women can act as God's agents on earth, whether prophets like Pearlie, or true priests like Mrs. Cavers' mother. Mrs. Cavers tells Braden to speak to her mother for comfort and absolution: "Tell her all about it — she'll understand, just like your own mother would — these dear old mothers are all the same" (SC, 359). Braden enters the parlour. "What passed between them no one ever knew, but an hour later Sandy Braden went out from the little white cottage with a new light shining in his face, and the peace of God, which passes all understanding, in his heart" (SC, 359).

McClung's treatment of Braden's reconciliation is stylistically melodramatic, and could be dismissed as sentimental on those grounds. However, it is important to distinguish here between style and content. Sandy Braden has sinned against the human community, partly through ignorance, and partly through lack of active care. His negligence results in a death, for which he feels guilty and for which he tries to make restitution. His early offers are rebuffed, because it is necessary for him to experience some of the suffering he has caused. Just as the Cavers family was broken apart, so too Sandy Braden must be set aside from the human community until he acts unselfishly rather than to ease his own pain. While his repeated financial aid to Libby Anne and Mrs. Cavers might seem excessive, in McClung's moral economy it is only just, for Braden's wealth derived from men like Cavers; in helping Mrs. Cavers he is in reality only giving back what should have been hers in the first place. Finally, once he has accepted the justice of his punishment, he can be truly healed. It is fitting that a mother, symbol of home and family and the core of the human community, should act as the agent for the dispensation of God's grace, for in McClung's religion it is in human interrelation rather than in the institutional church that God primarily resides.

McClung's understanding of religion is stated explicitly in the chapter entitled, "Pearl's Philosophy," wherein Pearl provides the impetus for Sandy Braden's salvation. Faced with Braden's leaden remorse after Bill Cavers' death, Pearlie assures him that God "always knows what He's doin'" (SC, 231). Justice is achieved in the end, and even the worst sinner can be saved. In response to Braden's declared lack of faith, Pearlie assures him: "Oh, don't worry about Bill Cavers now . . . Bill's still in God's hands, and God has a better chance at him now than He ever had . . . God would do good things for people if they would only let Him, but He has to have a free hand on them" (SC, 231).

Not only is there, apparently, salvation *after* death, God also makes up undeserved suffering with good fortune in this life. However, this divine recompense is not administered supernaturally, but through the loving action of caring neighbours. The Watsons, for example, contribute $200 to the Cavers for the use of their farm land. The act of giving benefitted all, as Pearlie notes: "She didn't want to take it, but was really glad of it, and Pa and Ma and all of us have been feeling better ever since" (SC, 232). Once again, McClung shows that love begets love, and multiplies in the giving, and this is why the refusal of care is such a devastating punishment.

Pearl concludes her ministering to Sandy Braden with a sermon on women, and a plan for him to be reconciled to God. Braden's assertion that he didn't see much in religion, but he certainly wouldn't hit a woman (SC, 232), is met by Pearlie's quick reply that if it weren't for religion, he wouldn't know that. He is not a bad man, she assures him, and in most countries he would be considered an "awful good man," but "If it wasn't for the Bible and Christ we wouldn't know how good a man should be" (SC, 233). While this passage could be read as sheer apologetic, McClung's intention might be read more subtly. That is, McClung recognizes that Christian tradition has allowed the abuse of women, but in her view this is a deviation from the true teachings of Christ and the Bible. McClung constantly harkens back to Biblical roots in order to shame people into actually practising what they claim to preach.

In Braden's case, he has fallen away from the faith, and Pearl's preaching in itself falls short of the mark. Theology, McClung seems to be saying, cannot convince the unbeliever, no matter how passionately it is espoused. What has to be reclaimed is the experience of religion, which in its most fundamental form is found in a mother's unconditional love. When Braden denies knowing the Bible, Pearl responds, "Well, I bet you a dollar some one read it and passed it on to you" (SC, 233). Braden falls into a reverie:

> He saw his mother sitting in a rocking-chair, with a big Bible on her knee, and by her side was a little boy he knew to be himself. He saw again on her finger the thin silver ring, worn almost to a thread, and felt the clasp of her hand on his as she guided his finger over the words she was teaching him; and back through the long years they came to him: "Love one another as I have loved you." (SC, 233-4)

Again, though portrayed in the form of melodrama, McClung's message is not necessarily sentimental. She is affirming that love is expressed through action, and thus Pearlie shows Sandy Braden a way out of his misery. She tells him that he has stopped doing wrong, but has not yet started to do right, and that is the most precarious position of all for his soul. Hence her remedy: "If you'd just get busy helpin' people you'd soon get over bein' sad and down-hearted . . . don't let the chances all go by you" (SC, 235-6). She reinforces the point with a reference to Jacob Marley in *A Christmas Carol*, doomed to wander the earth witnessing the misery he caused but is now unable to alleviate.

Like all McClung's novels, *The Second Chance* ends happily. Sandy Braden is reconciled with the human family through Mrs. Cavers' acceptance of him and, through her mother, with God. The Watsons are now happy and successful farmers, and though they are far from rich, the stage is now set for the realization of Pearlie's ambition to become a teacher. Martha, too, receives her reward, but only when she has given up all hope of achieving her heart's desire in Arthur's love. Betrayed by his English fiancée, Arthur Wemyss has returned to England in despair, leaving Martha with her affections undeclared. Months pass, Arthur's letters stop, and Martha resolves to make "a fight, a brave fight, with an unjust world. She would study — she would fit herself yet for some position in life. . . . Surely, there was some place where a woman would not be disqualified because she was not beautiful" (SC, 366). Through Pearlie's help, Martha has become a survivor, not merely a subsister. Arthur's unannounced arrival and his subsequent declaration of love are not to be understood as necessary for Martha's fulfilment. She has become a whole person in herself, independent and patient and courageous. In fact, it is only when Martha has become so, when she has ceased being self-effacing and subservient, that her true beauty can shine through. That beauty is appropriately described by Arthur as the beauty of the prairie, "the sunshine, the bird-song, the bracing air, the broad outlook, the miles of golden wheat" (SC, 369). Though austere, the prairie is resilient and, like the beauty of Martha, it is well worth the effort of cultivation. In presenting Martha as a symbol of the prairie, and charting her transformation and ultimate happiness, McClung offers hope to those struggling under difficult conditions for sheer survival, and it is through this inspirational literature that McClung is attempting to give them hope for their own "second chance."

The Pearlie Watson trilogy is completed by *Purple Springs*, a 1921 publication which reflects McClung's personal and political development through the suffrage battle and the war. The cosy anecdotal approach characteristic of the first two books is here replaced with a

refined, almost sophisticated attitude which is reflected in the character of Pearlie herself. If we are to consider Pearl (as she is now called)
as a prototypical McClung, this shift in atmosphere is instructive. In
Sowing Seeds in Danny and *The Second Chance* Pearlie's faith, and the
inspiration arising therefrom, are sufficient to win the day. Her enemies are ignorance and lack of care, problems which can be resolved
on a personal, individual basis. If there are external structures of
injustice, such as those created by prejudice, these can be overcome
through enthusiasm and active example. By changing one's "mental
attitude" one can change the world.

By *Purple Springs*, McClung has learned much of the ways of the
world, and this is reflected in her writing. While there are elements
which recall her early humour, such as the gossiping Mrs. Crocks and
her stablehand Bertie, the main text of *Purple Springs* is a thinly disguised retelling of McClung's own political career. Too, the straightforward sermons of the earlier books have become more like political
analyses. This transition is evident even in chapter titles. Where *Sowing Seeds in Danny* speaks of "The Faith That Moveth Mountains" and
"Saved," and *The Second Chance* of "Spiritual Advisors" and "The
Contrite Heart," *Purple Springs* has "The Power of Ink" and "Peter's
Report." Selfishness and ignorance have attained corporate propor-
tions, and must be attacked on that level. While individuals still may
be converted, such as the young Conservative party hack Peter Neelands, who, in an interesting twist of a traditional theme, falls in love
with Pearl and becomes a Liberal women's rights activist, the problems Pearl encounters are the result of specific social structures. Individual moral regeneration is still necessary in a spiritual sense, but it
is insufficient to change the total situation for the better.

Too, if moral regeneration is not forthcoming, McClung is prepared to sacrifice Christian patience to expediency. As one brother
describes Pearl's attitude to wrong-doers, "Make them repentant — or
dead!" (PS, 24). McClung is not arguing for the slaughter of the opposition here. Rather, her experience on the hustings has made her
somewhat more cynical about the intrinsic goodness of human nature,
and the power of example and exhortation to achieve conversion.
Direct action is necessary at the institutional level; legislation of public
morality is preferable to continued abuse.[29]

All three volumes of the Watson trilogy are structured in a similar
fashion. McClung creates a small-scale fictional world wherein several
dynamics interconnect. As we have seen, incidental actions can have

profound consequences; a casual remark inappropriately uttered, or an unobtrusive act of kindness can affect the community far beyond their original intent. McClung is reaffirming the interdependence of all persons, and each one's importance as a moral actor. In *Purple Springs*, this dimension of moral agency is relocated at the corporate, governmental level. Individual action remains important, but the locus of McClung's concern has become the broad structures which inhibit or enhance those actions.

The source of this "broader view," which is one of McClung's abiding ideals, is in part education. At the end of *The Second Chance*, McClung has Pearl, then 15, receive a ring from Dr. Clay, with the promise that on the first of May, three years hence, he will "ask her a question." In the interim, rather than doing fancy-work for her trousseau, or preparing to be a "good wife," Pearl has gone to Normal School to become a teacher, an experience of McClung's own which she describes in *Clearing in the West*.[30] She has also become politicized. Here McClung deviated from her own life, imbuing her character with a sophisticated activism which emerges, apparently self-evidently, from education and direct observation of the political process. When Pearl returns to her family in Millford, she is deeply committed to both temperance and woman suffrage, to the point that she is willing to risk censure by speaking out on these issues in a public lecture, an event which threatens to jeopardize her teaching career.

In the meantime, Dr. Clay is being courted by the local Liberal association to run in the upcoming provincial election against George Steadman, whose greed and misplaced sense of self-importance have placed him firmly in the Conservatives' pocket. Unfortunately, just prior to being asked to run, Clay is informed that he has a serious illness which demands that he avoid all over-exertion. (McClung leaves the ailment unnamed, to great melodramatic effect.) His colleague Dr. Brander, whom McClung presents as someone who would currently be termed a chauvinist, advises against marriage. In his view, "St. Paul was right when he advised men to remain single if they had serious work to do. Women, the best of them, grow tiresome and double-chinned in time" (PS, 41). (To which McClung has Clay reply, "I like that . . . a man with a forty-two waist measure, wearing an eighteen inch collar, finding fault with a woman's double chin. You are not such a raving beauty yourself" [PS, 41].) Nevertheless, Clay is convinced that it would be unfair to Pearl to take on an invalid for a husband, and on the day he had anticipated proposing to her, he instead gives her a noble-sounding but ambiguous speech about her youth and worth, and leaves the matter ultimately unresolved.

The ensuing complications provide McClung with ample opportunity to hold forth on a variety of subjects. We will direct our attention to three levels of concern, beginning with McClung's understanding of politics, addressing the character of McClung's feminism as expressed through Pearl Watson, and concluding with the understanding of religion which emerges from the narrative. It should be noted, however, that McClung does not separate these factors, but presents religion, feminism and political activism as logically integrated elements of a compassionate, responsible life.

As much as McClung was a life-long supporter of, and an occasional candidate for, the Liberal Party of Canada, in *Purple Springs* she presents both Liberals and Conservatives as essentially the same in moral terms. Both parties "play politics." She has the Liberal field organizer, Mr. Summersad, say to Clay:

> Politics is a game of wits . . . the smartest one wins, and gets in and divides the slush money. The other side howl — because they didn't get any. . . . Both parties have the same platform, too, there is only one principle involved, that is the principle of re-election. (PS, 116)

He continues his cynical tale, assuring Clay that he need not be concerned with actual reforms promised by the party, and responds to Clay's shock by replying, "You can be as full of moral passion as you like — the fuller the better. The Opposition can always be the Simon-pure reformers" (PS, 118). These comments notwithstanding, McClung does believe that a committed individual can make a difference, and she eventually has Clay throw caution to the wind and run for office.

There are two points to be made here. First, McClung herself was "not a good party woman," by her own admission and as this description of Summersad's politics implies (SRF, 172). She had no intrinsic faith in institutions, although her involvement with both church and government indicates her recognition of their importance and power. Her early optimism and faith in human nature, so evident in *Sowing Seeds in Danny* and *The Second Chance*, is here informed by the practical experience of working within institutional structures for change. The result is a somewhat jaundiced view of the political process as a whole, also evident in an underlying tone of bitterness in her later articles and autobiographies. At the time of *Purple Springs*, however, she retains enough of her early liberalism to believe that individual action can transform the institution from within.

Second, McClung has Clay change his mind about his candidacy out of love for Pearl. In this radical reversal of the masculine stereotype, echoed in *In Times Like These*'s call for "brave women and fair men," it is Clay who is vulnerable to his passion for Pearl; his actions are not guided by sexual desire, but out of a need to earn her love and respect in fighting for the vote he knows she deserves. Too, he is influenced by Robert Gilchrist, President of the Political Club, who has met Pearl in action, and claims, "that girl can swing an election. No one can resist her arguments" (PS, 207). Clay does not have to be argued into political agreement with Pearl. He understands, instinctively, that voting is a woman's right. As he tells Summersad, "Women, although they are not so strong as men, do more than half the work, and bear children besides, and yet men have been mean enough to snatch power away from them and keep it" (PS, 119). Gilchrist's comment, that Pearl is disappointed in Clay for refusing the Liberal nomination, changes Clay's mind, and he defies Dr. Brander's warnings about his health for the woman he loves, not the least reason being to further her political career. As Clay boasts, "If women had the vote, what a power Pearl would be!" (PS, 208).

This reversal of stereotypes is of profound importance for McClung's use of literature as pulpit. As the reader identifies with Pearl, and rejoices in her success, so too does Dr. Clay's devotion to Pearl and her feminism become a plausible and desirable manifestation of masculinity. In the "noble character" of Dr. Clay, McClung legitimates male vulnerability in love, and refutes the notion that domination is intrinsic to the male character. Indeed, the proper relation of the sexes is one of mutuality. As Clay tells Dr. Brander, "Marriage is a mutual agreement, for mutual benefit and comfort, for sympathy and companionship. . . . Many a man has found himself when he gets a wife" (PS, 42). Thus McClung reverses the common stereotype, supported by both society and the church, that it is the woman whose identity marriage alone fulfils.

McClung employs unreversed stereotypes to her advantage as well. Dr. Brander, Clay's physician, represents a typical gentleman of the "old school." He cloaks his misogynism in scientific "fact," arguing that "old Dame Nature" dupes men into reproducing: "She makes women beautiful, graceful, attractive and gives them the instinct to dress in a way that will attract men. Makes them smaller and weaker than men, too, which also makes its appeal" (PS, 42-3). This "natural" inclination on the part of women to trap men nevertheless has negative moral implications, and Dr. Brander boasts that he has barely escaped the clutches of "these little frilled and powdered vixens" (PS, 43). Brander is contrasted with Dr. Clay, whose sense of self-worth does not depend upon feeling himself superior to women. Also, in having Dr. Brander bear the bad news of Clay's illness, which causes Clay and Pearl so much pain and difficulty, McClung ensures his character be received with even less sympathy than his unrelenting androcentrism would provoke. The subtle negativity with which McClung depicts Dr. Brander serves to deflate the scientific misogynist position he represents, at least as effectively as had McClung debated the point directly.

Political androcentrism is next engaged, in the person of George Steadman. The Steadmans had been established as cheap, unsympathetic folk in *The Second Chance*; in *Purple Springs* Mr. Steadman shows himself to be arrogant, ethnocentric, and condescending to women. These attitudes are reflected in his physical appearance:

> He was a stout man, with a square face, and small, beady black eyes and an aggressive manner; a man who felt sure of himself; who knew he was the centre of his own circle. There was a well-fed, complacent look about him too which left no doubt that he was satisfied with things as they were — and would be deeply resentful of change. There was still in his countenance some trace of his ancestor's belief in the Divine right of kings! It showed in his narrow, thought-proof forehead, and a certain indescribable attitude which he held toward others, and which separated him from his neighbours. (PS, 90)

As the Conservative member for Millford, and therefore a community leader, Steadman has been asked to introduce Pearl at the Chicken Hill School, where she is to speak on her experiences at Normal School in Winnipeg. Steadman's introduction turns into a political speech, as he waxes loquacious upon "woman's true place, the home." Carried away by the force of his own argument, he proclaims, "if the opposition ever get in power, the women and the hired men, and even the foreigners will run the country, and it will not be fit to live in" (PS, 94). Further, he opposes temperance legislation, attributing alcohol abuse not to availability, or social conditions, but to women's failure to provide "the right home training" to their children (PS, 94). In Steadman's world, the system works as it stands, and all problems should be attributed to those who refuse to "know their place."

Steadman represents all that McClung opposes, and his pomposity is thoroughly lampooned in Pearl's reply. Her humorous gibes are

direct quotations from many of the speeches given by McClung herself. For example, regarding the claim that women do not want to sit
in Parliament, McClung has Pearl reply: "He perhaps does not know
what it feels like to stand over a wash tub — or an ironing board — or
cook over a hot stove. Women who have been doing these things long
would be glad to sit anywhere!" (PS, 97). Pearl goes on to express
McClung's social philosophy: "no matter how fine we [are] as individuals, or how well we [do] our work, unless we [have] it in our
hearts to work with others, and for others — it [is] no good. If we
lack . . . social consciousness, our work [will] not amount to much"
(PS, 99). The liquor traffic must be outlawed, for it endangers the
whole social fabric. Women should have the vote, not because they
are morally superior, but out of fairness, and to allow them to "do
their share" in the world's work. Social consciousness, not misplaced
individual egoism, is the core of the suffrage movement. Finally, this
social consciousness must extend to all members of society, including
the foreign-born. While McClung may be cited as speaking paternalis-
tically by current standards, for example, in her use of the term "our
foreign people," her attitude is better understood in the following:

> We have many foreign people in this country, lonesome, homesick
> people — and sometimes we complain that they are not loyal to
> us — and that is true. It is also true that they have no great reason to
> be loyal to us. We are not even polite to them, to say nothing of
> being kind. Loyalty cannot be rammed down any one's throat with a
> flag-pole. (PS, 101)

Building Canada is a cooperative venture. In contrast to Steadman's rather xenophobic conservatism, Pearl/McClung emphasizes
non-hierarchical cooperative effort. Pearl concludes:

> To keep what we have, we must improve it from year to year. And to
> that end we must work together — fighting not with each
> other — but with conditions, discouragements, ignorance, prejudice,
> narrowness — we must be ready to serve, not thinking of what we
> can get from our country, but what we can give to it. (PS, 101)

One specific material condition which requires change in the light
of social consciousness is the legal disability of women in Canadian
society. McClung illustrates the problem via two examples. The first
involves Annie Gray and her small son Jim, who settle near the town
and give Purple Springs its name. "Mrs." Gray is apparently unmarried; the resulting gossip and community censure drive her son from
school, and threaten to terminate Pearl's teaching career through a

boycott when Pearl decides to board with them, all other homes being closed to her in protest of her feminist activism. McClung shows at length the insensitivity and outright cruelty women can show to each other in maintaining conventional notions of sexual propriety. More radically, when Pearl is challenged by a neighbour woman, who says an unmarried woman like Annie Gray "has no right to have a child," Pearl replies, "Why not if she wants to? . . . Having a child is nothing against her" (PS, 241-2). In McClung's view, legal marriage is of far less import than how a woman actually treats her child.

The further point McClung wishes to make, however, is that women like Annie Gray accept social scorn out of necessity, to retain custody of their children, for at the time of McClung's writing, women could only be legal guardians of bastards. Fathers could will away custody of even unborn children to whomever they chose. In a fitting complication of the plot, McClung has Annie Gray's father-in-law be precisely the kind of arrogant, judgemental person who would take the child on the grounds of his mother's "immorality"; she also makes him "Mr. Graham," Conservative party leader and Premier of Manitoba, a barely disguised version of her old enemy, Sir Rodmond Roblin. McClung is intent to show that, pious rhetoric about love and respect for women (for which Roblin was famous) aside, in practical fact women had absolutely no legal protection in the event of male vindictiveness. Even the highest authorities cannot be trusted to treat women fairly if it is in their own interest not to do so. In a truly democratic, cooperative country, women's rights cannot depend upon men's whims to grant them.

As great a threat to women's security as wilful malice is the ignorance and insensitivity which prevent men from even recognizing the sources of women's discontent. To illustrate this situation, McClung recounts the story of one Mrs. Paine, whose husband has decided to sell the family farm and buy the local hotel in town. She panics, both at leaving the farm and at the prospect of entering the liquor trade, but her husband informs her that she is powerless to stop him: "I'll sell the bed out from under you — I'll break you and your stuck-up ways, and you'll not get a cent of money from me — not if your tongue was hanging out. . . . You've got no one to turn to, so you might as well know it — I've got you!" (PS, 166-7). His anger is kindled by what he perceives as her pride and hostility, but he is unaware of the extent to which he himself has been responsible for her attitude. Specifically, both she and the children are poorly clothed, barely fed, and living isolated, deprived lives in a crude house, virtually empty of comfort, on the barren prairie. He, on the other hand, travels often, dresses well, and has $15,000 in the bank from his cattle trading, over which he exercises total control.

Paine is an unpleasant, selfish man, who believes marriage depends on male authority, and sees every independent thought of his wife's as an attempt to usurp his rightful place as head of the family. He is bitter and defensive, and it seems his interest in selling the farm lies less with his desire to run a saloon than in demonstrating his power to do so, should he choose. His attitude of belligerence extends to other aspects of life as well. McClung describes him sitting "in front of the stove, smoking and spitting, abusing the country, the weather, the Government, the church. Nothing escaped him, and everything was wrong" (PS, 169).

Given his attitude, it is not surprising that Mrs. Paine tells Pearl never to marry, for "Marriage is a form of bondage — long-term slavery — for women." She goes on, "It isn't the hard work — or the pain — it isn't that — it's the uselessness of it all" (PS, 125). There is no moral order which guarantees that people will get what they deserve. Mrs. Paine has worked all her life running the farm while her husband has been away buying and shipping cattle, but she has no control whatsoever over the products of her labour. The bitter reality of her helplessness has destroyed not only her faith in marriage, but her faith in God. She brushes off Pearl's assurance of God's justice with the comment, "I'm not God, but I take responsibility for my children. . . . But God does not stand by me" (PS, 127).

McClung here shows that injustice on earth can destroy faith in the justice of heaven. Many women have no reason to believe in God or God's care, for the practical experiences of their lives have been characterized by the abuse of power at the hands of men who have made the world to suit themselves. Moreover, they justify the situation by giving scientific, political and religious reasons for the necessity of keeping women "in their place" (PS, 126-7).

To attribute to men the ability to destroy faith utterly is a serious charge, and one might conclude from this that McClung considers men evil, or morally deficient. Certainly she considers the system which reinforces male power over women to be so, but she disputes Mrs. Paine's argument that marriage will destroy her:

you are wrong in thinking that all men are mean and selfish. My
father is not. We've been poor and all that, but we're happy. My
father has never shirked his share of the work, and he has only one
thought now, and that is to do well for us. There are plenty of happy
marriages. (PS, 129)

In McClung's view, men have abused a system made to their advantage, but if the system changes, abuse will be minimized. Further,
there are good men, like Pearl's father, Dr. Clay, and Robert Gilchrist,
who refuses to buy the Paine farm without Mrs. Paine's approval,
men who see the present injustices to women, and will work to end
them. Too, there are young men, like Peter Neelands, who come to
look beyond their own youthful arrogance to recognize the call of
common justice.

Men like these notwithstanding, McClung is aware that the actual
abuse of women in marriage profoundly challenges the validity of
that institution. So long as women suffer under grievously unjust
laws, actions such as Annie Gray's are not only tolerable, but laud-
able. In McClung's view, God makes marriages, not the government,
and women have no reason to put faith in either until they are given a
fair deal.

The character of McClung's feminism is not "doctrinaire," in the
sense that she takes a unilateral position "against" marriage, or "for
the home." Rather, human life is filled with possibility, depending
upon the characters of the persons involved and the contexts within
which they are allowed to act. Unjust social structures thwart good
characters and help to create bad ones; they therefore must be
changed. McClung's feminism is one which recognizes that women in
particular have suffered injustice, although there are ways in which
some women help to perpetuate women's plight (for example, the
gossiping women of Purple Springs, or the anti-suffrage busy-body
Mrs. Crocks). While men overall are either ignorant of or insensitive
to this injustice, there are good men who see the truth, who will put
aside male privilege and work for the benefit of all. In any case, this
sense of "fair play" can always be learned. As Pearl insists to herself
in a moment of frustration: "It is a good world . . . God made it, Christ
lived in it — and when He went away, He left His Spirit. It can't go
wrong and stay wrong. The only thing that is wrong with it is in
people's hearts, and hearts can be changed by the grace of God" (PS,
73). However, as we have seen, this change in perspective does not
occur miraculously, but through human action. The chapter closes
with an end to Pearl's despair: "A sudden feeling of haste came over

her — a new sense of responsibility — there were so many things to be done. She roused the fat pony from his pleasant dream, to a quicker gait, and drove home with the strange glamour on her soul" (PS, 73).

Once again, religious conviction is the source of social action. Too, social action has a religious character in itself, as is indicated in Pearl's reply to Mrs. Paine, who has begged her to keep up her campaign for suffrage instead of marrying and ending up like her, "tied down with a bunch of kids and . . . dulled with work and worry" (PS, 129). Pearl tells her not to despair: "Wherever two or three gather Pearl Watson will rise and make a few remarks unless some one forcibly restrains her" (PS, 129). (Pearl's feminist activism is here implicitly imbued with the spiritual authority of Matthew 18:20: "where two or three are gathered in my name, there I am in the midst of them.")

In the light of Mrs. Paine's predicament, and insistent concern that Pearl avoid the bondage of marriage from which she herself suffers, Pearl consciously reflects upon what she is coming to understand as her calling. She struggles with her sense of duty to work for other women, and tries "to harden her heart and fill it with ambitions, in which love and marriage had no place" (PS, 130). She knew from the day of her speech at the Chicken Hill School that she had the power to "move people to higher thinking and nobler action" (PS, 131). She asks herself:

> Could it be that she was being called of God to be a leader in a new campaign against injustice? Was it her part to speak for other women? . . . Was it possible that God was calling her to declare a message to the people, and could it be that it was for this reason her sweet dreams [i.e., marriage to Dr. Clay] had been so suddenly broken? (PS, 130-1)

Pearl exhibits the typical reluctance of the prophet in accepting what is understood as a call to preach against injustice, with all the personal sacrifice this entails. Should the reader miss the allusion, McClung underscored the significance of Pearl's decision: "The whole world seemed to be holding its breath expectantly, in a waiting, quivering silence. It was as if her name had been called; the curtain had rolled up and a great audience waited" (PS, 131). Pearl's reply importantly illustrates McClung's understanding of feminism, social activism, and God. Pearl's simple acceptance of prophetic responsibility would imply several things. First, that women do have to make a choice between marriage and a career,[31] with all that that implies about the deleterious effects of marital commitment upon personal autonomy. Second, having the power to do something is sufficient moral justification for the exercise of that power. Pearl knew she could move an audience with her speeches — although she expresses appropriate trepidation about the responsibility that implies. Finally, that God speaks unambiguously and directly to persons chosen to do God's will.

McClung rejects all these alternatives in Pearl's anguished reply: "I can't do it!... Don't ask me, Lord, I can't! I can't do it alone — but give me the desire of my heart, oh, Lord, and I will never tremble or turn back or be afraid. I will declare the truth before kings!" (PS, 131). This pained, and painful response should not be misunderstood as contending that women are nothing without marriage, wherein women's "true work" resides. Everything McClung has written to this point indicates her profound recognition of the real disabilities many women suffer as wives and mothers. Rather, McClung is illustrating a deeper point, and one with serious religious implications. That is, service of God, even in the cause of feminism, does not require the sacrifice of human love. Feminism does not demand the rejection of men, although their works may be suspect, and subject to evaluation. As McClung's political activism implies, God's work is done in this world, and is enhanced — in fact, constituted — by loving relation. Further, this relation is embodied, in the fullest sense of the word. As McClung states elsewhere (ITLT, 85-6), there are legitimate reasons why women refuse to marry, when the price is self-abnegation. However, this is a violation of God's true purpose in marriage, which is that of mutual, and equal, benefit. In a man-made world, God's plan for creation is thwarted in the service of male interests. In having Pearl insist upon her "heart's desire" to empower her, McClung is issuing a powerful challenge to religious and secular understanding alike, both of which relegate women who marry to a kind of "ladies auxiliary" confined to the sidelines, while others carry out the world's "real" work.

As her treatment of Annie Gray and Mrs. Paine amply illustrates, McClung did not consider marriage, *per se*, as unambiguously good, or even necessary, for women, given the reality of women's current situation. It is surprising, therefore, that her critical stance with regard to this institution has so little informed the popular assumption, expressed by Veronica Strong-Boag, that "McClung never really came to terms with women whose major function would not be motherhood."[32] A similar misconception exists with regard to McClung's understanding of class. Much has been made of McClung's alleged "agrarian bias," and what is taken to be a corresponding inability to "appraise industrial problems realistically."[33] While there may be some truth to the charge that McClung was not a sophisticated industrial economist — although it is unclear, given her other myriad accomplishments, why she should be required to be so — it is not the case that McClung was indifferent to, or ignorant of, the issue of class. McClung herself was the child of poor immigrant farmers, who moved west to make a better life for their children. Despite years of hard, honest labour, in the eyes of "polite society" the Mooneys were definitely of the lower classes. In *Purple Springs*, McClung has Pearl address this subject with such frequency and passion that McClung's view of the issue can neither be overlooked nor misunderstood.

When Pearl's romance with Dr. Clay is interrupted by his concern over his illness, the gossiping Mrs. Crocks suggests to Pearl that his sudden coolness is due to his political ambitions. She tells Pearl:

> Of course now he will settle down no doubt, everyone thinks he will anyway, and marry Miss Keith of Hampton — the Keiths have plenty of money, though I don't believe that counts as much with the doctor as family, and of course they have the blue blood too, and her father being the Senator will help. (PS, 66)

Pearl is shaken, and asks herself if this can really be the case, that Clay would reject her because her family was "socially impossible." Pearl's response is appropriate to quote at some length, as in it McClung's position on social class is brought to the fore.

First, Pearl experiences a flash of rage, prefigured in an earlier incident when she overheard her parents described as "common people":

> "'Common,' are they?" she said, with eyes that darted fire; "not half common enough — decent people that do their work and mind their own business — helpin' a friend in need and hurtin' no wan — it would be a better world if people like them were commoner! 'And the mother washed for ye,' did she, you dirty trollop? Well it was a mercy that some one washed for you, and it was a good clane washin' she did, I'll bet — and blamed little she got for it, too, while you lay in your bed with your dandruffy hair in a greasy boudoir cap, and had her climb the stairs with your breakfast. And you'd fault her for washin' for you — and cleanin' your house — you'd fault her for it!" (PS, 9-10)

The memory which triggers Pearl's anger after speaking to Mrs. Crocks is similar, in that a "miserable little shrimp" of a schoolmate had "flung it at her that her people were nothing and nobody — her mother a washer-woman and her father a section hand" (PS, 69). Amazingly, Pearlie's reaction, which was to wash the girl's face in the snow, was not chastised by the schoolteacher; rather, the whole incident was turned into a lesson that "all work is necessary and all honorable" (PS, 70). Further, the next day the teacher instituted a new grace, because "all that we enjoy in life comes to us from our fellow workers, and he was going to have a new grace, giving the thanks to where it belonged" (PS, 70).

However satisfying this was to Pearlie as a child, the adult Pearl is concerned:

> She began to wonder now if Mr. Donald had been right in his ideal-istic way of looking at life and labor. She had always thought so until this minute, and many a thrill of pride had she experienced in think-ing of her parents and their days of struggling. They had been and were, the real Empire-builders who subdued the soil and made it serve human needs, enduring hardships and hunger and cold and bitter discouragements, always with heroism and patience. The farm on which they now lived, had been abandoned, deserted, given up for a bad job, and her people had redeemed it, and were making it one of the best in the country! Every farm in the community was made more valuable because of their efforts. It had seemed to Pearl a real source of proper pride. . . . But since she had been away, she learned to her surprise that the world does not give its crowns to those who serve it best — but to those who can make the most people serve them. . . . It was quite a new thought to Pearl, and she pon-dered it deeply. The charge against her family — the slur which could be thrown on them was not that of dishonor, dishonesty, immorality or intemperance — none of these — but that they had worked at poorly paid, hard jobs, thereby giving evidence that they were not capable of getting easier ones. (PS, 71-2)

McClung wishes to make several points here. First, work in itself is honourable, whatever its form, and particularly so when bravely done in the face of adversity. Second, this perspective is not shared by those in power, who look down on those whose labours feed their ease. A system is thereby enforced wherein those who deserve it least gain the most in the eyes of the world, at the price of their characters and, McClung implies, perhaps even their souls:

> It was a mistaken way of looking at life, she thought; the world, as God made it, was a great, beautiful place, with enough of everything to go around. . . . What had happened was that some had taken more than their share, and that was why others had to go short, and the

> strange part of it all was that the hoggish ones were the exalted ones,
> to whom many bowed. . . . (PS, 72)

Class inequality, and the differences in social status which accrue
thereby, violate God's egalitarian intention for Creation. McClung is
enough of a liberal to want to reward individual initiative, insofar as
those who work hard are benefitted by their labours; what she is criti-
cizing here is a system of inherited privilege which sees the power to
abuse others as a sign of superiority. It is a perspective which informs
her feminism as well.

It is also instructive to note that it is Pearl's reflection on class
which serves to trigger her political activism. In her recognition that
God does not intend injustice, and that the world can be changed,
Pearl is overcome by "a new sense of power — an exaltation of the
spirit" of such visionary character that she likens the experience to
"Elisha's servant at Dothan when he saw the mountains were filled
up with the horses and chariots of the Lord!" (PS, 73). Pearl experiences a political epiphany, "a new sense of responsibility" for social
transformation. In having Pearl's next act be the speech at the Chicken
Hill School, McClung once again effectively reinforces the intercon-
nections between religion, feminism and social activism, using the
narrative to convey this understanding to her readers.

Purple Springs concludes with the reconciliation of the community,
and Pearl's obtaining her "heart's desire," Clay's love. At Pearl's insti-
gation, ex-Premier Graham is reunited with his grandson and daugh-
ter-in-law, and returns to Purple Springs with them, where he publicly repents of his prior behaviour. His gratitude to Pearl for helping
to bring about his change of heart is so great that he even claims,
"when she runs for the Legislature, I promise I will get out and campaign for her" (PS, 306). The community's minister follows suit, apol-
ogizing for their censorious behaviour towards "Mrs. Gray." In an
interesting turn, McClung has the minister attribute their poor attitudes to "our religion [which] has been too stuffy, too mouldy, too
damp, too narrow" (PS, 307). As an antidote to the pious self-righteousness which McClung implies is encouraged by the traditional
church, the community decides to espouse "outdoor religion,"[34]
wherein propriety becomes secondary, and the embodied joy of God's
creation is experienced in direct contact with the world. In reply to
Mrs. Watson's concern that too much happiness will make people
"lose their religion," Pearl assures her that there is no danger:

> Any neighborhood that could treat a stranger [i.e., ex-Premier Gra-
> ham] the way they did! But I do believe the sunshine and blue sky,
> the flowers and birds, and the getting together, along with the words
> of the sermons and the hymns they'll sing, will make them a lot more
> human. I never can think it would hurt God's feelings a bit to see
> children playing, and neighbors happy together on His day. (PS, 309)

McClung's conclusion demonstrates her conviction that, while individual repentance may be necessary, it is only in reconciliation with
the community that God's will is truly done.

An entry in one of McClung's diaries, dated 12 March 1900,
describes her involvement in a debate.[35] The topic: "Resolved that
women exert greater influence for good than men." McClung argued
for the negative, citing as reasons the "narrowness of woman's
sphere," which leads to self-centredness, narrow understanding, and
harsh judgements. As the women of Purple Springs demonstrate,
petty lives can create petty, though proper, women; as she argues in
the debate, a far preferable model for women would be the political
activist Frances Willard, President of the Women's Christian Temperance Union and originator of its "Do Everything" policy. *Purple
Springs* is a thoroughgoing embodiment of this perspective. Through
Pearl Watson, McClung shows that women can change the world —
but they must do so directly. Moral suasion is only effective in concert
with political activism; on its own, it merely allows women to be held
responsible for the continuance of the very conditions from which
they are trying to escape. George Steadman's argument that drunken-
ness was a direct result of inadequate moral teaching on the mother's
part was one heard often by McClung as she campaigned against the
liquor traffic and for woman suffrage.

In fact, it is the demonstrable impotence of moral suasion which
demands feminist activism. Pearl explains her involvement in the
Woman's Parliament to Premier Graham, where she gave the speech
which brought down his government and lost him his seat:

> Yes . . . it was me; and when the women of the city here, who had
> come to you and tried to break down your stubborn prejudices, tried
> to reason with you, but found it all in vain; when they told me that
> first night to think of some sad case that I had known of women who
> had suffered from the injustice of the law and men's prejudice, and
> strike without mercy, I thought of your daughter-in-law and all that
> she had suffered . . . and the rest was easy. There was no other way,
> sir; you would not listen; you would not move an inch — you had to
> be broken! (PS, 295-6)

Feminism is a response to male prejudice and male intractability; in an egalitarian world it would be unnecessary.

Through the narrative, McClung is able to convey her feminist perspective in an unthreatening, persuasive way, winning the reader over through Pearl's likeable character and humorous outlook. As the story unfolds, the reader learns what it is like to see the world through feminist eyes, long before any specific political arguments are made. This is a particularly effective technique for circumventing conventional prejudice; it is easier to reject an unfamiliar argument than a character with whom one has come to identify.

McClung is also provided with the opportunity to establish new role models for both men and women. Just as Pearl Watson and Annie Gray are "new women," loving, independent and courageous, so too Dr. Clay stands as an example to men, fair-minded, honest, and living proof that sympathy with women's cause in no way diminishes one's maleness. Indeed, self-assured men such as Clay can even stand rather dramatic role reversals, as when Pearl sweeps away his somewhat traditional concerns for her youth and his own ill health:

> It's all settled — I'll just marry you without being asked. The covenant between you and me was made before the foundations of the world. You're my man. I knew you the moment I saw you. So when I say, "I, Pearl, take you, Horace," it's not a new contract — it's just a ratification of the old. . . . You see dear, you just can't help it — it's settled. (PS, 321-2)

Pearl's marriage to Clay is apparently "made in Heaven" in a literal sense. It is appropriate to note, however, that even divine sanction requires personal initiative for its achievement. Once again, McClung reinforces the point that women must act to change their lives.

Purple Springs, and the Pearlie Watson trilogy in general, confirm this point, that it is through action — active, practical care — that God is made present in the world. And as the world's primary active caregivers, women stand in closest proximity to God, as both priests and prophets of true religion. It is important to realize, however, that while women in general perform this function, there are exceptions for both sexes. Mrs. Crocks and the neighbourhood ladies are no closer to God than self-centred men like George Steadman, while Dr. Clay and Mr. Watson are sterling examples of competent caregivers. It is not gender, but behaviour and perspective which are the crucial elements in McClung's religion. As her narrative confirms, fair and loving men do exist, and they stand side by side with women such as

Pearlie. No small part of her purpose in writing these stories was to convert others to this cause.

In sum, the Pearlie Watson trilogy is intentionally didactic. McClung sets up a tension between the world "as is" and the world as it could be, and through the actions of her characters shows her readers how that better world is to be achieved. The harsh realities of life are not avoided — Mrs. Paine's despair of marriage is real, and has been experienced by many women — but, McClung continually assures us, there is always the possibility of change for the better, if we only act to achieve it. As the title of the last chapter of *Purple Springs* proclaims, "There is Nothing Too Good To Be True."

In writing the Pearlie Watson trilogy, McClung's religious purpose and vision is made plain. Her "sermon in disguise" contains a blueprint for transformation, both personal and social, presented in such a manner as to inspire its achievement. While this is not strictly "realism" it can be extremely effective politically, as indeed was McClung's avowed intent, and any adequate assessment of her literature must be cognizant of that fact. As continued examination of McClung's central writings will show, while style and format vary in response to her context, her political — hence, religious — purpose remains constant. In further demonstration of this contention, it is to McClung's last novel we shall now turn.

Notes

1 From an article discussing *Sowing Seeds in Danny* and *The Second Chance* entitled "Coming Fiction," *Town Topics* (Winnipeg, Man.), 27 August 1910: McClung Papers, Add. MSS 10, n.v.

2 Book review of *Purple Springs, Boston Transcript*, 18 March 1922, 6: McClung Papers, Add. MSS 10, Vol. 28.

3 Mark McClung, "Portrait of My Mother," transcript of a speech given 27 September 1975 at the Nellie McClung Conference, University of Guelph, Guelph, Ontario, 14. One wonders how much McClung's style owed to the revivalist preachers of her youth.

4 Cook, *The Regenerators*, 150.

5 Letter to the "Vegreville Observer," dated 8 December 1915: McClung Papers.

6 The Canadian stereotype of "Our Nell" has often obscured the extent to which McClung was an important international figure in the struggle for women's rights. Her personal papers abound with telegrams from across the United States urgently requesting her presence prior to state votes on the suffrage question; one speaking-tour itinerary, dated 3 November-5 December 1916, has her in 23 cities, from New York to Galveston, Texas. Perhaps most revealing is a request from the Susan B. Anthony Memorial Library of California, dated 6 March 1944, requesting further information on McClung, in which it was noted, "She was not only active in Canada, but lectured quite extensively in the United States. I have accounts of her speak-

ing in Wisconsin, Minnesota and West Virginia and also touring in the Texas locality with three or four of our women. Think that was 1917. She was described as a very entertaining speaker." Letter to Hester MacKay, dated 6 March 1944, McClung Papers. Hitherto uninvestigated material such as this raises important questions regarding the international character of first-wave feminism. It further reflects upon the development of "national histories" which marginalize women's experience which cuts across the boundaries of their already established, male-defined categories.

7 *The Stream Runs Fast*, 77.

8 Margaret Ecker Francis' article "Nellie McClung," *Canadian Home Journal*, October 1947, notes that *Sowing Seeds in Danny* had enjoyed forty years of continuous publication to date. McClung Papers, Add. MSS 10, n.v.

9 Schieder, "She Came to the Rescue," Pt. II *passim*.

10 Desmond Pacey, "The Novel in Canada," *Canadian Novelists and the Novel*, ed. D. Daymond and L. Monkman (Ottawa: Borealis Press, 1981), 160-5.

11 Pacey, 162.

12 Pacey, 162, 163.

13 Joanne Hedenstrom, "Puzzled Patriarchs and Free Women: Patterns in the Canadian Novel," *Atlantis*, 4, no. 1 (Autumn 1978), 2-9.

14 Hedenstrom, 2.

15 Ibid.

16 Hedenstrom, 3.

17 In a chapter entitled, "Feminist Fiction and the Rejection of Realism," Patricia Stubbs suggests that feminist fiction is often intentionally inspirational, written with a specific social purpose. Speaking of one author, "George Egerton" (Chavelita Dunne), she notes, "It is this vision — of new possibilities, of different ways of living — which makes her work important. It provided alternative models on which women could focus and which could act as a measure of both their achievement and their potential." Patricia Stubbs, *Women and Fiction: Feminism and the Novel, 1880-1920* (London: Methuen, 1979), 113. McClung's own work reflects this concern for the creation of new models for women, while quite realistically portraying the actual conditions of many women's lives. What may be perceived by some as unrealistic is the way in which McClung portrays God working through women to empower them to challenge the conditions which oppress them.

18 McClung, *The Stream Runs Fast*, 70. Also given as a speech at a Canadian Authors' Convention as "The Writer's Creed."

19 "The Writer's Creed," rough draft, typewritten and amended, McClung Papers, Add MSS 10, Vol. 24, f. 3.

20 Ibid.

21 Frontispiece, *Sowing Seeds in Danny* (Toronto: Thomas Allen, 1965). Subsequent references will be given parenthetically in the text.

22 Working in the public sphere was for McClung no guarantee of "liberation." She has Camilla note in her diary: "Farewell, oh Soulless Corporation! A long, last, lingering farewell, for Camilla E. Rose, who used to sit upon the high stool and add figures for you at ten dollars a week, is far away making toast for two kindly souls, one of whom tells her she has brains and virtue and the other one opens his mouth to speak, and then pushes fifty cents at her instead" (SSD, 140).

23 Nellie McClung, *Purple Springs* (Toronto: Thomas Allen, 1921), 9-10, 70-2. Subsequent references will be given parenthetically in the text.

24 This condemnation of the respectable, but otherwise unloving person is a constant theme throughout McClung's work.

25 When "Bugsey" Watson confesses to Mary Barner that he "sassed" old Mrs. McGuire, she solemnly chastises him, forgives him, then sends him home happy, "shriven of his sin. . . . Better still, he went, like a man, and made his peace with Mrs. McGuire!" (SSD, 58-9).

26 Letter to McClung from her father-in-law, 1908, cited in Candace Savage, *Our Nell*, 62.

27 Nellie McClung, *The Second Chance* (Toronto: Briggs, 1910), 13. Subsequent references will be given parenthetically in the text.

28 For example, see Claudia Black, *It Will Never Happen to Me* (Denver: M.A.C. Printing and Publishing Division, 1981).

29 See Nellie McClung, "The Land of the Fair Deal," in *In Times Like These* (Toronto: University of Toronto Press, 1972), 95-105, for a fuller discussion of this topic. Subsequent references will be given parenthetically in the text.

30 Nellie McClung, "Winnipeg in 1889," *Clearing in the West* (Toronto: Thomas Allen, 1935), 247-56.

31 McClung refutes this position in her article, "Can a Woman Raise a Family and Have a Career?" *Maclean's Magazine*, 15 February 1928, 10, 73-5.

32 Veronica Strong-Boag, "Introduction," *In Times Like These*, xix. It is difficult to reconcile Strong-Boag's analysis with statements such as: "When women are free to marry or not as they will, and the financial burden of making a home is equally shared by husband and wife, the world will enter upon an era of happiness undreamed of now" (ITLT, 86).

33 Strong-Boag, "Introduction," *In Times Like These*, xv.

34 For a later treatment of this theme, see "Outdoor Religion," *Edmonton Bulletin*, 18 July 1936.

35 McClung Papers, Provincial Archives, Victoria, B.C.

II

The Importance of Discernment:
Painted Fires

In a chapter entitled "Our Present Discontents," Candace Savage casually dismisses *Painted Fires*, McClung's final and most complex novel, with the following comment: "What can one say about a book in which the villain is struck dead by lightning just in time to prevent the hard-pressed heroine from doing him in?"[1] Although *Painted Fires* is partially redeemed for Savage by the strength of its female characters, overall the "vicissitudes of the plot" render it ridiculous. As she remarks amusedly, "poor Helmi does have her difficulties — everything from unfair imprisonment to unemployment and single motherhood!"[2]

There is some justification in Savage's charge that McClung's plot is contrived. As earlier discussion has shown, this control of events and consequences is part of McClung's intention as author, and consonant with her understanding of literature as a vehicle for religious and moral edification. Considered within this framework, the question of whether or not the plot is totally "realistic" loses much of its significance. Indeed, it is precisely at the points where McClung seems to be stretching for resolution that the disguise falls away from the sermon, and McClung's moral is made plain.

In this chapter we shall be exploring the narrative of *Painted Fires* in relation to four foci, namely, class, ethnicity, gender and religion. As with all of McClung's work, these factors function as parts of an interrelated whole. However, in an interesting stylistic shift, McClung isolates at least two of these elements, namely, class and religion, for

---

Notes to Chapter II are on pages 81-4.

specific commentary. As a closer examination of the context of *Painted Fires* will reveal, McClung was beginning to find it necessary to "preach her text" in an increasingly explicit way. Indeed, the very structure of *Painted Fires*, with all its anachronisms and implausibilities, reinforces an underlying sense of frustration on McClung's part at getting her message across. Questions of style or strict historical accuracy were of little significance compared to having her readers receive the intended import of the text as a whole.

In *The Stream Runs Fast*, McClung describes what led her to write the story of Helmi Milander, the heroine of *Painted Fires*: "For years I had wanted to write an immigration story in the form of a novel. I wanted to portray the struggles of a young girl who found herself in Canada dependent upon her own resources with everything to learn, including the language" (SRF, 237). Her original intention had been to write about a Ukrainian girl, as there were so many books available about Ukrainian culture. However, she eventually decided upon a heroine of Finnish extraction, not the least reason being Finland's "advanced attitude to women." As she notes: "Finnish women received the vote and sat in Parliament long before any other women, and I wondered about this and what quality of mind had brought it about" (SRF, 237). The resulting character of Helmi Milander was so convincing that *Painted Fires* was translated into Finnish, published in Helsinki, and run in virtually all the Finnish papers in North America as a serial (SRF, 241).

There were other confirmations of the accuracy of McClung's portrayal. Her personal papers reveal a long and laudatory correspondence with her Finnish publisher, Dr. Eino Railo, who had two oil paintings by the Finnish artist Arthur Heickell sent to her as part of her royalties. Even the Finnish government acknowledged McClung's work, sending her a book about Finland, "with the best wishes of all Helmi's countrymen" (SRF, 241). McClung truly struck a chord, exercising her skill in character delineation, if not plot development. As she concludes: "I was particularly pleased to receive letters written in Finnish, telling me that although I had not a Finnish name, they felt sure that I must have Finnish blood to be able to enter into their spirit. Could any author ask for more than that?" (SRF, 241).

Painted Fires was favourably reviewed in the general community as well, remaining in print for at least 20 years after its original publication in 1925 (SRF, 241). One reviewer notes that critics in the United States and Canada "invariably agree" that *Painted Fires* was

McClung's best effort to date.[3] Another confirms: "It is good to have this first wholly imaginative novel from Mrs. McClung. There is no question that with the freer scope thus gained she has written a bigger book than 'Sowing Seeds in Danny' or 'Purple Springs.'"[4] While reviewers of the time were aware of the occasional anachronisms and implausibilities which negatively affect Savage's assessment, most do not consider these central.[5] Where strong opinion is evident, its origin seems less *Painted Fires'* intrinsic literary merit than the esteem in which McClung herself was held by the author of the piece. For example, consider the following two reviews. The first describes McClung in this manner:

> She is renowned not merely as a story-writer, but as a leader in political, social and religious activities over a wide area, and is highly esteemed and much in demand as one who can always be depended upon to say something worth saying in such a way as to command attention. Her platform addresses, besides being rhetorically effective, are never lacking in wise counsel and sound common sense, which she has skill enough to make palatable by a judicious admixture of choice wit and humor.[6]

After praising McClung for the accuracy of her portrayal of farm life, the reviewer concludes:

> When so much is said, it is hardly necessary to commend her literary efforts in book form. They are uniformly excellent, and depend for their appeal to thousands of readers perhaps less upon their artistic treatment of theme and plot, and their admirable character weaving, than upon her unique personality which colors agreeably most of what she has written.[7]

The second review, "Nellie McClung's Heroine Has Very Narrow Escape," describes an altogether different book and author. The dynamics of the plot are highlighted and disparaged, and McClung's underlying political perspective drawn into serious question. The reviewer exclaims:

> But as to Helmi? Surely her experiences cannot be typical of all immigrant girls? . . . Surely the heads of detention homes are not cruel and narrow-minded; surely Justices of the Peace do not conspire with designing men to betray ignorant immigrant girls; and surely the social service workers of the west are not hypocrites.[8]

"G.M.," then, accuses McClung of writing in a sensational manner to draw attention to herself, attributing her popularity to her skill at self-aggrandizement. Of *Painted Fires* it is said, "it is certain of a good sale;

for Mrs. McClung's books always get that, through advertising, personal and otherwise."[9] In the final analysis of this reviewer, McClung's work was both overblown and irrelevant. Damning with faint praise, "G.M." concludes: "Mrs. McClung writes well enough; but she does not seem to pick upon anything important or national, as one might expect from a Canadian writer who gets so much favorable advertising."[10] Given the importance of immigration to the emerging Canadian nation, one wonders what topics this reviewer would consider to be of national significance.

The range of opinion brought forth by these reviewers indicates in part a polarization of attitude triggered by McClung's political activism. For those who thought McClung's cause just, the story of Helmi was eminently believable, and well written in the bargain. To the "unconverted," McClung was a dealer in caricature, for what are implied to be the basest of motives. Neither, of course, is entirely accurate. There are exaggerations and inconsistencies in *Painted Fires*, just as there are moments of fine, crisp writing. While not all magistrates are struck down by lightning, as McClung's is, injustices did occur, and many immigrant girls were unfairly treated in an alien and unsympathetic court system, as McClung's good friend Magistrate Emily Murphy could well attest. Whatever the relative merits of each perspective, however, what is important to note is the disparity with which McClung's message is being received. The increasing didacticism of her later works was an attempt to convey her "sermon" to those who no longer instinctively shared her vision of the world, and were thereby impeded from absorbing the moral of her story directly through the narrative.

Too, the range of opinion expressed by past and current critics suggests that, in many ways, *Painted Fires* is McClung's most difficult book. It is certainly the most complicated. The plot is convoluted, tracing Helmi's adventures from her arrival in Minnesota to her ultimate destination of Eagle Mines, Alberta. In the interim, she moves to Winnipeg, where she works first as a hotel maid and then as a domestic servant. She is taken under the wing of one "Miss Abbie," who sends her to the C.G.I.T., but who unfortunately lives across the street from a beautiful but unscrupulous heroin addict, Eva St. John. Helmi is duped by St. John into going to buy her "medicine," and is captured in a raid. She is thereupon sent to a reformatory, the Girls' Friendly Home, where she languishes for almost a year. Fearing that Helmi will reveal her as the person who sent her for the drugs, St. John helps

Helmi escape, putting her on a train for Alberta. Helmi passes through Edmonton to Eagle Mines, where she gets work as a waitress, and eventually falls in love with and marries a young miner by the name of Jack Doran.

All is not well, however, for Jack has been lured by a business partner into prospecting for gold, and he leaves Helmi soon after their marriage in order to make their fortune, little suspecting that Helmi is pregnant. A series of betrayals (a lying magistrate, a thieving "friend," local gossip) convince Jack that Helmi has deserted him, and he goes off to war, angry and heartbroken. Meanwhile, Helmi has been struggling to survive as an unemployed single mother in Edmonton, where she nearly loses her child, Lili, to scarlet fever.

In a series of coincidences rendered only slightly less improbable by the fictional device of the war, Jack ends up in a prison camp with Arthur Warner, the former neighbour at Eagle Mines whom local gossip had identified as the man who had stolen Helmi's affections. Warner confirms Helmi's steadfast love for Jack, then joins in an escape attempt in which he sacrifices his own life so that Jack may return to her. In so doing, Jack passes through London, where he encounters his sister, Eva St. John, who has given up her drug addiction to nurse the wounded. Despite a variety of other complications, Jack Doran eventually returns to Eagle Mines, where he is reunited with his strong and stalwart wife. The book concludes with a tribute to Arthur Warner, whose self-sacrifice embodied the high moral character and sincerity of purpose which McClung saw post-war society as so sadly lacking.

As even this superficial retelling of the plot indicates, McClung has come a long way from the cosy community of Millford, Manitoba, which she portrays in the Pearlie Watson trilogy. Many of the more obvious differences are due to changes in McClung's own life. At the time of the writing of *Painted Fires*, McClung had been a published writer for almost 20 years. She had also established herself as a feminist and a politician, facts strongly reflected in *Painted Fires*' scathing portrayal of the treatment of women within social and legal institutions. The shift from homily to corporate critique evident in the last volume of the Pearlie Watson trilogy is here taken one step further. In *Purple Springs*, one can "change the government" by voting a newer, better party into office; in *Painted Fires*, the whole structure is corrupt. Simple reform had ceased to be a possibility, and, as we shall see, McClung is somewhat at a loss for a viable political alternative. It comes as no surprise that her heroine achieves peace and happiness only when she abandons the artifice of urban life and retreats to the frontier environment of the Alberta foothills. After her ultimately unsatisfying stint as an Alberta M.L.A., one suspects McClung would have longed to have done the same.

With this in mind, the "divine intervention" which Savage ridicules might be read not as an expression of naive supernatural faith, but as an angry and frustrated response on McClung's part to her increasing political ineffectiveness. Disabused by her experience as an elected official of the notion that rhetorical excellence is sufficient to change bureaucratic hearts, McClung resorted to fictional overkill to satisfy her outraged sense of justice. Nor are drunken magistrates the sole targets of McClung's wrath. Religious conservatives, "pillars of the community," society ladies, and the otherwise apolitical all come in for heavy-handed treatment. The gentle irony of McClung's earlier fiction has here given way to her impatience, and her considerable irritation with a self-indulgent post-war society which cared little for the "loving service freely given" which lay at the heart of her religion. If society could not longer be easily mobilized, however, it could still be lectured, and McClung uses the many trials and tribulations of young Helmi Milander to underscore her point. That these trials were so many suggests that McClung considered society's sins to be very grave indeed.

The underlying moral of *Painted Fires* is the necessity of distinguishing truth from illusion, and of developing the kind of character which allows one to do so. As McClung noted in *The Stream Runs Fast*, she took her title from a poem fragment: "We cannot draw from empty wells / Nor warm ourselves at painted fires" (SRF. 241). Helmi Milander's odyssey is McClung's fictional vehicle for pointing out what she considered to be the many "painted fires" of post-war society. Superficially pleasing and economically affluent, the 1920s rang hollow for McClung, who saw in the luxury of city life a loss of the moral proving ground of simple hard work. Even her politically progressive characters, such as Reverend Terry and Miss de Forrest, retain a kind of "old-fashioned" personal integrity reflective of McClung's central concern of active care. It is entirely in keeping with this agenda that McClung resurrects the central characters of 1912's *Black Creek Stopping House*, Maggie and "Da" Corbett, to rescue Helmi from Edmonton's evil "big city" ways.

Indeed, this tension between truth and illusion, between superficiality and integrity, is the source of many of the anachronisms noticed by McClung's reviewers. Although the story is set just prior to World War I, McClung describes the urban environment of the 1920s, complete with "flappers," middy dresses, bridge parties and the C.G.I.T. The worth of the cultural changes McClung depicts is illustrated through their effect, for good or ill, upon Helmi's life. McClung is thus able to alert her readers to the dangers inherent in their society, while pointing out which social developments do, in fact, have a solid foundation and are worth cultivating. Nor is this appeal purely theoretical. Once again, McClung uses her skill at making the reader identify with the character, so that the behaviours and perspectives which make Helmi's life a misery will be shunned. With this in mind, we now turn to the text itself, to explore the causes of Helmi's difficulties, and the means by which her happiness is finally achieved.

Painted Fires opens with 13-year-old Helmi's excited determination to join her vivacious Aunt Lili in North America, following her aunt's enthusiastic endorsement of the "new country." Employed as a waitress, Aunt Lili has been able to earn enough money to travel, to buy marvellous clothes, and to bring exotic gifts back to her family in Finland. Helmi is overwhelmed by such luxury, but is equally drawn by her aunt's description of women's lot in her new-found home:

> "You work too hard here," she said, "and you never play. We work in America, but we have good times, too. This country is all right for men, but what is there for women but raising children and work? . . . It is all just giving in, and giving up for women, until at last they give out. I wouldn't live here if you gave me the whole country. I couldn't stand it now I have seen what a good time American women have!"[11]

Helmi is entranced by the thought of such independence, having rejected early the traditional "womanly" values of self-abnegation and subordination to men. Indeed, "she had once been severely whipped by her father for saying that if her man ever dared strike her she would kill him with a bossa and throw his body into the flood" (PF, 144). After four long years of waiting, Aunt Lili finally sends Helmi her passage, and, at the age of 17, Helmi sets off to make her fortune in the new world.

To her dismay, upon her arrival she finds that her once independent aunt, "the Great Person who had brightened her childhood" (PF, 4), was married, overcome with illness, and fighting a losing battle for

her life. Aunt Lili begs Helmi to return to Finland, with a fervent plea
which underscores McClung's concerns:

> It's a good country, Helmi ... only men are so bad. ... Men just
> want their own pleasure. Mike was good to me while I could sport
> around and dance, and while I did not say a cross word to him for
> what he did to men when they got drunk. He takes their money,
> Helmi; I can't stand that. I threatened him I'd go and tell, and then
> he struck me with a chair. ... Helmi, men are queer and all for self.
> The trouble started when my little Helmi was on the way. I had her
> named for you. Men do not like kids, they're too much trouble. He
> was mad and cross at me because I was not smart and was some-
> times sick, and when little Helmi came she only lived a day, and he
> was glad. Then I hated him, Helmi — I hate him now, and that's bad.
> It's wicked to hate when one is going to die, but I cannot help it,
> Helmi, I wanted to warn you not to get mixed up with men — they
> break your heart. (PF, 5)

Once again, *Painted Fires* describes a situation significantly worse than
that described in *Purple Springs*. Mr. Paine was merely selfish, and abusive through neglect. He entertained the idea of running a saloon, but
was persuaded without much difficulty by Pearl Watson that he should
really try to reach a compromise with his wife on the matter. Mrs.
Paine's despair of marriage is thus not absolute, and men's "conversion" a very real possibility. In contrast, Aunt Lili's husband is a vile
man. He owns a bar, and steals from his patrons. He physically abuses
his wife, and is glad when his female first-born dies. He is also a lecher,
attempting to seduce Helmi on the very day of his wife's funeral.

Further onslaughts against Helmi's virtue are offset by the cook,
Miss Kenny, who bundles Helmi off to her sister in Winnipeg, then
coolly informs her employer of what she has done, and why. McClung's
observation is bitter, and to the point: "Mr. Laine could not reply to
Miss Kenny's accusations and threats of exposure by hitting her over
the head with a chair. Such crude methods of dealing with women can
only be safely used inside the hallowed precincts of matrimony" (PF, 7).
This stark assessment of male perfidy, and its sanction by societal institutions, is pronounced throughout *Painted Fires*. McClung is pointing
out that the protection of women through convention is a fiction, as
again and again men are willingly abusive of women while their fellows
look the other way. Indeed, as *Painted Fires* goes to great lengths to
show, the abuse of women is presupposed by societal convention, reinforced through pious rhetoric, and sustained from generation to generation by the inaction of otherwise "nice" people who are content to support the status quo without question.

A particular target for McClung's anger is the sexual double standard. As she illustrates in *In Times Like These*, many trusting immigrant girls were betrayed into a life of prostitution by being sexually used against their wills, and thereafter stigmatized as "fallen women" (ITLT, 77-8). McClung addresses this issue at length in *Painted Fires*, most thoroughly in relation to the Girls' Friendly Home to which Helmi is eventually sent. The Home's Board epitomizes all that McClung despised about well-meaning conventionality. It is composed primarily of ministers, whose religious sentiment is displayed in their propensity to give flowery speeches about "the lost lambs of the flock, pierced by many a thorn; the white lily, bruised and broken and crushed in the dust of life, the lost piece of silver which caused such a household upheaval" (PF, 71). Their numbers were augmented by others of McClung's foes, "that type of middle-aged portly gentlemen who are usually alluded to as 'solid business men'" (PF, 71). No women were allowed on the Board, although their efforts at fundraising were appreciated so long as they asked for no part in the Board's decision-making.[12]

McClung challenges the status quo in the person of the Matron, a younger, independent woman whose understanding of reform led her to run the Home on the merit system, and to try to rehabilitate her charges through a program of responsible active care. The Board balks at the removal of punitive measures, arguing that "there should be some differences in the way well-brought up girls and fallen girls are treated" (PF, 72-3). The Matron's reply seethes with McClung's anger:

> the Matron interrupted him to ask him to retract the word "fallen." She gave the Board members positive chills by the things she said about the double standard of morals which was made by men to shield men, and went on to tell them that many of her girls were innocent young things from the country who had come to work in the city to help the family at home, and who had fallen victims to men's lust and hypocrisy. The very men who had led them astray, fathers of families some of them, and regarded as respectable men in society, no doubt spoke of these girls as "fallen women." It was most embarrassing. She also hinted that there should be women on the Board and questioned the ability of men to quite understand the problems of rescue work. (PF, 73)

As McClung acidly concludes, "Any one can see from this what sort of woman the Matron was and why the Board dismissed her. The girls had loved her and had done their best to carry out all her wishes" (PF, 73).

The Matron's active care for her charges, and their growing self-respect, undermines a double standard which flourishes by "blaming the victim." Even those who might be considered technically "guilty" of wilful unconventional behaviour would be little served by further punishment, for they have already been stigmatized by polite society. A much more effective program of reform, in McClung's view, is one which empowers by turning energy to more positive tasks. Just as Martha Perkins learns to care for herself in *The Second Chance*, so, too, do the inmates of the Girls' Friendly Home. Under the Matron's care, "they had scrubbed and washed and polished the Home until it sparkled; they had planted a garden and made flower-beds; they had sewed and crocheted and embroidered; they had studied, sung, prayed and bravely tried to live a useful and happy life" (PF, 73). In McClung's moral universe, it is far more effective to teach people to want to be good than to punish them for being bad.

That most of the girls had had sexual experience is not an issue for McClung, even in the case of those who were not at all innocents in the matter. The character of Rose Lamb is a case in point. A long-time resident of the Home, Rose boldly instructs the girls on birth control, although Helmi virtuously refuses to listen (PF, 80). Apparently, Rose enjoys debauchery for its own sake. Risking severe punishment, she entertains the girls by mimicking the new warden; then "she cake-walked around the room, singing, 'I'm a little wrinkled prune, I am not stewed yet but will be soon'" (PF, 89). Despite her wildness, Rose is a thoroughly likeable character, a cheerful, good-hearted girl who straightforwardly admits what she wants, and has no illusions about it.[13] She knows how to survive in the world, and is willing to impart that knowledge to others. While she might not choose what McClung would consider the "highest" road, she is positively depicted as one who knows the difference between a "painted fire" and the real thing.

This quality of discernment is central to McClung's assessment of character in *Painted Fires*. The persons of whom she approves are those who see through convention and are willing to question the status quo, at best in the service of moral reform. Here, McClung's "good women" are not wives and mothers, but women like Miss Abbie, the spinster who takes Helmi in, or Miss Rodgers, the leader of the C.G.I.T., or, most of all, Miss de Forrest, the teacher at the Girls' Friendly Home who disrupts Eva St. John's elegant benefit Tea to challenge the women there to more concrete forms of social activism.

Using her powers of description to the full, McClung paints a rich and detailed picture of the Tea, vividly rendering its lush decadence:

> The ladies came in gaily colored throngs, high-heeled, silk-lined, per-
> fumed. Mrs. St. John, who stood inside the drawing-room door,
> received her guests, in an American Beauty cut velvet dress. The
> roses on the table, in a bowl sitting on a mirror and so doubling their
> number, were of the same shade. . . . Very slim young ladies served,
> scantily clad in dresses which were low in the neck, high in the hem,
> and niggardly in width. There were stuffed olives, rolled sandwiches
> tied with baby ribbon, tiny biscuits . . . blanched almonds, more
> sandwiches, pimiento filled, in harmony with the color scheme.
>   Then the ices! . . . Pink roses they were, set in the palest of green
> leaves. The guests were rapturous. Angel cake, white and of fairy
> lightness, and then white creams in disks, flavored with peppermint;
> rose disks, flavored with wintergreen, more almonds, more disks. . . .
> (PF, 99)

Into this atmosphere, virtually opiated with excess, strides Miss de
Forrest, "large deep-chested, deep voiced, dominant. When she spoke,
her voice boomed" (PF, 100). The whole room is soon shocked to
attention, as she castigates the women present for falling prey to a
"dull, selfish age" (PF, 100). In an attempt to spark their concern, she
recounts Helmi's plight, concluding her lecture with the rather sarcas-
tic observation: "Some of you women should be on the Board and try
to get some sense into its wooden head. I now know the origin of the
word 'Board.' That's how to help wayward girls, though I admit it's a
lot more fun to go to teas and eat olives on their behalf" (PF, 100-1). It
is no surprise to the reader that Miss de Forrest, too, has been
dismissed by the Board, reflecting perhaps the kind of marginaliza-
tion that reformers like McClung were beginning to experience in the
1920s. Opposition to the "cause" is here depicted by McClung not as
ignorance, as in the Pearlie Watson trilogy or even in *In Times Like
These*, but as a consequence of lazy, self-satisfied self-indulgence, a triumph of individual excess over a sense of social responsibility.

Interestingly, virtually none of McClung's positive characters in
Painted Fires is married. Maggie Corbett from *Black Creek Stopping
House* is an exception, a remembrance of an earlier time. Even Helmi
is only with her husband a few weeks before he goes off prospecting
for gold, leaving her to fend for herself. This focus on women alone
continues in McClung's short stories and essays. While it is doubtful
that McClung lost her faith in marriage per se, it is possible that the
rapidly changing social realities sparked by the war left her without
an adequate model from which to work.

Part of the difficulty in depicting married life positively may be
due to what appears to be McClung's increasing disgruntlement with

the male character. *Painted Fires* is replete with villains, from the lecherous "Uncle Mike" to Tom Keith, the seducing and betraying gold prospector, to the evil Magistrate who fails to record Jack and Helmi's marriage to save Jack, an Anglo-Saxon boy, from being tied down to an immigrant girl. Jack himself is a problem, for while he does not actively abuse women, he is immature, and is easily influenced by town gossip and the overblown army recruiter, Col. Blackwell, into thinking that his wife betrayed him. Jack eventually returns to Helmi, but McClung is seemingly beyond trying to reform men through a good woman's influence. It takes the war, and the death of his new-found friend Arthur Warner, to bring Jack to a recognition of the truth. Masculine "drinking hall" camaraderie is here revealed as yet another "painted fire."

Good men do appear in *Painted Fires*, but they are usually single, and likely to remain so. Arthur Warner is a recluse, who leaves his cabin at Eagle Mines only when he discovers England is at war. Old "Sim," the crippled railroad man who also befriends Helmi, is a likewise sympathetic character, although McClung uses him to preach an alternate message to Warner's patriotism:

> Everyone in the war loses — no one wins — everyone blames someone else. No one knows for sure what it is about, but just while it is on no one cares. To these fightin' men any war is better than no war. Then it gets done when every one is dead or lame or blind or tired enough to talk sense, and the world tries to pay the debts, builds up the burnt cities, gets the sick fellows well, buys crutches for the one-legged men and glass eyes for the blind and provides for the widows and orphants! (PF, 179)[14]

That McClung could portray two characters with such different positions on the war with equal sympathy suggests that her own position had been rendered more ambiguous through her personal experience of it. Patriotism had its place, when informed by noble sentiment rather than jingoism, as did a profound scepticism with regard to patriotic rhetoric. For McClung, the only truly unacceptable stance was to live as if the war had not happened, and to forget the hard-won lessons of its moral proving ground. McClung's anachronistic depictions in *Painted Fires* are the fictional means by which she is able to remind those of a "dull, selfish age" of the very real sacrifices which had been made for them, in the hope of converting them to the path of social responsibility.

The "Jazz Age" at its worst is epitomized by McClung in the character of Eva St. John, a lovely but thoroughly spoiled, indolent wife. Eva is a thrill-seeker, a woman who has learned to love the taste of luxury and is willing to sacrifice anything, and anyone, in the service of her self-indulgence. Her brother Jack describes her to Helmi somewhat more charitably:

> She is so good to look at, and she is so frankly selfish. . . . She loves beauty more than anything on earth, and would sacrifice principle for it. Now she may love this husband of hers — I hope she does — but I know this that if he had been poor she would not have looked at him. (PF, 164)[15]

It is appreciation for Helmi's beauty, rather than any concern for another's welfare, which leads Eva St. John to offer to provide the young girl with English lessons. In contrast to Miss Moore's pious homilies, such as "honesty is the best policy," however, Eva's lessons are little more than instructions in decadence. A typical example of Eva's vocabulary follows:

> The lady is beautiful.
> She has an elegant coat.
> Will you go for a drive?
> Have a chocolate?
> I adore chocolates. (PF, 48)

Unknown to her physician husband, Eva has become a heroin addict, a diversion McClung seems to consider only slightly more serious than the endless round of bridge parties in which Eva and other 1920s "sophisticates" indulged.[16] It is Eva who sends the unwitting Helmi to pick up her "medicine," abandoning her when she is caught in a drug raid in order to protect her own reputation. Her superficiality is such that when her soldier brother Jack is preparing to leave for the Front, Eva attempts to turn his leaving into a party event for her friends, an act which kindles her husband's anger so deeply that he finally sees her for the "painted fire" she is.

McClung draws a striking contrast between Eva St. John and Dr. St. John's mother to illustrate her point. Noting that his wife held bridge parties on the same night his mother used to go to prayer meetings, Dr. St. John reflects:

> His mother had spent years on a treadmill, her days laid out for her in regular lines. Work stared at her from morning till night, and she did it, and held her head above it all. She was always sweet-tem-

> pered, interesting, sympathetic. Eva having nothing to do, did noth-
> ing, and doing nothing, degenerated, grew shallow, selfish, cross-
> grained and hard. (PF, 273-4)

Nor, as McClung takes pains to point out, is the doctor's sexual attraction for his wife a sufficient reason to stay with her.[17] In the long run
it, too, is a "painted fire," and no substitute for the warmth of the
hearth which St. John's mother represents.

Eva St. John, mistress of illusion, is sharply brought down by
McClung's hand. A lover of beauty all her life, so much so that she
easily gave up heroin once she saw the "pasty-faced, dead-eyed,
mouth agape" visage of a long-term addict (PF, 310), the lovely Eva
St. John is hideously disfigured during a London air raid. McClung
allows her an appropriate repentance:

> It's all right, Jack . . . better women than I have been blown to pieces.
> Maybe God is giving me a few more years to atone for what I have
> done. . . . I will go to France. Maybe I can take the place of some bet-
> ter and happier woman, and when the shell comes marked for her, it
> will take me instead. And Jack . . . you will tell Helmi all of this and
> ask her to think as kindly of me as she can. She loved me once with
> all a young girl's adoration. (PF, 309-10)

In McClung's new, harsher moral economy, however, repentance is
not enough to make things right, and restitution is not always possible. She underscores her point with Jack's concluding reflection
upon his sister's confession:

> He could not reproach her — there was no need, but his own heart
> was aching with the sorrow of it all. Sin and sorrow — the age-old
> partnership — sin and sorrow! By one man sin came into the world,
> and death by sin; but the one who sins is not always the one who
> suffers. (PF, 310)

The sin is further compounded, in McClung's view, in that it is
another woman who brings Helmi so much grief. In her selfish disregard for others, the heroin-addicted Eva St. John is no better than the
myriad male drinkers who populate McClung's fiction. The bitterness
of this insight, i.e., that women can be as irresponsible as men if given
the chance, pervades the novel, and may help to explain why this is
McClung's last. The very human — albeit socially irresponsible —
reaction of many women to the increased affluence and freedom of
the 1920s undercut McClung's central fictional dynamic, the triumph
of good, strong, political womanhood over male-created situations of
evil. With external goals such as suffrage having been won, McClung

has nothing to fall back upon to explain women's failure to mobilize to transform the world. It makes sense, then, that the heroine of *Painted Fires*, Helmi Milander, is an immigrant pioneer who must make her way in Canada "from scratch." This is a story McClung understood and told well. If the villains she encounters are more evil, and the betrayals she experiences more profound than anything depicted in McClung's earlier fiction, it is perhaps that in the belief in the simple, educable perfectibility of the human spirit, McClung came to recognize her own "painted fire."

As noted above, political realities also became more complex for McClung in the 1920s. Although she seems less sure about what political perspective ought to be adopted (in contrast to her support of the Liberal Party in *Purple Springs*, for example), she is alert to which aspects of the post-war political ferment ought to be rejected. A case in point is the issue of class and class warfare, to which she devotes chapter 2 of *Painted Fires*. The theme is not developed further in the text, save to the extent to which Helmi, as a foreign-born, apparently single mother, suffers economic hardship and prejudice in her employment as a domestic labourer. In chapter 2, however, McClung is concerned to show the folly of the kind of soap-box street-corner activism which creates, rather than resolves, social unrest. She does so through the person of Anna Milander, a Finnish waitress in Winnipeg's Yale Hotel, who becomes caught up in "the Union" during her two years in Canada.[18]

Anna spouts "Union" rhetoric constantly, remarking upon Helmi's imminent arrival: "she's nothing to me — merely another wage slave coming to take a job. . . . We're opposed to immigration . . . the Government dumps in people here, just to keep wages down. It's the capitalists again. You haven't sense enough to see it" (PF, 10). Her attitude is challenged by Maggie Kenny, the Irish cook, who serves to illustrate McClung's objections to the ideology of class warfare. She responds to Anna with a shocked, "My God . . . is that the brotherhood you learn at your meetin's?" She goes on: "For all the brazen, selfish lumps I ever saw it's you, Anna. When you came here two years ago all you could say was 'Yiss.' Who showed you how to make a bed and comb your hair and garter up your stockings? . . . Did you never hear of the Golden Rule, do as you would be done by?" (PF, 10). Anna's retort includes a blanket condemnation of the Government and the "capitalists," scorn for the "soothing sirup" of religion, and a denunciation of workers who are too weak to "throw off their chains" and wrest the world from the owning class (PF, 10-11). Later, she manages to get arrested for throwing a rock at a policeman, an event which pleases her mightily. McClung thinks of it somewhat differently, as her tone reveals:

> She had struck a blow in Freedom's cause. It was all rather vague in Anna's mind. She was rather favorably disposed to policemen as a class, but having joined the Union she was determined to become "class conscious." Policemen were enemies; so were employers; everyone was an enemy except members of the Union. So Anna having a clear program in her mind, sat on her narrow bed in her warm cell, well content. Her picture would be in the paper; she would be praised by the speakers. She had risen from the dull, gray, dusty depths of obscurity. . . . (PF, 14-15)

McClung plainly had little sympathy for an organized workers' revolt. Anna's parroting of slogans, and her thirst for notoriety, make it obvious that what is at stake here for McClung is not a genuine, thought-out political position but the seduction of the gullible by the promise of something for nothing. Like Eva St. John, Anna Milander wanted gain without effort, and like Eva St. John she found her own opiate, here, the rhetoric of a workers' revolution. McClung describes her in her jail cell:

> Anna dreamed pleasantly of the golden age of which the street corner leaders told, when there would be leisure and luxuries for the workers and confusion for the capitalists; when railways and streetcars and theaters and all the sources of pleasure would be free as air, and tiresome, disagreeable drudgery would be gone forever. . . . So Anna sat on her narrow bed, a prisoner before the law, but not cast down or desolate. She, too, had her own little painted fire, and she had not yet found out that there was no heat in it. (PF, 15-16)

In her rejection of Anna Milander's brand of socialism, it was not that McClung was opposed to workers' rights, or was unaware of the severe economic hardship caused by unrestrained, unlegislated capitalism. Her own actions, such as dragging Sir Rodmond Roblin into the sweatshops of Winnipeg's garment district, are ample proof of her commitment to the betterment of the worker's lot. McClung's objections rested upon what she perceived to be the polarized, conflictual mode of militant unionism, its threat of violent social revolution, and its uncompromising "us against them" attitude. In general, McClung was always willing to offer the possibility of change, the "second chance" which figures so prominently in all her work. The ideology of class warfare denies the possibility of this sort of conciliation, and cooperation toward the achievement of a common goal,[19] and as such was anathema to McClung's political outlook.

It is important to note in this context that McClung was opposed to a certain form of socialist activism, but not to socialism per se. Her position is more nuanced than the commonly held stereotype of her "bourgeois liberalism" admits at present, and deserves to be spelled out at some length.

As has become abundantly clear in this examination of her writing, Nellie McClung was an ardent supporter of properly rewarded hard work. The sustained effort of working toward a realisable goal provided, in her view, a moral proving ground which created character and helped build the community. She had little patience for sweeping theory, advocating instead that people "get the thing done" through legislation and cooperative action. This being said, McClung recognized that external constraints such as laws only serve to curb the worst abuses of power. In an apparently unpublished essay on the Winnipeg General Strike she notes that "it has been by strikes that the working man has gained most of the privileges he enjoys today. But for strikes he might still be working twelve hours a day."[20] Too, she criticizes the "old system whereby a firm of textile manufacturers may make 72% on their capital . . . and quite frankly rejoice over their handsome profits and disclaim all responsibility for the high price of clothing. . . ."[21] Throughout this piece, it is evident that McClung understood the workers' dilemma, and sympathized with their sense of desperation in the face of rising costs. At the same time, she rejected both the radical's call for a workers' revolution, and the moderate's total reliance on governmental legislation. Neither would yield lasting change, in McClung's view, without a significant change in people's attitudes. As she says: "Legislation is not enough — it is not new laws we need, it is a new spirit in our people — it is sometimes called a change of heart. No law or set of laws can bring peace to a world of grabbers."[22] In being seduced by the promise of a better world without effort, Anna Milander of *Painted Fires* reveals herself as one of the "grabbers," and she is properly punished by McClung by being left to languish in her jail cell, surrounded by her illusions.[23]

McClung's failure to resolve the political question in *Painted Fires* stands in marked contrast to the drama of judgement and reconciliation enacted with Premier Graham in *Purple Springs*. Her intervening experience as a Member of the Legislative Assembly for Edmonton had substantially challenged her optimism regarding the ease of government-led social transformation, once the "right" people were in power. Although she felt certain enough of which political directions were not desirable, her loss of political naiveté seems to have undercut her ability to preach her political text in the affirmative. In fictional terms, it is entirely in keeping with this view that the misguided radical Anna Milander is abandoned by chapter 3, and that Helmi, the heroine of the tale, while as determined, hard-working and intelligent as Pearlie Watson ever was, is nevertheless totally apolitical.

McClung devotes somewhat more attention to the question of ethnicity in *Painted Fires*, although less than might reasonably be expected, given that the tale centres upon the experiences of an immigrant girl in Canada. In some respects, this is an omission with positive import. The stereotyping of racial and ethnic groups was commonplace in the face of the waves of immigration to Canada in the early part of this century, and was, in the main, pejorative. J.S. Woodsworth's *Strangers within Our Gates* amply illustrates many of the presuppositions of otherwise well-meaning, socially conscious Canadians to cultures other than their own. For example, J.W. Sparling's Introduction to the text warns:

> *there is a danger and it is national!* Either we must educate and elevate the incoming multitudes or they will drag us and our children down to a lower level. We must see to it that the civilization and ideals of Southeastern Europe are not transplanted to and perpetuated on our virgin soil.[24]

Sparling's prejudicial attitude is ameliorated by the text proper, but even so, it is clear that only northern Europeans are considered truly worthy and acceptable new members of the Canadian family. While no direct racial slurs are made, the writer's perspective is reflected in his tone, which is alternately laudatory or patronizing. (For example, Icelanders are "sober, industrious and thrifty"; Swedes are "naturally religious." "The Italian," on the other hand, "is gay, light-hearted, and, if his fur is not stroked the wrong way, inoffensive as a child."[25])

In the face of such biases, McClung's treatment of the Finnish "national character" is mild indeed and, as we have seen above, met with the approval of the Finns themselves. Where McClung does note ethnic or racial differences, she does so for positive comment, rather than to patronize or condemn. As her eloquent rhetoric in *In Times Like These* emphasizes, McClung felt deeply the injustice meted out to new immigrants because of the prejudice and power of Canada's earlier settlers. She castigates her audience severely, making her own position plain:

> in our blind egotism we class our foreign people as ignorant people, if they do not know our ways and our language. They may know many other languages, but if they have not yet mastered ours they are poor, ignorant foreigners. We Anglo-Saxon people have a decided sense of our own superiority, and we feel sure that our skin is exactly the right color, and we people from Huron and Bruce feel sure that we were born in the right place, too. (ITLT, 53)

Another way McClung challenged prejudicial attitudes was by positively depicting members of minority groups in her fiction. For example, when Helmi arrives at Maggie Corbett's North Star Rooming House in Edmonton, apparently unmarried and about to give birth, it is Maggie's Jewish neighbour, Mrs. Kalinski, who helps with the birth and generously donates blankets and other necessities for the infant, even though she is going to give birth soon herself. Later, when Helmi is searching for work, it is she who points out the aid provided by the Hebrew Association of Women, causing Maggie Corbett to exclaim, "Ain't the Jews wonderful to think of things?" (PF, 263). While modern readers might be uncomfortable with Mrs. Kalinski's tendency to talk about her husband's shrewdness as a merchant,[26] or with the pervasive assumption of several characters that it is a disgrace for a white girl to work at a "Chink's," when taken in the context of the literature of the time, McClung's characterizations are benign, if not always explicitly laudatory. Too, it is important to consider not only what her characters say, but what her characters do. Mrs. Kalinksi may talk about bargains, but her actions are generous and neighbourly. Likewise, while McClung accurately depicts the contemporary prejudice against the Chinese, she shows Helmi's boss, Sam Lee, to be a kind and fair employer, and eventually a good husband to Rose Lamb.

In the main, McClung's treatment of the ethnicity question is typically "liberal," insofar as she is concerned with individual effort and character rather than any group's alleged characteristics. Her "Land of the Fair Deal" differed significantly from the Canada J.S. Woodsworth envisioned when he wrote that the ideals of Canadian well-being must never be lost sight of, and to that end, "[e]ssentially non-assimilable elements are clearly detrimental to our highest national development, and hence should be vigorously excluded."[27] Too, McClung was more concerned with ethnic *women* than with ethnicity per se. She saw within women's common experience a link between cultures, and fictionally depicted female solidarity in the face of a common male oppressor.

McClung illustrates her view in a small scene which takes place after Helmi's baby daughter is born. A doctor has come to check them and, upon finding out that Helmi is foreign born, notes the frequency with which Canadian men trick immigrant girls into false marriages, and remarks to Mrs. Corbett, "It is disgusting how easy these girls are!" (PF, 220). He goes on to castigate women's organizations for failing to keep immigrant girls from unwed pregnancy, claiming his "utmost sympathy for these unfortunate girls" (PF, 221). Maggie Corbett's reply is gentle, but incisive:

> I see what you mean, Doctor, and I know it's a grand thing to always be able to lay all the blame on the women. You see the Lord lets her bear all the pain, and we see to it that she gets all the shame; so why not let the rest of the women bear the blame—there's no use spreadin' it any farther. (PF, 221)

She further advises:

> "Get busy on the men. . . . Leave the women to women—it's women who look after women, anyway."
> The doctor interposed: "Now, Mrs. Corbett, I cannot agree with you there. You must have noticed that women are very hard on women." He was pulling on his gloves now, rubbing out the wrinkles carefully.
> "No, I haven't noticed it, but I've heard it—I've heard a lot of men say it." (PF, 221)

Immigrant girls may suffer more acutely than the native born because of their ignorance of Canadian customs and the English language, but both are equally the potential victims of "men's lust and hypocrisy." In the face of this common foe, whatever ethnic differences existed between women are minimal, and easily overcome.

One further anecdote must be cited in support of this point, illustrating as it does McClung's delightful and subtle wit. The scene takes place at a meeting of the C.G.I.T., where the girls are discussing Miss Rodgers' suggestion that they invite "a girl of foreign birth" to a supper meeting. Some of the participants are in favour, but others are concerned about the potential violence of their proposed guest:[28]

> Dorothy Moss was afraid. "The foreigners quarrel so among themselves," she said, "and they're so fierce. Our washerwoman's sister killed her man up at Gimli, and when she was in jail at Stony Moun-

tain my mother went to see her and asked her if she wasn't sorry, and she said she was, and mother thought that was a good sign, and maybe she was going to repent and find pardon but she went right on and said she was sorry she had not killed him long ago. Mother did not know what to say. But Mrs. Karaski said she believed in God all right, if that's what mother wanted to know. 'God was all right, you bet,' she said, and she was thankful, too. God had been good to her and let her find the ax just when she was getting the worst of it. Mother came home all shaken up." (PF, 39)

One can sympathize with Mrs. Moss' confusion, but it is evident where McClung's sympathies lie!

McClung concludes the episode by having Miss Rodgers instruct the girls in the lesson McClung herself wished to teach her readers: "Remember . . . foreign girls are just like us. They feel, see, are hurt or are pleased, just like us. It just happened that they were born in another country" (PF, 40). Nor does everyone want to have been "born British," given the option. McClung identifies this view as complacent and insensitive to the realities of others' lives. In fact, as Miss Rodgers points out: "every one likes her own country best. Here I am, an American, and I like my own country best. But we are making a new country here in Canada, and we will love it best of all because we are making it" (PF, 40).[29] This united effort towards a common goal has no room for petty prejudice and "one-upmanship" based on one's country of origin. Ethnicity is an accident of birth and, as such, is worthy of neither praise nor blame. What is important for McClung is one's willingness to cooperate in the task of "making paths and laying foundations" in the creation of Canada's future (PF, 40).

The final narrative cornerstone of *Painted Fires* to be considered is religion. As with her treatment of class, ethnicity and gender, McClung's meditations upon religion are not uniformly well integrated into the flow of her text. It appears that she is beginning to find herself in an unfamiliar world, one which does not necessarily reflect progress towards the single vision her earlier novels espoused. The cohesive organic order of turn-of-the-century Millford has been lost, and with it much of McClung's easy confidence in human perfectibility. The religious world of *Painted Fires* reflects this shift, manifest in a sharp dichotomy between those who would uphold a Law of Love and those who advocate a Rule of Fear. At least part of McClung's task is to expose the latter as a "painted fire" of the most serious sort, and she does so by exploring the experiences and circumstances which shape Helmi's developing religious understanding, affecting her life for good or ill.

As mentioned above, the Pearlie Watson trilogy tends to depict a rather conventional theological worldview, wherein God acts directly in human life, through nature (e.g., the hailstorm in *The Second Chance*) and through the transformation of the human heart. Even McClung's treatment of women as priests and prophets of God does not present a serious deviation from the mainline Victorian assumption that religion was part of "woman's proper sphere." At this point, McClung's integrated religious world is still intact. By *Painted Fires*, however, divisions have become discernable, and possibly irreparable. The Social Gospel vision of building God's Kingdom on Earth had been seriously undermined by intra-denominational political conflict. Radicals such as J.S. Woodsworth were leaving, or being encouraged to leave the church. The war had split many Christians on the question of pacifism, and the social upheavals of the late 'teens such as the Bolshevik revolution had added to a general feeling that the old order had passed. While all these elements are not directly traceable in McClung's work, it is certainly true that the world of *Painted Fires* is far more divisive and conflictual than any other in her fiction. The reader senses that a crisis point has been reached, and that hard and specific decisions will have to be made. While initially McClung employs her old technique of humour to influence the choice, eventually, as with the magistrate, she resorts to fictional overkill in an effort to reestablish the moral order.

In the first instance, however, McClung paints one of the funniest characters in all of her fiction, a crusty old church warden named Mr. Sims. Sims is a perfect representative of those "pillars of the church" who are faithful attenders and good at heart, but for whom ongoing theological reflection is an alien experience. Critical of change on principle, Sims' idea of a good church is one where the pomp and ceremony of social hierarchy is made visible and celebrated. His world is a secure one, where everyone has a place and knows it, and God's intention for humanity is expressed through a dedicated maintenance of the status quo. Gently, McClung allows Sims to poke fun at himself. She sets the stage by having him grumble about cleaning up after another of those "new-fangled" religious projects, the C.G.I.T.:

> "There's no respect for the sacred edifice anymore. I can't get used to rioting and mirth in God's house, an the cleanin' up after it is fearful; and my word! this swimmin' pool that he's goin' to put in is a wicked thing to me. The house of God is for the cleansin' of hearts. 'Cleanse your hearts and not your garments,' says Job. 'Whited sepulchres, makin' clean the outside of the cup and platter while the

inside is full of ravenous wolves' — ain't it the livin' truth? But no one listens to me now — my ways is out of date. It's all youth, youth, and I wouldn't mind so much if he brought in only our own young people. I buried their fathers and mothers, some of them, and christened them, but this man brings in every tag end he can find — odds and ends — odds and ends — what does he care? The church had a name before he came. More cars and better cars stopped at our curb than at any church in town. What now? Baby carriages, mothers' meetings, bean feeds. I find broken garters, table napkins rolled into wads, sandals, comforts, babys' [*sic*] bottles. 'Servin' the neighborhood,' he says. It's grand to be a sinner these days — there's so much done for them — and even at that he don't believe in hell! I asked him, and what did he say? Says he, 'I wouldn't like to take the responsibility of hell, Mr. Sims.' He says. 'Take hell away from our religion,' says I, 'and where are we?' says I, and he went out laughin' like an overgrown schoolboy — laughin' because he could not answer me.

"Religion ain't what it used to be. There's no way of warnin' the wicked now. Where's the good old hymns we used to sing — 'We'll hear the wicked wailin', wailin', wailin', we'll hear the wicked wailin' in that great day!' That was a grand hymn to bring conviction to a stony heart and to such as be of perverse countenance. Now it's all 'Love o' God, Love o' God, Jesus the Friend.' Soft I call it, and too easy.

"These young ones that come here — tell me they are Christians? 'Did you ever repent' I says. 'Lots of times,' says they. Is that religion?" (PF, 36)

Sims' fractured theological recollections, and his palpable longing for a world he used to understand enjoin the reader's sense of sympathy for him personally, however much his view of religion is obviously to be rejected. For McClung, it is precisely in the direction of "bean feeds" and "Jesus the Friend" that the church ought to travel, as she implies at the end of *Purple Springs* with the Sunday service and picnic, and as she develops in *Painted Fires* through the character of Reverend Terry.

The Reverend Terry, whose social conscience proved so vexing to Mr. Sims, is a strong, energetic young fellow with "the physique of a light-weight boxing champion" (PF, 59). He is the epitome of a good man, reminiscent of Dr. Clay of the Pearlie Watson trilogy, innately fair and willing to fight for justice. Despite his minimal acquaintance with Helmi, he defends her in court after she is arrested for possession of heroin. Further, he does so out of a sense of theological conviction (PF, 60). Reverend Terry embodies, then, all the qualities of the church that McClung wishes to recommend to her readers — socially active, theologically open, and supportive of women in the service of justice. His treatment of Sims is also indicative — gentle, indulgent, he humorously accepts his warden's foibles and ignores his theological meanderings.

Other persons, however, are not so benign. Mr. Sims is treated affectionately because he is harmless. His theological conservatism and old-fashioned outlook are curiosities which befit him as an eccentric old man. McClung's concern arises when persons of like perspective actually have jurisdiction over the lives of others. A theology of judgement rather than mercy is a dangerous temptation to fallible human beings, McClung seems to be saying, and can be extremely destructive if not expressed in an overall context of mercy. Further, those espousing this traditional perspective tend to be particularly harmful to women, who labour under the yoke of longstanding church-supported prejudice and condemnation.[30] For all her confidence in Reverend Terry and his fellows, McClung is distressed that their "wave of the future" will be overcome by the undertow of the past, fictionally depicted here as Mr. and Mrs. Wymuth, the new directors of the Girls' Friendly Home. Their unsavoury behaviour and sheer unpleasantness leave the reader with no doubt that their world is at best a "painted fire" — and at worst a literal hell for those over whom they have authority.

McClung describes them thus:

> The Wymuths were of exactly the same type, — black-eyed, pale, anaemic, with lusterless thin black hair, through which a bloodless scalp showed blotchily; false teeth — no, not false — every one could see what they were — artificial, rather — so white they were almost blue. They believed in hell and spoke of the "world" in a tone which implied both horror and contempt. They knew that Christ was coming soon to take His own out of the world, leaving the other odd millions to their well-merited punishment. (PF, 74)

Mrs. Wymuth is an especially repulsive character. Subservient to her husband in public (PF, 74), manipulative and cruel in private, she rules her petty kingdom through lies and fear. When one of the girls is in the agonies of childbirth, the others are forced by Mrs. Wymuth to hear her screams, because "it was well for the girls to know the wages of sin" (PF, 80).[31] She reads all the girls' mail, and withholds incoming letters to coerce her charges into confessions of further guilt and wrong-doing. Her repeated prayer meetings blister with hell-fire and denunciations of sin, with a particular focus upon minute disciplinary infractions. McClung remarks:

> She had a way of tattling on the girls, telling God everything she had noticed all day that was in any way unpleasant. "And oh, dear, gracious God, we ask Thee to forgive Mary, who came to the table to-night with filthy hands. Teach her that clean hands are pleasing in Thy holy sight. And soften Helmi's hard heart, dear Lord, we pray. Oh, bring down conviction like a rain of fire, so that her poor sin-stained soul may not be eternally lost and cast away to burn forever and ever. Teach Minnie to know that authority must be respected. . . ." (PF, 83)

For McClung, this is the very antithesis of religion. Her anger at the Wymuths' abusive, self-righteous theology bristles through the chapter, as she chronicles episode after episode of cruelty and deceit. Their alleged dedication to "evangelistic work" notwithstanding, the Wymuths are virtual demons who fawn before the authorities in public and destroy souls in private. Indeed, their evil is so great that, with a fine melodramatic flourish, McClung is driven not only to violence, but to the only expression of profanity in all her fiction:

> Something broke in Helmi then. . . . One moment she had been perfectly calm, tight-lipped, composed, mistress of herself, determined to bear all things: the next moment she was a flaming fury, with murder in her eyes. She hurled Mr. Wymuth from her with a swinging blow that sent him crashing into the china cabinet, and the words she said were words she had not known she knew. In the hotel in Saint Paul she had heard the cook say them to a persistent peddler at the door, "You go to Hell!"
> Mrs. Wymuth screamed in genuine, honest fright. (PF, 85-6)

McClung's point is reinforced throughout the text by anecdotes related to Helmi's religious development. True religion empowers, engendering love and trust. The care given by the C.G.I.T. girls, for example, sustains Helmi in the face of the Wymuths' abuse, and reassures her that "She was not alone, not a prisoner, not a disgrace — her friends loved her" (PF, 91).[32] Maggie Corbett is another sustainer, protecting Helmi's reputation by slipping a wedding ring on her finger. When asked by a fearful Helmi, "Will God be mad with you for telling a lie for me?" Maggie expresses McClung's conviction:

> "No fear! God ain't as touchy as lots of people try to make out. It isn't as if I lied to be mean or to hurt some one, and I'll tell you how I've got it sized up. It's a sort of a treat for Him to hear some one lie for a woman instead of to her, or about her if you can get what I mean. . . ." (PF, 223)

Even Cleo, Arthur Warner's dog, becomes a means by which God's loving friendship is extended, comforting Helmi with her puppies after the wretched night when the magistrate was struck down by lightning (PF, 184-5).[33]

These experiences set the stage for Helmi's conversion, but it is the discovery that in fact she had not been responsible for the magistrate's death which tips the scale:

> Then the soul of Helmi was born anew in thankfulness to God, and in a faith in His goodness that never again wavered, for God had saved her from sin. God had intervened to save her when her heart was farthest from Him. God was her friend. He loved her — He would not let her sin! With His own arm He had saved her. (PF, 285)

McClung acknowledges that this is a "simple theology,"[34] but nevertheless maintains the strength of Helmi's conversion, and the peace which it brings her, throughout the remainder of the novel. The traditional emphasis upon conversion and a personal relationship with God is reinforced, but in connection with a larger social religion which makes these experiences possible. The Wymuths' exclusive focus upon individual sin and repentance ignores the circumstances which bring people into difficulty, and lends itself far too easily to a punitive, judgemental approach to other human beings. Right religion, on the other hand, is epitomized by Maggie Corbett, who helps first and asks questions later, and who is always willing to extend the benefit of the doubt without sacrificing her own excellent qualities of discernment.

However "untheological" this might seem to the conservative, McClung is once again arguing that the active care expressed through bean feeds and mothers' meetings is the true locus for Christian faith. As she said to the 5th Ecumenical Methodist Conference in London in 1921 about the Canadian church's encounter with new immigrants:

> In our preachers and workers we are not so strong on fine points of doctrine as we are on the spirit of service. Our W.M.S. women try to interpret the love of God to our people from distant lands; our new Canadians by building hospitals and boarding-schools for the children in the far distant districts. Linen sheets, loving and skilful hands, seem to be a good way to interpret God's love. It is effective. It works. It gets the message over. The people come to us so strange, so lonely, so homesick. It gives the opportunity for showing the spirit of love. Our workers are not so intent on making Methodists out of these people as they are on interpreting God's love to them. Indeed, our Methodists forget they are Methodists, so intent are they on their big work. Their theology might not get by the Ecumenical Conference, but it has vitality; it brings joy in heaven.[35]

This spirit infuses *Painted Fires*, as McClung uses her gift of story-telling to express her understanding of God to her readership. Though fraught with implausibilities of plot and inconsistencies of style, *Painted Fires* is an important barometer of McClung's own perspective. It is not surprising, therefore, that her initial tale of an immigrant girl's courage in building a new life in Canada is virtually overwhelmed by her need to instruct her readers about the evils with which she considered her society to be rife. Prejudice, injustice, indolence and self-righteousness all come under attack, as McClung shows their cruel effect on her innocent heroine. The intensity of McClung's depictions and her outlandish convolutions of plot and character only reinforce the sense that for McClung, things had reached a crisis point, and there were serious decisions to be made. Read another way, McClung's underlying desperation could be reflective of the extent to which she herself felt powerless in the face of a rapidly changing post-war world. In either case, *Painted Fires* remains an important part of the McClung corpus, embodying her most sustained meditation upon truth and illusion in both the material and spiritual life, and the absolute need to choose that which empowers and expresses God's active care.

Notes

1 Savage, *Our Nell*, 169.

2 Ibid.

3 McClung Papers, Add. MSS 10, Vol. 28.

4 Austin Bothwell, "A Canadian Bookshelf," McClung Papers, Add. MSS 10, Vol. 28.

5 Bothwell's review notes that McClung's discussion of birth control is out of place, as "this scene took place before the war. Marie Stopes and Margaret Sanger were then unknown to fame ... in Winnipeg." His other criticism in an otherwise positive review is that "'Painted Fires' would have been just that more convincing ... had Helmi's misfortunes not been so many and so trying."

6 Review of *Painted Fires*, published in *World Wide*, 9 January 1926. McClung Papers, Add. MSS 10, Vol. 28.

7 Ibid.

8 "Nellie McClung's Heroine Has Very Narrow Escape," by "G.M.," McClung Papers, Add. MSS 10, Vol. 28.

9 Ibid.

10 Ibid.

11 Nellie L. McClung, *Painted Fires* (Toronto: Ryerson Press, 1925), 2. Subsequent references will be given parenthically in the text.

12 McClung also makes this point in the poem which introduces the chapter "Women and the Church" in *In Times Like These*, 67.

13 For example, Rose eventually marries an old Chinese restaurant owner in anticipation of inheriting his fortune. She explains her decision to a troubled Helmi in this way: "Kid, I couldn't work. I hate dishwater and I couldn't scrub — it always made

my nose sore. I hate work and what could I do? If I had lots of money I'd run straight. Old Sam is not so bad, and the gray car is a pippin" (PF, 260). Aware of her limitations, Rose has made a reasonable choice, far preferable in McClung's view to the life of prostitution which Rose implies would be her alternative.

14 Compare "Old Sim's" views with Arthur Warner's reasons for volunteering: "The British Empire is my country . . . I was born beneath the British flag, and so were my people for generations back. I love it. The British Empire is in trouble and has called. I do not reason, I go. It's like your mother calling — would you wait to question if your mother called? If you knew your mother was attacked by a bully would you hang back to see first if she had been to blame in any way — would you? My mother couldn't be wrong — not to me. That's what I mean" (PF, 187).

15 A somewhat different, though no less reprehensible version of feminine indolence is given in the minor character of Maudie Herriott, a "pretty, plump-faced girl of twenty-three" (PF, 265). Maudie's only response to her child's diagnosed scarlet fever is irritation, lest her bridge and curling schedule be interrupted by the illness. Her selfishness appalls McClung, who describes her in sinister terms: "Plump and pink and white, with a baby smile, was Maudie Herriott, the petted child and wife, but hard and cruel as any toothless old crone" (PF, 269).

16 McClung describes the poisoned atmosphere of Eva St. John's bridge parties from her husband's perspective: "tinkles of laughter, high-pitched and nervous, shot through the velvety murmurs of conversation.

   The doctor had listened to such conversation many times, and knew the little razor-sharp points of antagonism it held and which seemed to pop out like needles from a squeezed pin-cushion, thin, sharp, unexpected. . . . They had no community of purpose — they were pursuing no particular trend of thought, they were time killers, sensation hunters. He knew the very odor of the room — sachet powder, cigarette smoke, flesh of women too scantily clad, perfume heavy and exotic, a sweet smell, yet not wholesome — like good apples wanting air" (PF, 273).

17 See Sheila Jeffreys, *The Spinster and Her Enemies: Feminism and Sexuality, 1800-1930* for a provocative argument linking antifeminism and the "eroticizing" of the married woman by sex reformers such as Havelock Ellis. Jeffreys contends that the sex reformers were concerned to enforce women's subordination within heterosexual marriage "by introducing a new binding ingredient in the form of women's sexual response to sexual intercourse, to compensate for the lost legal and economic restraints" (167). She quotes the Dutch sexologist Van de Velde's immensely popular 1926 text, *Ideal Marriage*, which states that the most important element of marriage is "a vigorous and harmonious sex life" (167). Contrast this with McClung's 1915 statement of the issue: "marriage is a divine partnership based on mutual love and community of interest . . . the pleasant glowing embers of comradeship and loving friendship give out a warmer, more lasting, and more comfortable heat than the leaping flames of passion, and the happiest marriage is one where the husband and wife come to regard each other as the dearest friend and the most congenial companion" (ITLT, 33). If one accepts Jeffrey's hypothesis, McClung's anger at Eva St. John becomes more understandable, in that through her very indolence and sexualized allure Eva serves to undermine the feminist aspiration for full, responsible personhood for women.

18 McClung does not specify here which "Union" she means, although it is possible she is referring to the One Big Union, or "Wobblies" who figured prominently in Winnipeg's post-war political scene. (For a discussion of the O.B.U.'s influence on the 1919 Winnipeg General Strike, see Allen, *The Social Passion*, 87-98.) It is equally possible, however, that McClung had no specific group in mind, lumping together as the "Union" all those of a socialist stripe with whom she disagreed.

19 Veronica Strong-Boag makes a similar point in her Introduction to McClung's *In Times Like These*, xv. She regards McClung's rejection of "socialism" as a logical outgrowth of her notions of Christian stewardship. However, Strong-Boag fails to acknowledge the variety of forms socialism, and stewardship, can take. McClung rejected socialisms which espoused an ideology of inevitable conflict and class warfare, just as she rejected notions of Christian stewardship which demanded the paternalistic governance of women by men. She did embrace what she called "Christian socialism," a cooperative, non-hierarchical perspective compatible with a democratic system of government. For a description of her view of Christian Socialism, see "The World of Tomorrow," *Winnipeg Free Press Magazine Section*, 2 August 1941, 5.

20 McClung Papers, Add. MSS 10, Vol. 12.

21 Ibid.

22 Ibid.

23 McClung discusses her view of Christian socialism in her newspaper columns of the 1930s and '40s. The "right" kind of socialism allows for the moderate ownership of private property, but calls for state funding of all social services, including education and free health care. (See "The World of Tomorrow," cited in n. 19.) She further clarifies her objections to radical socialism in "No Classes on a Lifeboat," McClung Papers, Add. MSS 10, Vol. 52: "I do not like to hear anyone try to draw a sharp line between 'workers' and 'owners' as the radical speakers used to do in days gone by. Surely it is not wrong for a man to 'own' his home, or his factory. . . . Nor do I like to term 'working people' applied exclusively to those who work for wages. I believe one weak spot in our democratic way of life is the way we draw lines between different kinds of work, counting some higher than others in the social scale." McClung's point regarding the status of certain kinds of work recalls her discussion of class in *Purple Springs*, where Pearlie Watson fears Dr. Clay will not marry her because her parents are only common labourers. While it is possible to see McClung's objection to differential status as a way of reconciling "the oppressed" to their lot, it is equally possible to hear in her complaint a rather revolutionary call for the reevaluation of our society's understanding of work. She goes on in the article to relate an anecdote about a young woman forced by her fiancé to give up her job as a domestic and take work in a laundry because of the higher social status accruing to work outside the home, despite the fact that she much preferred her original source of employment. In her high valuation of women's traditional forms of labour, and her rejection of wages as the sole gauge of economic productivity, McClung reflects an important feminist insight which has been too often omitted by dominant socialist analyses.

24 J.S. Sparling, "Introduction" to J.S. Woodsworth, *Strangers within Our Gates* (Toronto: The Missionary Society of the Methodist Church, Canada, 1909), 4.

25 Ibid., 97, 91, 165.

26 This alleged racial characteristic is preserved in a pejorative phrase denoting hard bargaining to one's own advantage, i.e., "jewing someone down."

27 Woodsworth, *Strangers within Our Gates*, 278.

28 Here McClung took occasion to poke fun at her own heritage. Facing the possibility of a "fighting foreigner," "Lucy Powers at this cried out, 'Oh, gee, wouldn't that be fun?' She was of Hibernian extraction" (PF, 39).

29 McClung makes a parallel argument in *The Next of Kin* (Toronto: Thomas Allen, 1917): "We must love our own country best, of course, just as we love our own children best; but it is a poor mother who does not desire the highest good for every other woman's child" (211). Loyalty and commitment need not lead to self-righteousness and prejudice, just as self-affirmation need not lead to the denigration of

others. This approach to difference in the construction of the Canadian identity is consonant with current government emphases on multiculturalism, and distinguishes McClung from the assimilationist policies of Woodsworth and others.

30 McClung's description of the magistrate before whom Reverend Terry must argue Helmi's case highlights this point. Prejudiced, punitive, he has judged Helmi guilty before even seeing her, on the grounds that "Finns are naturally red [i.e., communist] . . . and in every case the women are the worst" (PF, 61).

31 McClung's distress is conspicuous in the following quotation: "The Girls' Friendly Home had been built by Christian people. The men who sat on the Board were convinced that they were doing a noble thing. Faithful women sewed and baked and sold tickets to maintain it. O God! O God! what cruel things are sometimes done in the name of Thy compassionate son!" (PF, 80-1).

32 Indeed, the C.G.I.T. Blue and Gold Book is even cited to exonerate Helmi from hitting Mr. Wymuth (PF, 91-2).

33 This section contains a rather odd and ambiguous episode, wherein Helmi's physical agony at abruptly weaning her child is relieved in some way by one of Cleo's pups, possibly by her suckling it. In any case, as the episode makes clear, the shared bond of motherhood is so strong as to transcend even differences of species.

34 "Life had changed for Helmi. The demon of revenge which had embittered her heart had been laid to rest by the hand of God, her friend. In her simple theology God had actually reached down His hand through the blackness of the storm and struck the magistrate dead because he had brought such evil upon her, and to prevent her from committing the crime of murder. God would be her friend forevermore; she would trust Him now whatever came" (PF, 287).

35 "The Awakening of Women," 260.

III

In Times Like These:
The Anti-Feminist Context

> Sane opinions temperately expressed, illustrated by humorous incidents and anecdotes based upon her broad experience in fighting for decency and the safety of the home.[1]

> Hysterical and fantastic bunkum.[2]

The world into which *In Times Like These* was received upon its publication in 1915 was one intensely divided around the question of woman suffrage. Despite the range of topics addressed in the text, "the vote" was almost the exclusive focus of its reviewers. Later historians have similarly emphasized the centrality of the suffrage, often reducing the myriad aims of first-wave feminism to this single goal. The problems inherent in this approach have been alluded to elsewhere.[3] Our purpose here is to investigate both the text and the context of what is currently McClung's most famous piece of writing,[4] with a two-fold purpose. First, the context of *In Times Like These* will be explored with an eye to illuminating the factors which influenced McClung to couch her arguments for woman suffrage, temperance, women's ordination, and other issues in the way that she does. As the introductory quotations indicate, McClung was not writing for a neutral audience. A highly politicized environment influences the way in which one advances one's ideas—and indeed, often the ideas themselves. In this chapter, therefore, an attempt will be made to clarify

---

Notes to Chapter III are on pages 124-35.

McClung's context through a consideration of the reviews of the text, and the anti-feminism of three important opponents of women's rights: Sir Almroth Wright, Stephen Leacock, and Manitoba Premier Sir Rodmond Roblin. A second chapter will be devoted to the text of *In Times Like These* itself, and will lift up and clarify McClung's arguments around suffrage, temperance and other issues, and thereby attempt to revise the current stereotype of McClung as a "bourgeois, liberal, maternal" feminist.

1. The Reviews

Even negative reviews of *In Times Like These* generally conceded that McClung wrote well. The "anti-suffragist" in the Boston *Advertiser* review of 4 December 1916, for example, allows that "the humor of the book [is] clever enough,"[5] although he[6] goes on to note that it "is frequently no more than biting sarcasm; and sarcasm is generally conceded to be more harmful and [sic] helpful."[7] What is perceived by more congenial reviewers as a "causticity [which] reaches the mark without giving offense"[8] is here understood as a rather ill-tempered attack, and ill-bred in the bargain. The "anti-suffragist" concludes, "The book has style, if you like the flamboyant, loud and independent kind. There is nothing calm or steady about it. . . ."[9]

This "lack of balance" is a common complaint of the opposition. The "anti-suffragist" states, "the whole style reeks of smashing head-long protestations instead of logical reasons,"[10] and a particularly aggressive reviewer for *Saturday Night* complains, after calling McClung's work "fantastic and hysterical bunkum": "The volume is merely typical of a great deal of wrong-headed and bitter propaganda now being conducted by women, and that is my excuse for devoting so much space to a book so entirely superficial in thought and crude in statement."[11] Again, while conceding McClung shows "some thought," *In Times Like These* is cited for its "fallacies" and "sweeping generalizations," particularly regarding women's character and capabilities.

The tone of these reviews is one of irritability and offended sensibility, of the astonishment and outrage engendered when "time honoured truths" come suddenly under attack. Certainly the reviewer for *Saturday Night* exhibits these characteristics, lashing out at McClung in his first paragraph:

> Mrs. McClung was formerly known as a writer of popular tales of the sort Sunday-school superintendents give to particularly assiduous pupils. Recently, however, she has become even better known as a spell binder for moral reform and patriotic purposes — also half the collection. She has even won quite a tidy local fame in Toronto through the publicity given her endeavors to collect what she regarded as her share from a committee of ladies who thought more ought go to an army field kitchen. God forbid I should express an opinion![12]

It is clear that these writers perceived McClung as a threat. Even where her arguments are addressed directly — for example, the *Saturday Night* reviewer challenges McClung's argument that woman suffrage will lead to substantial improvement in social welfare — there is an underlying defensiveness of tone which suggests that the real problem with *In Times Like These* for these writers does not reside primarily in its alleged deficiency in argumentation.

In contrast, positive reviews of *In Times Like These* praise McClung for her "sanity," evident in the thoroughness of her argumentation. The "suffragist" opines:

> The very fact that such a book as this, — expressing ideas and proving opinions in favour of woman suffrage, has been accepted by a firm of men for publication, would argue that it must be a just and logical exposition of fact written in a temperate yet forceful style.[13]

While it might be argued that this reviewer was predisposed to accept the logic of McClung's views, other less obviously biased writers concur with the "suffragist's" positive judgement. As the Toronto *Globe* notes: "Whether the reader agrees with all these thrusts and lashings, there is no question about the brilliance, wit and pungency of these pages, and Mrs. McClung will widen her already great circle of admirers by this novel collection of opinions."[14]

One contributory factor to this assessment was McClung's ability as a writer. Several reviewers note, as does "the Bookman," that McClung had "a great talent for epigram and a real genius for the illuminating anecdote," calling her style "conversational, piquant, colloquial."[15] A more significant element in the book's appeal, however, was McClung's personality itself. As one reviewer notes: "The author of *Sowing Seeds in Danny* has ceased to be a mere entertainer. She is a propagandist, whose charming personality fortunately reveals itself in travel now and then to remove the illusion which her arguments suggest."[16]

McClung had the power to persuade, even in the face of prejudice. Further, her writing empowered others to both personal and social transformation. As one reviewer comments: "None can come under the spell of Mrs. McClung's delightful sense of humor, her sane arguments, and her ever present wit without feeling glad to be alive and able to do something to make the world better."[17]

McClung had indeed found her pulpit in *In Times Like These* — nor had her image as preacher escaped her readers. The "Bookman" compares her to Alexander Grant, Spurgeon and Moody, all great evangelical preachers, both for her wit and her effective use of anecdote.[18] Another reviewer is even more explicit: "In her pages we are brought into contact with a soul on fire with earnest purpose, and astir with genuine ethical ferment.... She is a sayer of wise things, and her work will do good like a tonic."[19]

To focus solely upon McClung's arguments in *In Times Like These*, as have many of her detractors, past and present, is to miss much of the book's import. *In Times Like These* is not a philosophical treatise, but a collection of impassioned, revivalistic sermons, geared to the common person with the conscious intent to convert. Taken within that context, the defensiveness of her negative reviewers becomes more understandable, for they, too, recognized her power to sway, even shape, public opinion. Her status as a famous and much admired Canadian novelist combined with her passionate conviction and genuine gift for public speaking to produce a formidable political agent for change — all the more so as she employed the rhetorical, anecdotal style of evangelist preaching with which much of her audience would have already been familiar. Once again, McClung used conventional form to convey unconventional content,[20] to empower, convert and transform.

2. The Anti-Feminist Context

As indicated by the reviews explored above, McClung wrote *In Times Like These* with a highly political intent for a politically divided readership.[21] Scholars have tended to focus on one half of this dynamic, the supporters of and arguments for suffrage, but very little scholarly attention has been directed to the often quite intense pronouncements of the anti-suffrage camp.[22] It is essential these be investigated. McClung's speeches — the various chapters of *In Times Like These* — are often constructed in the form of a debate, and are crucially dependent upon the arguments mounted by the other side. It is clear, therefore, that accurate evaluation of McClung's feminist activism must take these into significant account. With this in mind, this section will consider the anti-feminist context of *In Times Like These* through an exploration of various materials, primarily the anti-feminist writing of two figures, Stephen Leacock and Sir Almroth Wright. These have been chosen for two reasons. First, both were well known and authoritative figures whose views on the issue of suffrage would carry weight with the public, and second, both were challenged by McClung in print. Brief consideration will also be given to McClung's well-publicized clash with Sir Rodmond Roblin, as his dogged opposition to woman suffrage is engaged by McClung in a particularly vivid way. Overall, I wish to show that in the speeches which became *In Times Like These* McClung was forced, for political reasons, to address the suffrage question in a way already pre-determined by the opposition. Any reading of *In Times Like These* which does not take this factor into account runs the risk of confusing political rhetoric with McClung's genuine and long-standing beliefs, as embodied in her novels.

a. Sir Almroth Wright

Sir Almroth Wright (1861-1947) was a pioneer in vaccine therapy at St. Mary's Hospital, Paddington, London, and is chiefly known today in his connection with Sir Alexander Fleming, the discoverer of penicillin. In McClung's day, however, he was also known for his thoroughgoing opposition to woman suffrage, evident in his 28 March 1912, "Letter on Militant Hysteria" to *The Times*, London, and in his longer exposition of the topic, *The Unexpurgated Case against Woman Suffrage*,[23] in which the letter appears as an appendix. Although McClung addresses Sir Almroth directly only once in *In Times Like These*, in response to his claim that "there are no good women, though there are some women who have come under the influence of good men,"[24] his arguments against woman suffrage inform much of the line of attack which McClung chooses in her demand for the vote. It is appropriate therefore to discuss his position in detail.

Sir Almroth begins by challenging the feminist contention that one ought not generalize about women. Drawing upon his authority as a scientist, and sprinkling his argument with snippets of French, Latin, classical quotations and technical terms like "diacritical judgement,"[25] Sir Almroth tries to show that generalizations are not only possible about women, but necessary. Moreover, since "logical proof is obtainable only in that comparatively narrow sphere where reasoning is based — as in mathematics — upon axioms" (16), it is legitimate to take a more personal, experiential route in the formulation of these generalizations. He describes the process as follows:

> When I venture to attempt a generalization about women, I endeavour to recall to mind without distinction all the different women I have encountered, and to extricate from my impressions what was common to all, — omitting from consideration (except only when I am dealing specifically with these) all plainly abnormal women. (18)

The next step is to submit the generalization to investigation by another, whose task it is to go through the same "mental operations, review [the] judgement, and pronounce his verdict."[26] Should the other concur, "that particular generalization will . . . go forward not as a datum of my individual experience, but as the intellectual resultant of two separate and distinct experiences. It will thereby be immensely fortiifed" (17-19). In effect, Sir Almroth is arguing that the more men [read: males] who believe a thing, the more likely it is to be true. Moreover, he is regarding his subject, women, much as he would bacteria, the focus of his own scientific research. Externally observable and subject to the experts' taxonomy (note his unsubstantiated categorization of "plainly abnormal women"), women are best known and understood by men of science like Sir Almroth, whose systematic scholarly approach gave clear evidence of his "objectivity."

The rest of the text makes hard reading for those accustomed to accepting women's full humanity. It is all the more important, therefore, to consider his arguments with some care, as many of the assumptions undergirding his approach are employed in current scholarly discussion to dismiss or discredit a gender-critical approach to a variety of issues. While much of Sir Almroth's text may appear extreme, there remains a significant continuity which has informed current scholarly treatment of suffrage and other feminist concerns.

Sir Almroth begins his attack by asserting "the Woman's Suffrage Movement has no real intellectual or moral sanction" (21), for two reasons. First, regarding the movement's moral claims, he states, "the preponderating majority of women who claim the suffrage do not do so from motives of public interest and philanthropy," but because they resent "that woman should be accounted by man as inherently his inferior in certain important respects," hence receiving justifiably, in Sir Almroth's view, a reduced portion of the world's good, both social and material (21-2). Women desirous of suffrage are driven by resentment and pretension to claim what is not rightfully theirs —

hence the movement has no "moral prestige." Secondly, the move-ment's intellectual prestige resides solely in the advocacy it has received by "a certain number of distinguished men" (22), men who are either "cranks" or who, like John Stuart Mill, have been deluded into thinking a common humanity supersedes sexual difference (25).[28] In fact, Sir Almroth devotes several pages to refuting Mill and his works, juxtaposing appeals to conscience (e.g., "no upright mind can fail to see that the woman who lives in a condition of financial dependence upon man has no moral claim to unrestricted liberty" [26])[29] with demonstrations of his own erudition.[30] He concludes with a casual dismissal of the third type of man who supports woman suf-frage, "an idealistic dreamer: one for whom some woman's memory has become, like Beatrice for Dante, a mystic religion" (30).

By the end of his Introduction, Sir Almroth has established, by definition, the complete illegitimacy of any claim for woman suffrage. In good scholarly fashion, however, he elaborates his point, refuting first the various arguments put forward in support of woman suf-frage, then turning to his own reasons for wishing to refuse to extend the parliamentary suffrage to women. He concludes with his own set of "palliatives or correctives for the discontent of women," offered as an alternative to suffrage. These sections will be addressed in turn, as they yield important insight into the enormity of the prejudice — and indeed, the enmity — facing women who chose to challenge the status quo. Further, works such as *The Unexpurgated Case* illustrate the imperviousness of the anti-suffrage mind to systematic counter-argu-ments from the feminist side. As will become apparent, women *by def-inition* are seen as incapable of reasoning adequately; the rare woman whose intellectual skill is undeniable is summarily delegitimized with the label "plainly abnormal," much in the manner of Dr. Johnson's dancing dog.[31] Thus defined out of the scholarly court, feminists such as McClung found humour, anecdote and rhetoric far more effective weapons than sheer argumentation against "authorities" like Sir Almroth. Indeed, by shifting the ground of attack, feminist wit was able to undercut the appeal of the conservative position by making men like Sir Almroth — and in McClung's case, Sir Rodmond Rob-lin — appear pompous, rather tedious examples of a dying breed.[32]

This dimension of the suffrage battle was lost on Sir Almroth. His arguments proceed in an orderly, systematic fashion, building through "scientific" observation and argumentation toward what, the reader becomes sure, was for him the inescapable conclusion that the call for votes for women was a moral outrage which, if implemented, would result in no less than the utter destruction of western civilization.

The text proper begins with a consideration of the various arguments put forward to support woman suffrage, namely, the argument from natural rights, the argument from "the intellectual grievances of women," and the argument that the vote is necessary for instructional purposes. To the first, he replies that justice does not demand that men and women be treated equally. Such a view misunderstands the fundamental meaning of "right," which is not a concept pertaining to the individual, but a creation of the community: "A right is created when the community binds itself to us, its individual members, to intervene by force to restrain any one from interfering with us, and to protect us in the enjoyment of our faculties, privileges and property" (35-6). While a right may be independent of and antecedent to law, such as the right to freedom, or to personal property (36), the communal notion of right remains central. It is further borne out in Sir Almroth's notion of justice, which must "be conformable to the principle of utility and directed to the advantage of society" (39-40). Everywhere, he tells us, "The conception of Justice is thus . . . interfused with considerations of utility and expediency" (40).

Opposed to this view is the suffragist "Principle of Egalitarian Equity," a scientifically unsupportable and socially irresponsible notion which espouses that "all distinctions depending upon natural endowment, sex, and race should be effaced" (41). Sir Almroth reacts with horror at the thought:

> we have here a principle, which would make of every man and woman *in primis* a socialist; then a woman suffragist; then a philo-native, negrophil, and an advocate of the political rights of natives and negroes: and then, by logical compulsion an anti-vivisectionist, who accounts it *unjust* to experiment on an animal; a vegetarian, who accounts it *unjust* to kill animals for food; and finally one like the Jains, accounts it *unjust* to take the life of even verminous insects. (42)

This connection of woman suffrage with a plenitude of other evils is by no means unique to Sir Almroth. In a pamphlet entitled "What is Feminism?" found in McClung's personal papers, the Pennsylvania Association Opposed to Woman Suffrage fearlessly links feminism, socialism and physical degeneracy, and show their combined effect in criminal behaviour, divorce, and the overthrow of the church.[33] Like

Sir Almroth, they invoke scientific authority to support their views. Citing Lombroso (whom Sir Almroth in fact rejects), the pamphleteers claim:

> the higher in civilization men and women rise the more different from each other they become. The female acquires softer lines, a more feminine character; the male develops stronger features, a deeper voice, more inventive ability and greater ambition. Among savages . . . women are inclined to angular forms, square, masculine jaws, and deep voices, while the men rarely grow beards and are lazy and less ambitious than civilized men. Civilization develops the differences of the sexes; in Science as well as Romance, the manly man and the womanly woman are the best representatives of the race.[34]

Although they argue their point differently, both the authors of this piece and Sir Almroth Wright connect feminism with the obliteration of sexual difference and the downfall of civilization. The exhortations of McClung and others that feminism would in fact *improve* the race need to be understood in relation to these claims. Much of McClung's alleged "maternal" feminism in *In Times Like These* takes on a decidedly different cast once the reader realizes her opposition's attempt to cast suffragists as epicene degenerates bent on the destruction of the home. As the following chapter will show, McClung's affirmation of women's traditional domestic and child-rearing roles is less "naive maternalism" than shrewd political strategy. While she certainly considered these things valuable, she nevertheless understood the equal necessity for their reform.[35]

Sir Almroth next attacks the suffragist claim that women are unjustly subject to "taxation without representation" (44-5), pointing out that, economically speaking, women are so dependent upon men that, "the very revenues which the Woman Suffrage Societies devote to man's vilification are to a preponderating extent derived from funds which he earned and gave over to women" (47). Operating on the principle of "All yours is mine, and all mine's my own" (50), the suffragist agitates for women's greater economic and political freedom and refuses to acknowledge the true source of anything which pertains to her:

> And so we find the women who want to have everything for nothing, and the wives who do not see that they are beholden to man for anything . . . in short, all the ungrateful women — flock to the banner of Women's Freedom — the banner of financial freedom for woman at the expense of financial servitude for man. (52)

Sir Almroth's conclusion is succinct, and extremely revealing, *to wit*, "The grateful woman will practically always be an anti-suffragist" (55).

The ungrateful woman, the grasping woman, the rude and self-aggrandizing woman, on the other hand, will fight belligerently for suffrage, thus abrogating chivalry, the very law upon which higher civilization is based. Sir Almroth's definition of the term is quite clear:

> When a man makes this contract with a woman, "I will do you reverence, and protect you, and yield you service; and you, for your part, will hold fast to an ideal of gentleness, of personal refinement, of modesty, of joyous maternity, and to who shall say what other graces and virtues that endear woman to men," that is *chivalry....* And the contract is infringed when woman breaks out into violence, when she jettisons her personal refinement, when she is ungrateful, and, possibly, when she places quite extravagantly high estimate upon her intellectual powers. (56)[36]

Further, contrary to the suffragist claim that chivalry is insulting to women's dignity, chivalry is nothing less than men "serving woman without reward" (56).

As Sir Almroth develops his argument, the source of the vehemence with which he denounces woman suffrage becomes clear. Women are plainly inferior, he states, physically, intellectually, and morally. The "womanly woman" acknowledges this fact, and is accordingly grateful to men for their beneficence.[37] Feminists, however, refuse to recognize this reality, and attribute the learned judgements of even distinguished men like Sir Almroth to "prejudice." In so doing, they are flying in the face of reality, and challenging "objective" scientific authority in the bargain. Feminist claims, therefore, are both absurd and impudent.

This being said, Sir Almroth nevertheless takes some pains to refute the charge of prejudice. First, he notes that it is a convenient rhetorical tactic to dismiss any "unwelcome generalization" as prejudice (56-7). We must generalize, he argues, if we are to learn anything from experience. While it is certainly true that "if our generalization happens to be an unfavourable one, we shall necessarily have prejudged the case of those who are exceptions to their class" (60), the reverse is equally the case. Further, while it is possible that generalizations may be erroneous, "when a generalization finds wide acceptance among the thoughtful, we have come as close to truth as it is possible for humanity to come" (61-2). Just such a generalization is that of women's inherent inferiority to men. He states that "experience with regard to the capacity of woman has been accumulating in all climes and through all times . . . the belief of men in the inherent inferiority of women in the matter of intellectual morality and in the power of adjudication, has never varied" (62).[38]

This same rational objectivity pertains to the laws which govern society. Suffragists are wrong to call them "man-made," implying that their formulation in any way reflects male self-interest:

> In reality the law we live under . . . descends from the past. . . . More- over, we, the present male electors — the electors who are savagely attacked by the suffragist for our asserted iniquities in connexion with the laws which regulate sexual relations — have never in our capacity as electors had any power to alter an old, or to suggest a new law; except in so far as voting Conservative or Liberal we may indirectly have remotely influenced the general trend of legislation. (64-5)[39]

Further, he rejects the argument, employed by many a social reformer, that social laws may embody past prejudices which are inappropriate to the current "enlightened" age. On the contrary he states:

> It will be obvious to every one who considers that the draughting of statutes and the formulating of legal decisions is almost as imper- sonal a procedure as that of drawing up the rules to govern a game; and it offers hardly more opportunity for discrimination between man and woman. (65)[40]

This description of social life as a game, and its legislation as the game's rules clarifies the intellectual underpinnings of what might otherwise seem biased rationalization. That is, if in fact rules can be generated "objectively," without the taint of self-interest or prejudice towards others, it follows that not everyone need have a direct say in establishing those rules. That task is best left to the "experts," whose superior knowledge and skill befit them to the task:

> But in reality, whether it is a question of the rules of a game, or the reciprocal rights and duties of members of a community, it is, and ought to be, to every reasonable human being not a grievance, but a matter of felicitation, that an expert or a body of experts should have evolved a set of rules under which order and harmony are achieved. (67)[41]

Sir Almroth's emphasis upon "order and harmony" is illustrative of his argument against woman suffrage as a whole. If women would only recognize their true place, as established by those best qualified to determine it, society would return to an equilibrium which would benefit all. This conservatism, evident in other anti-suffragists of the period as well, presented a fundamental challenge to supporters of women's rights, who were forced to argue, in contrast, that social change was needed to achieve the "harmony and order" which Sir Almroth imagined to exist in the pre-feminist past. What are often perceived as feminists' overly utopian visions of a post-suffrage future are better understood as a necessary counterbalance to the conservative push to restore the patriarchal status quo. McClung and others attempted to show both that following the "rules of the game" would *not* necessarily lead to harmony and order,[42] and that a better, fairer, and more peaceable game could be established.

The "order and harmony" understood by Sir Almroth, however, is the equilibrium of the battlefield where, quite literally, the best man wins. He states: "an electoral contest partakes of the nature of a civil war . . . to give [women] the parliamentary vote would be to reduce all those trials of strength which take the form of electoral contests to a farce" (71). While women suffragists may claim, naively, that the vote is necessary for women's protection, or as an educative tool so that women may attain full intellectual stature (72-6), the call for the vote is nothing more than a rallying cry, borne out of selfishness, for "every . . . woman who wants to apply the screw to man" (75). The only advantage of granting the suffrage, or even extending the principle "and for instructional purposes make of a woman . . . a judge, or an ambassador, or a Prime Minister," would be "by these means once and for all to bring home to man the limitations of woman" (76).[43]

That such a move would bring the world to the brink of disaster is in Sir Almroth's mind never in doubt. In the second section of *The Unexpurgated Case against Woman Suffrage*, the various disabilities pertaining to women are carefully outlined to substantiate this conclusion. As one reads this material, Sir Almroth's desire to contain women within the private sphere of the home becomes fully understandable for, it appears, women are dangerous creatures indeed.

He sets the stage for his discussion of women's character by noting that "we should in legislating guide ourselves by consideration of utility and expedience" (80).[44] Abstract principles such as "equality" and "liberty" should be disregarded because they "are not all of them guides to utility" and because they are "open to all manner of private misinterpretation" (80). His task, then, is to determine "whether the state would, or would not, suffer from the admission of women to the electorate" (80).

To do this, it is necessary to determine the nature of "woman" herself. Drawing upon his authority as a scientist, Sir Almroth claims that women are simply not physically strong enough to warrant the vote. They lack the "moral prestige," directly derived from physical force, which is necessary to determine whose ideas will hold sway. Domestic politics would be thrown into complete disarray.[45] Moreover, the whole empire would be endangered. Sir Almroth explains:

> Now it is by physical force alone and by prestige — which represents physical force in the background — that a nation protects itself against foreign interference, upholds its rule over subject populations, and enforces its own laws. And nothing could in the end more certainly lead to war and revolt than the decline of military spirit and loss of prestige which would inevitably follow if man admitted woman into political co-partnership. (83)

Sir Almroth is adamant on this subject: "no military foreign nation or native race would ever believe in the stamina and firmness of purpose" (82-3) of the British Empire should women get the vote, for "there cannot be two opinions on the question that a virile and imperial race will not brook any attempt at forcible control by women" (82).[46]

Here Sir Almroth begins an argument, developed further in his "Appendix on Militant Hysteria," which is central to understanding the depth of the challenge which the call for woman suffrage posed. Far from being the inevitable conclusion of an enlightened age (although often presented as such, for political effect, in suffragist rhetoric), woman suffrage met with serious, determined, and at times violent opposition. While Sir Almroth does not explicitly state that, should women obtain the vote, men ought challenge them to define their positions physically, violence against women becomes a very thinly veiled threat throughout the remainder of the text. This element merits further consideration for two reasons: first, because it challenges the ahistorical assumption that women's rights have been and are established through coherence of logical argument, and second, because it highlights the tactical dimension of McClung's use of humour in dealing with the anti-suffragist. Realizing that reason alone had no power to cure the "mental strabismus" of prejudice,[47] McClung made the opposition laughable, transforming what might otherwise have been seen as the claim to authority into the appearance of blustering pomposity. It is testimony to McClung's power as a writer that current analysts of this historical period have been tempted to dismiss the anti-suffrage opposition on the assumption that such rhetorical portraits were in fact mere descriptions to which everyone might accede.

Returning to Sir Almroth, the appeal of his argument becomes more apparent once his understanding of women and violence is investigated. To begin, he states, "woman does, and should, stand to physical violence in a fundamentally different relation to man" (87). When women resort to violence, as did the militant suffragists, they violate the "unwritten, and unassailable, and irreversible commandments of religion" (179). These Sir Almroth describes somewhat obliquely as: "that code which forbade us even to think of employing our native Indian troops against the Boers; which brands it an ignominy when a man leaves his fellow in the lurch and saves his own life; and which makes it an outrage for a man to do violence to a woman" (178-9).

Elsewhere he reveals the grounding of this code in social reality. He describes human society as a series of concentric circles with the legitimacy of exercising physical violence continually decreasing as one penetrates toward the centre. The most external ring is "the realm of uncompromising violence such as exists when human life is endangered by wild animals, or murderous criminals, or savages" (129).[48] One then proceeds through rings of "civilized war," humanity in general vs.animals, humanity and pet animals, then "those who belong to the white race," then those of one's own nation, then women and children in general vs. white men in general, then relatives and friends vs. strangers, then the family, then finally at the centre of all the circles, "women of our own households" (129-30). Nor is this ranking accidental. He tells the reader: "The course of civilization and of the amenities, and the welfare of the nation, of the family, and of woman, are all intimately bound up with faithful adherence to this compromise" (130-1). In asking for the vote, and even exercising violence toward that end, women are violating the fundamental order of civilization:[49] "it is this solemn covenant, the covenant so faithfully kept by man, which has been violated by the militant suffragist in the interest of her morbid, stupid, ugly and dishonest programmes" (181). Moreover, he queries: "Is it any wonder if men feel that they have had enough of the militant suffragist and that the state would be well rid of her if she were crushed under the soldiers' shields like the traitor woman at the Tarpeian rock?" (181).[50]

Sir Almroth's irritation is compounded by the intrinsic incapacity of women to reason clearly, and so to understand the force of his arguments. Unlike men, who are in the main creatures of logic, "woman looks upon her mind not as an instrument for the purpose of truth, but as an instrument for providing her with creature comforts in the form of agreeable mental images" (88). This disregard for the truth is congenital, as women have a "physical yearning for such comforts" (88-9). Precisely this need to disregard reality in favour of "congenial images" is what causes the suffragist to concoct her totally unrealistic view of the world. Sir Almroth is prepared to allow women some mental capacity, however, although he is quick to discount its significance. Speaking of certain of women's "indisputable" mental attributes, he notes:

> it is not so much a quick memory or a rapid power of apprehension which is required for effective intellectual work, as originality, or at any rate independence of thought, a faculty of felicitous generalizations and diacritical judgement, long-sustained intellectual effort, an unselective mirroring of the world in the mind, and that relative immunity to fallacy which goes together with a stable and relatively unresponsive nervous system. (92)

Women's nervous systems, in contrast, are notoriously volatile. At least in part this is due to the fact that "the sexual products influence every tissue of the body" (81), to such a degree that "unsatisfied sexuality is an intellectual disability" (93).[51] The unmarried feminist suffers a double burden—not only is she physiologically unsuited for rational moral thought by virtue of being female, her reasoning processes are further impaired by her (presumed) lack of sexual satisfaction. Once again, the contribution of happily married mothers like McClung to the suffrage movement becomes apparent, as they stood in visible contradiction to the stereotype of feminist as unfulfilled spinster. This being said, it is doubtful that such would be accepted as serious counter-evidence by persons such as Sir Almroth, who notes of women's claims to have "progressed" beyond the pattern of deficiency that he describes: "the educated native too has advanced in all these respects; and he also tells us that he is pulling up level with the white man" (97).[52] That anyone external to the group attain the same level of achievement or capacity as white males was in Sir Almroth's view clearly impossible.

Finally, Sir Almroth seeks to establish women's deficiency in the matter of morality. Women are particularly suited, he says, to the private sphere. Their morality is a domestic one, concerned with the personal and the demands of the ego (100-1), and is so instinctive as to be "almost . . . animal" (109). In a way, women's moral deficiency is an extension of their intellectual deficiency, as in either case there is an overriding need to extract comfort and pleasure from the immediate circumstance.[53] To allow the vote to persons of such limited capacity for discernment would indeed be "pernicious to the State" (98), for they would never be able to transcend personal concerns to consider the abstract principles upon which civilization is based (100).[54] Public morality is the proper domain of the male, whose altruistic perspective (100-1)[55] and "comparatively unresponsive nervous system" best befit him to make the larger judgements necessitated by national life.[56]

The point which Sir Almroth is making with regard to gender difference in moral discourse is one which has received serious attention in recent years. In particular, Carol Gilligan's *In a Different Voice* explores women's characteristic tendency to organize moral energies around "caring" rather than "justice" concerns, and argues that *both* generate legitimate languages of moral discourse.[57] She would agree in the main with Sir Almroth's statement that "woman feels no interest in, and no responsibility toward, any abstract moral ideal" (108), but would understand in that statement the failure of the "abstract ideal" to support the web of caring connections which are constitutive of women's lives. Ethicist Karen McCarthy Brown would go even further. In a provocative article entitled "Heretics and Pagans: Women in the Academic World," McCarthy Brown addresses the problem of women's moral experience and its significance for debate on public and private ethics. Like Gilligan, she wishes to affirm that between men and women "fundamentally different experiences underlie our speaking in the world,"[58] with this difference providing the material base for divergent languages of moral discourse. Individually, for Gilligan this is acceptable; however, for McCarthy Brown, problems arise once the question of the values of the public sphere are considered:

> The complicating factor here is that the institutions of our society without exception are constructed out of the world-as-taken-for-granted by men. I say without exception and I mean without exception, for even the family is dependent on the male worldview internalized (although never completely so) and enacted by the female.[59]

Men feel more "at home" in the public sphere than do women precisely because the values of that sphere, embodied in its institutions, are generated out of male experience. Women, on the other hand, are forced to operate in an alien and often openly hostile world.

For Sir Almroth, who assumes the neutrality and objectivity of those structures, women's sense of "dislocation" in the public sphere is a clear sign of moral deficiency. For contemporaneous feminists like McClung, however, who recognized the "man-made" character of the shared social world,[60] women's alleged "disabilities" were either imposed or non-existent. Further, it was a moral imperative to remove those imposed constraints through the restructuring of society so that the male world of the public sphere became a truly human world. McCarthy Brown concurs: "The answer lies in a radical redefinition of the basis of all moral thought, that is community, and especially community in its most rudimentary form, the intimate relationship between two persons."[61] Women's "moral deficiency" thus becomes the very sign of male privilege and injustice toward women which necessitates the social activism Sir Almroth so deplores.

The remainder of the text treats a variety of concerns, as Sir Almroth turns his attention from "woman in general" to the specific social circumstances which have generated the call for woman suffrage. Not surprisingly, he rejects outright the "Mental Outlook and Programme of the Female Legislative Reformer," with its emphasis upon equal treatment for men and women in the public sphere, and its rejection of violence as the foundation of human society. Unlike women, whose moral malleability and physical incapacity render them incapable of discerning and implementing genuine legislative reforms, says Sir Almroth, the rational (male) legislative reformer recognizes that violent power must be wielded in the state's interest — although, as he cautions, "man should put responsible limits to the amount of suffering he inflicts . . . *always requiring for the death and suffering some tangible advantage*" (122).[62] Violence in and of itself is both inevitable and (for men) ethically neutral, a position which McClung sharply challenged.[63]

The rational legislator also defers to authority, and would "always take expert advice as to whether the desired object [i.e., legislative reform] could be achieved by legal compulsion" (116-17). This observation is entirely in keeping with Sir Almroth's general confidence in the expert's neutral exercise of rational judgement, but also serves, in practical terms, to reinforce an androcentric, hierarchical status quo.

As we have seen earlier regarding Sir Almroth's commentary on "grateful" women, one constant thread which runs through his discussion is women's refusal and/or inability to appreciate male authority.[64] On this point, women's education is to blame:

> The girl who is growing up to woman's estate is never taught where she stands relatively to man. She is not taught anything about woman's physical disabilities. She is not told . . . that child and husband are to woman physiological requirements. She is not taught the defects and limitations of the feminine mind. One might almost think that there were no such defects and limitations; and that woman was not always overestimating her intellectual power. . . . (158-9)

Neither do women's objections that equal education has proven them men's intellectual equals hold any sway, for "Practically every man feels that there is in woman — patent or hidden away — an element of unreason which, when you come upon it, summarily puts an end to intellectual discussion" (142).[65] This common opinion held by men, which has already been identified as "as close to truth as it is possible for humanity to come," further justifies women's exclusion from any education toward public responsibility; indeed, in the main, such efforts would prove fruitless. The rare woman whose competence, in male terms in the male sphere, is undeniable, serves in no way to contradict this general approach to the education of women, for not only is such a woman plainly unnatural, an aberration, her exceptional ability does not "abrogate the disqualification of belonging to an inferior intellectual caste" (161).[66]

That women are so marked as an inferior caste offsets what might be the logical conclusion to this discussion, that is, if women are not educated into submission, they will not submit, thus disproving the "naturalness" and inevitability of women's subordination. *By definition*, women belong to an inferior group, marked by their difference, as defined and adjudged by men. That McClung and others found far more rhetorical power in their redefinition of the *nature* of women's differences, rather than in the denial of difference altogether, is not surprising, given what is here an absolutely entrenched conviction in a dual-nature, hierarchical humanity. By maintaining the conventional *form* of the argument, and substituting unconventional *content* (e.g., women's self-defined "superior nature," male "particularity" vs. "female universalism" in the matter of the public good, etc.), McClung was able to highlight some of the more preposterous claims of her opponents, meanwhile conveying in a positive, affirmative way women's unique perspective and contribution toward the building of a better world.

While it is tempting to read Sir Almroth, in opposition to McClung, as an untroubled defender of the status quo, such in fact was not the case. He recognized the source of "woman's discontent," issuing in the call for woman suffrage, as grounded in social reality, specifically in the growing numbers of "surplus" (i.e., unmarried) women.[67] The agitation surrounding women's political rights had two sources, a dearth of marriageable men who might provide a legitimate focus for women's energies, and the "intellectual disability" suffered by women through (hetero)sexual inactivity. In searching for a "palliative or corrective for the discontents of woman," Sir Almroth proposes three possible courses of action.

First, as many "surplus women" as possible should emigrate to the colonies to find husbands. This would serve both as an individual cure for the women involved, and as a social boon, inasmuch as the Empire would be strengthened through colonization and England itself cleansed of a disruptive social group. Those women unwilling to emigrate are instructed to "go out from the social class [in which] they are not self-supporting and into a humbler social class" (157), a move which would afford them the opportunity to find the kind of unskilled jobs for which they are alone qualified. Finally, a woman "can forsake conditions in which she must remain a spinster for conditions in which she may become a mother" (157).[68] Sir Almroth's delicate language does not make explicit which indelicate occupation he is recommending, but it is clearly one which involves the rendering of sexual services to obtain an income. Any other solution to the "Woman Question" is misguided, based on a failure to respect the experts' determination of public utility and women's intrinsic inferiority.

Sir Almroth's text concludes with his "Letter on Militant Hysteria," included here as Appendix D. Therein he considers the types of women who agitate for suffrage, and offers his comments upon the proper resolution of this unrest. As we have seen, it is axiomatic for Sir Almroth that "there is mixed up with the woman's movement much mental disorder," the source of which lies in "physiological emergencies" borne out of insufficient heterosexual intercourse (168). In addition to this general condition of distress, there are five more acute manifestations of women's imbalance, characterized by the following types of militant feminists. First "come a class of women who hold, with minds otherwise unwarped, that they may, whenever it is to their advantage, lawfully resort to physical violence" (116). While these women are not mentally ill, precisely, their folly lies in usurping the male prerogative of using violence in the service of social utility, thereby violating the law of chivalry established for their protection. Next come "a class of women who have life-long been strangers to joy, women in whom instincts long suppressed have in the end broken into flame. These are the sexually embittered women in whom everything has turned into gall and bitterness of heart and hatred of men" (169-70). That is, these women have been so poisoned by their lack of sexual satisfaction that they have come to hate men, and are acting out their hostility through their militant feminism. A third category of militant feminist is that of the "incomplete," whose "programme is to convert the whole world into an epicene institution . . . in which man and woman shall work side by side at the selfsame tasks for the selfsame pay" (170). These insufficiently differentiated beings fail to recognize the differences which obtain between normal men and women, and wrongly suppose that, without socially differentiated spheres, humanity would come to reflect their own aberrant natures. Further, regarding employment, they fail to recognize that a man "can do his best work only in surroundings where he is perfectly free from suggestion and from restraint, and from the onus which all differential treatment imposes" (171). While it might well be the case that these women are able to perform certain tasks as well as men, their disruptive presence in the work-force undercuts male productivity and contributes thereby to the destruction of the social fabric (171).[69]

Equally dangerous is the fourth category of militant feminist, characterized by "the woman who is poisoned by misplaced self-esteem; and who flies out at every man who does not pay homage to her intellect" (172). Women like this are basically "ungrateful." Unimpressed with their "special nature" and true vocation of motherhood, they insist not only on intellectual equity, but on financial equity as well (173).[70] Their ultimate goal, apart from the beggaring of men, is to reduce the dignity of their parliamentary representative to such a level that "He humbly, hat in hand, asks for his orders from a knot of washerwomen standing arms a-kimbo" (173). This emasculation of the elected legislator would be a threat to both domestic and national security, as Sir Almroth elsewhere points out at some length.[71]

Finally, "Following in the wake of these embittered human beings come troops of girls just grown up" (173). Educated by unmarried suffragists into completely mistaken notions of "the intellectual, and moral, and financial value of women" (174), these young women demand "to be married upon their own terms. Man shall . . . work for their support . . . but they themselves must not be asked to give up any of their liberty to him, or to subordinate themselves to his interests, or to obey him in anything" (174).[72] While completely misguided, this category of militant suffragist is less threatening in Sir Almroth's view than the others, as the realities of economic dependency and women's intrinsic inferiority will soon defeat their youthful bid for autonomy. Nevertheless, they are still socially disruptive, and Sir Almroth is adamant that the "feminist indoctrination" which permeated their education be stopped as soon as possible.

In sum, then, there are no legitimate reasons for woman suffrage, nor can the conviction of its desirability be in any way construed as a moral stand. Persons taking this position are at best misguided and, at worst, an abomination to the order of nature and a threat to civilized life. Moreover, the solution to this enormous problem is painfully straightforward: women must simply accept the world as it is. Sir Almroth eloquently concludes:

> Peace will come again. It will come when woman ceases to believe and to teach all manner of evil of man despitefully. It will come when she ceases to impute to him as a crime her own natural disabilities, when she ceases to resent the fact that man cannot and does not wish to work side by side with her. And peace will return when every woman for whom there is no room in England seeks "rest" beyond the sea,[73] "each one in the house of her husband," and when the woman who remains in England comes to recognize that she can, without sacrifice of dignity, give a willing subordination to the husband or father, who, when all is said and done, earns and lays up money for her.[74]

b. Stephen Leacock

Anti-feminists also appealed to humour to reinforce their position. In Canada one of the more formidable practitioners of this approach was Stephen Leacock, McGill political economist and renowned writer and lecturer. Roughly McClung's contemporary (1869-1943), Leacock stood diametrically opposed to her on almost every issue. As early as 1905 he was establishing himself as an ardent spokesman for British Imperialism, eventually embarking on a world tour to preach his message.[75] Like Sir Almroth, his vision of imperialism was one which affirmed the superiority of the white male and reflected profound mistrust of the "lower races." As Alan Bowker notes:

> There was, however, a very ugly side to this sense of mission, a
> haunting fear of the coloured races which burst forth from time to
> time in Leacock's oratory. In a speech in 1908 he described world
> history as "the question of the Aryan civilization of the West and the
> uncivilized, or at best semi-civilized, people of the Orient. . . . There
> has never been harmony between them." The British Empire, includ-
> ing Canada, was the front line of the white race in this battle against
> Asiatic encroachment. Leacock denied that coloured peoples of the
> Empire had the same rights as whites.[76]

Leacock's view of the fundamental difference between races had
its counterpart in his understanding of men and women. While his
concern for "proper" gender roles continued throughout his life, sur-
facing in numerous pieces,[77] attention here will be paid to three specific essays. Two, "Apology of a Professor"[78] and "The Devil and the
Deep Sea,"[79] both published in 1910, illustrate the context of Leacock's
anti-feminism. The third, "The Woman Question,"[80] was originally
published in *Maclean's* magazine. *Maclean's* later solicited a reply from
McClung, "Speaking of Women," which will also be considered
below.

"The Apology of a Professor: An Essay in Modern Learning" is
Leacock's lament over the relativistic world of modern scholarship.
All certainty is gone, he says:

> There is no absolute sureness anywhere. Everything is henceforth to
> be a development, an evolution; morals and ethics are turned from
> fixed facts to shifting standards that change from age to age like the
> fashion of our clothes; art and literature are only a product, not good
> or bad, but a part of its age and environment . . . our formal studies
> are no longer burning quests for absolute truth. ("Apology," 35)

In addition to reducing modern scholarship to "resigned agnosticism"
(35), this loss of certainty has a further destructive effect in the emasculation of the scholar, who is now assumed, like the priest, to "prefer
tea to whiskey-and-soda, blindman's buff to draw poker, and a fresh-
men's picnic to a prize fight" (36).[81] Moreover, the fragmentation of
modern knowledge has created a situation wherein, wisdom having
been abandoned along with the quest for certainty, the professor cannot even put what little he does know to practical use: "Nor can the
professor make money out of what he knows. . . . A teacher of English
cannot write a half-dime novel, nor a professor of dynamics invent a
safety razor. The truth is that a modern professor for commercial purposes doesn't know anything" (37). Leacock is not here advocating
that the academic world embrace commercialism. Rather, he is decry-

ing that tendency in the world at large, and showing how, once adopted by the academy, it destroys from within, emasculating its practitioners and shattering time-honoured truths into bits and pieces of information which are not even commercially marketable. By "modernizing," therefore, the academy has sown the seeds of its own destruction.

Leacock's lament bears all the earmarks of a "paradigm break-down." Old certainties are challenged, facts proliferate independently of any meaningful context, and the world, as the British colloquialism would have it, "has gone to smash." Leacock confirms this assessment:

> if the mind as a speculative instrument has gone bankrupt [having no certain framework within which to speculate], if learning, instead of meaning a mind full of thought, means only a bellyful of fact, one is brought to a full stop, standing among the littered debris of an ideal that has passed away. (39)

It is instructive to note how Leacock concludes this piece, for only then does he name his "villain," the perpetrator of this intellectual and spiritual disaster. She is "the Woman with the Spectacles":

> The professor is passing away. . . . The male school-teacher is gone, the male clerk is going, and already on the horizon of the academic market rises the Woman with the Spectacles, the rude survivalist who, in the coming generation, will dispense the elements of learning cut to order, without an afterthought of what it has once meant. (39)

Since, as with Sir Almroth, it is axiomatic that women are incapable of rational, creative and sustained intellectual activity, their entry into the educational field can only spell the destruction of the enterprise itself. The non-traditional woman thus becomes for Leacock, in essay and in fiction, both the sign of social disintegration and, through her rejection of the past, the very perpetrator of it.

A similar process of disintegration was also taking place for Leacock within the moral realm, due to the substitution of "moral evolution" for the retributive function of the Devil. While "The Devil and the Deep Sea" is a witty, casual piece, underlying its jabs at pompous academics and silly women who go to fortune tellers is a genuine, and profound, concern for the loss of moral order which only the threat of eternal punishment could ensure.[82] While women are not singled out as responsible for this development, certainly feminism, religious and otherwise, challenged the moral order which

Leacock mourns. Charlotte Perkins Gilman, for example, directly attributed belief in the devil to a projection of the male mind upon the moral and social world, to the detriment of all:

> That which is true of the male creature as such is assumed to be true of life in general; quite naturally, but by no means correctly. To this universally masculine error we may trace in the field of religion and ethics the great devil theory, which has for so long obscured our minds. A God without an Adversary was inconceivable to the masculine mind. From this basic misconception we find all our ideas of ethics distorted.[83]

McClung likewise rejected the existence of the devil as necessary for the moral order, preferring a nurturing, educative approach to the problem of sin.[84]

For Leacock, however, this "New Morality" is self-indulgent and dangerous, and all its emphasis upon self-improvement is delusory. He states: "The vague and hysterical desire to 'uplift' one's self merely for exaltation's sake is about as effective an engine of moral progress as the effort to lift one's self in the air by a terrific hitching up of the breeches" (46). Physical self-improvement, such as that advocated by the W.C.T.U., was likewise foolish, a misdirection of energy toward an ultimately insignificant goal. The political dimensions of self-improvement are considered only regarding men, where Leacock speaks with some fear of "the new worship of the Strong Man, the easy pardon of the Unscrupulous, the Apotheosis of the Jungle, and the Deification of the Detective. Force, brute force, is what we now turn to as the moral ideal, and Mastery and Success are the sole tests of excellence" (49). In this he shares much with McClung, but he does not consider how, for women, "self-improvement" might lead to health rather than to domination. Rather, as Gilman suggests, Leacock assumes the male model of aggression and so laments the loss of the devil who alone is able to keep "man" in check.

The most concise statement of Leacock's anti-feminism is contained in his essay, "The Woman Question." Although couched in "humorous" terms, it resonates deeply with Sir Almroth Wright's argument against woman suffrage, most notably in its conviction of women's inferiority. While there are differences (Leacock is sure that women will obtain the vote, for example, but that they will do nothing with it), overall Leacock and Sir Almroth share a world wherein women have one true role, which is *not* political activism.

Leacock begins his essay by poking fun at the "Awful Woman" whose strident pronouncements on women's future influence drive Leacock's fictional companion to seek out a bar.[85] After showing that feminism achieves exactly the opposite of its alleged goals, Leacock proceeds to make a larger case. Women, he says, have no way of surviving in the world independent of men. This is the case because women are clearly, and totally, incompetent:

> The world's work is open to her, but she cannot do it. She lacks the physical strength for laying bricks or digging coal. If put to work on a steel beam a hundred feet above the ground, she would fall off. For the pursuit of figures her head is all wrong. Figures confuse her. She lacks sustained attention and in point of morals the average woman is, even for business, too crooked. (53)

At least part of women's moral inferiority is due to their inability to follow rules and to cooperate. Like Sir Almroth, Leacock appeals to the apparently inherently male capacity to follow the "rules of the game," claiming, "Women could never be a team of anything" (53). It is for this reason, and the fact that women are utterly unscrupulous, "that woman is excluded, to a great extent, from the world's work and the world's pay" (53). In fact, Leacock is so convinced of women's inferiority in this regard that he advocates removing all laws which would bar women from competing with men on equal terms. He observes:

> Here and there it is true there are things closed to women not by their own inability but by the law. This is a gross injustice. There is no defence for it. The province in which I live, for example, refuses to allow women to practise as lawyers. This is wrong. Women have just as good a right to fail at being lawyers as they have at anything else. . . . (57)

Those women who do not fail are "sports," biological oddities who in no way contradict his belief that "The ordinary woman cannot do the ordinary man's work. She never has and never will. The reasons why she can't are so many, that is, she '*can't*' in so many different ways, that it is not worth while to try and name them" (57).[86] That inherent inability, combined with the huge number of women attempting to enter the labour market, has created a situation wherein women who do work outside the home are poorly paid, receiving less than men for doing even the same jobs. There is inequality here, Leacock concedes, but it is not due to discrimination. Rather,

Women get low wages because low wages are all that they are
worth. . . . It is the sheer numbers of women themselves, crowding
after the few jobs that they can do, that brings them down. It has
nothing to do with the attitude of men collectively towards women
in the lump. (59)

Leacock recommends the development of social policy which
would acknowledge women's true vocation of marriage and motherhood, thereby accommodating their inevitable dependency: "If they
cannot be looked after by an individual . . . they must be looked after
by the State. . . . To turn a girl loose in the world to work for herself,
when there is no work to be had, or none at a price that will support
life, is a social crime" (60). The situation which Leacock would advocate, with all the motives of compassion and desire for social justice, is
that of a kind of permanent wardship for women. Like Sir Almroth,
Leacock recognized that feminism arose in response to a real social
problem, although both identify this as the proliferation of unmarried
women whose energies are misguided rather than as any fundamental flaw in traditional gender relations. However, unlike Sir Almroth,
rather than expecting women to fend for themselves in factory jobs,
domestic service and/or concubinage, Leacock suggests the institu-
tionalization of women's inferiority through a kind of State wardship.
It follows, although Leacock does not explicitly say this, that wardship status does not entitle women to the privileges of full responsible
citizenship, such as suffrage. In any case, even if women were to
receive the right to vote, women's intrinsic incompetence would
ensure that their exercise of this privilege would have no effect on
Canadian political life.[87]

Feminists who attempted to capitalize on women's growing discontent by advocating woman suffrage were dangerous, however, for
they would remove precisely those protective conventions which
sheltered women from a world in which they could not compete. Further, in advocating career choices for women, feminists endangered
the whole social fabric. For Leacock as for Sir Almroth, motherhood
was a necessity for women, although Leacock emphasized replenish-
ing the population and the moral education of children rather than
women's need for heterosexual satisfaction to ensure mental stability
as the most persuasive reasons for this vocation.

Finally, despite his humorous tone, Leacock retains his affinity
with Sir Almroth in his implied threat of violence against feminist
women. While he does not develop this point, and while his genuine
concern for the well-being of the "average woman" is evident, his

comments are nevertheless disturbing, particularly so since he obviously intended his readers to find his observations funny:

> Then there rose up in our own time, or within call of it, a deliverer. It was the Awful Woman with the spectacles, and the doctrine that she preached was Woman's Rights. She came as a new thing, a hatchet in her hand, breaking glass. But in reality she was no new thing at all, and had her lineal descent in history from age to age. The Romans knew her as a sybil and shuddered at her. The Middle Ages called her a witch and burnt her. The ancient law of England named her a scold and ducked her in a pond. But the men of the modern age, living indoors and losing something of the ruder fibre, grew afraid of her. The Awful Woman — meddlesome, vociferous, intrusive — came into her own.[88]

McClung's reply to "The Woman Question" is notable in its sober, thorough tone, as if she were willingly sacrificing her customary flamboyance to offset any invidious comparison with Leacock's "Awful Woman." Her argument is not unique; much of "Speaking of Women" is a toned-down version of sections of *In Times Like These*.[89] What is unusual is the care which she apparently is taking in not challenging Leacock head on, to such an extent that his name is not even mentioned.[90] Her response, then, is somewhat oblique, but no less effective for its strategic coloration.

McClung's central point is that, while "Men and women have two distinct spheres, when considered as men and women, . . . as human beings there is a great field of activity which they may — and do occupy. Now it is in this common field of activity that women are asking for equal privileges" (26). In response to the contention of Leacock and others that women are all somehow disabled regarding the franchise because of lesser physical strength, or because women "cannot lay bricks, nor string wire" (26), McClung makes two points: first, "The exercising of the ballot does not require strength or endurance" (25); and second, that many men cannot do women's traditional work either, and that does not disallow their voting privileges.[91] Drawing upon public sentiment against Germany, McClung chides her audience: "Surely the opponents of woman suffrage do not mean to advocate that a strong fist should rule; just now we are a bit sensitive about this, and the doctrine is not popular. Might is not right; without our heart's blood we declare it is not!" (25)

Indeed, says McClung, opposition to suffrage has its origin not in the doctrine of power, nor in concern for women's "frailty," but rather in the "deep-rooted fear, that change may bring personal inconvenience" (25).[92] Most are not honest enough to admit this, however, so they parade a variety of other plausible concerns:

> They say they oppose the enfranchisement of women because they are too frail, weak and sweet to mingle in the hurly-burly of life; that women have far more influence now than if they could vote, and besides, God never intended them to vote, and it would break up the home, and make life a howling wilderness; the world would be full of neglected children (or none at all) and the homely joys of the fireside would vanish from the earth. (25)[93]

By defining the problem as self-interested prejudice, rather than reason, McClung is able to argue all sides of the question at once. She nominally accepts women's physical "inferiority" and argues that voting is a "genteel" and lady-like way of expressing an opinion. Then in the following paragraphs she recounts the back-breakingly hard physical labour done by homesteading women, adding:

> No person objects to the homesteader's wife having to get out wood, or break up scrub land, or drive oxen, so long as she is not doing these things for herself and she has no legal claim on the result of her labour. Working for someone else is very sweet and womanly, and most commendable. (26)[94]

Likewise, McClung grants passing acceptance of the notion of "two distinct spheres" for men and women, then immediately points out:

> The exceptional woman can do many things, and exceptions merely prove *that there is no rule*. There is a woman in the Qu'Appelle Valley who runs a big wheat farm and makes money. The Agricultural Editor of the *Manitoba Free Press* is a woman who is acknowledged to be one of the best crop experts in Canada. Figures do not confuse her! Even if the average women is not always sure of the binomial theorem, that does not prove that she is incapable of saying who shall make the laws under which she shall live. (26)[95]

This juxtaposition of "conventional wisdom" and feminist counter-example heightens McClung's point regarding anti-suffragist prejudice, and effectively undercuts the appeal of their position for the average reader.

One final issue which McClung addresses is the question of the necessity of women's dependency upon men. She begins by pointing out that "this babble of marriage and home for every woman sounds soothing" (26), but in reality even before the War there were over 1.5 million more women than men in Britain. Moreover, the War was destined to increase that difference. She adds somewhat irritably, "One would think, to read the vaporings which pass for articles on the suffrage question, that good reliable husbands will be supplied upon request, if you would only write your name and address plainly and enclose a stamped envelope" (26). Furthermore, limiting women's sole useful role to the bearing and rearing of her own children diminishes society by depriving it of an invaluable resource:

> The strong, active, virile woman of fifty, with twenty good years ahead of her, with a wealth of experience and wisdom, with a heart mellowed by time and filled with that large charity which only comes by knowledge — is a force to be reckoned with in the uplift of the world. (26)[96]

Persons who do not recognize the full range of women's capacities and therefore oppose woman suffrage are living, in McClung's view, a sheltered life whose days are numbered:

> But time goes on and the world moves; and the ways of the world are growing kinder to women. Here and there in a sheltered eddy in the stream of life, where the big currents are never felt, you will find the old mossy argument that women are intended to be wageless servants dependent upon man's bounty, with no life or hopes of their own. But the currents of life grow stronger and stronger in these terrible days, and the moss is being broken up, and driven out into the turbulent water. (96)

The clean, healthy vigour of equal rights is contrasted with the swampy morass of prejudice, leaving the reader with a powerful image in support of change.

McClung's article ends with a reflection upon what women would do with suffrage. It is significant that she does not here make the sweeping claims which Leacock attributes to the "Awful Woman," i.e., that woman suffrage would prevent/end war, protect the abused, abolish poverty and injustice, etc. — claims indeed made by McClung in other contexts. Instead, in response to Leacock's "benevolent despotism" wherein women would be subject to State wardship, McClung argues that the extension of suffrage to women is necessary for true democracy. While not all women have suffered directly from their voteless state, their well-being has been entirely dependent upon the man who was their "ruler." Others, however, have suffered terribly, with no redress. True democracy would provide the necessary "checks and balances" to the social system to allow women to make their own mistakes, and to pay for them. McClung remarks "That will be nothing new — they have always paid for men's mistakes. It will be a change to pay for their own" (97). Indeed, having the leeway to make one's own mistakes, and to take responsibility for them, is one of the hallmarks of a democratic system, and a safeguard of it.[97] She concludes: "Democracy has its faults; the people may run the country to the dogs, but they will run it back again. People, including women, will make mistakes, but in paying for them they will learn wisdom" (97).[98]

McClung's reply to Leacock is an excellent illustration of her willingness to use a variety of rhetorical strategies to make her point regarding women's full humanity. Current readers frustrated by her "inconsistencies" — the ease with which she concedes "two distinct spheres" for men and women, for example, while simultaneously arguing against any formulation of what those might be — should reconsider the political realities of the suffrage struggle. Though the Canadian experience was in the main devoid of physical violence, anti-suffrage forces were not above using other tactics of dubious moral standing to thwart suffragist aims.[99] It is to this reality, in the person of Sir Rodmond Roblin, Premier of Manitoba, to which we now turn.

c. Sir Rodmond Roblin

In *Purple Springs*, the third volume of the Pearlie Watson trilogy, McClung describes a character known as "the Chief":

> The Chief was a man of perhaps sixty years of age, of florid countenance, red mustache, turning gray, splendidly developed forehead, dark gray eyes with wire-like wrinkles radiating from them, which seemed to have been caused more by laughter than worry; a big, friendly voice of great carrying power, and a certain bluff, good fellowship about him which marked him as a man who was born to rule his fellowmen, but to do it very pleasantly. (PS, 211-12)

He is Premier of the province, and approximately half of the novel is devoted to the newly-politicized Pearl's efforts to unseat him and his government. "The Chief" was in reality none other than Sir Rodmond Roblin (1853-1937), Conservative Premier of Manitoba from 1900 to 1915 and a staunch opponent of woman suffrage. McClung's physical description, above, matches Roblin's photographs; historical opinion might be more divided, however, on her characterization of his government:

> The government had been in power for many years and had built up
> a political machine which they believed to be invincible. They had
> the country by the throat, and ruled autocratically, scorning the
> feeble protests of the Opposition, who were few in number and weak
> in debate. Many a time Pearl sat in the Ladies' Gallery and listened
> to the flood of invective with which the cabinet ministers smothered
> any attempt at criticism. . . . They were so boastful, so overbearing,
> so childishly important, it seemed to her that it would be easy to
> make them look ridiculous, and she often found herself framing
> replies for the Opposition. But of course there was a wide gulf
> between the pompous gentlemen who lolled and smoked their black
> cigars in the mahogany chairs on the red-carpeted floor of the House,
> and the bright-eyed little girl who sat on the edge of her seat in the
> gallery. . . . (PS, 76)

Witnessing the complacency and corruption of "the Chief" and his
minions sends Pearl first into "the wordless rage of the helpless" (PS,
77), then, lethally for the government, to the Suffrage Society and
political activism.

That Roblin could have aroused such depth of feeling in McClung
that even six years after he was forced to resign from office she would
devote such energy to his fictional chastisement is testimony to his
intractability in the face of her persistent argumentation. Indeed, even
given the convention of melodrama employed in the text, McClung's
retributive justice borders on the extreme. "The Chief" is publicly
humiliated through a "Woman's Parliament" in which Pearl imitates
his behaviour in the Legislature with such devastating accuracy that
even his own party members are convulsed with laughter.[100] He
leaves the theatre a broken man, with "the echo of people's laughter
in his ears [as] bitter as the pains of death" (PS, 279). He is also pri-
vately humbled, and ends up begging forgiveness of his daughter-
in-law, whom he had terrorized and who had suffered years of hardship as a result. His role in the novel culminates in a public confession
wherein he not only thanks Pearl for removing him from office, but
offers to go out and campaign for her, should she ever decide to seek
election (PS, 306). Such a conversion definitely did not take place in
real life, although Roblin and McClung eventually became cordial
enough in their twilight years to exchange "pleasant messages . . . via
a mutual acquaintance."[101]

McClung's intense frustration with Roblin lay in his apparent dismissal of her — in public at least. Covertly, Roblin's Conservatives
seemed to consider her no small threat, to which they responded in
rather unsavoury ways. McClung's Papers contain an example of their

activities. In a newspaper clipping entitled "Orange Jingoes and Presbyterian Bull-dogs," the Manitoba Free Press reported a recent piece
found in the Conservative Ruthenian "organ" "Canada," in which the
Liberal party was defamed and McClung herself slandered.[102] Accusing the Liberals of buying the election, the piece declaims: "Mrs.
McClung . . . was paid by the Liberals $25 a day to insult, in babbling
storybook fashion, Premier Roblin throughout the province. The Liberals are sly. They know that whenever the devil cannot succeed a
women has to be employed." This sinister behaviour on McClung's
part was cited as simply one more element in a larger plot, contrived
by Protestants, Orangemen, and "women who walk the streets with
pet dogs and want to get into parliament" to destroy Ruthenian culture. Further, Roblin's response to McClung's suffrage delegation was
misrepresented so as to imply that the delegation's discontent with
Roblin issued out of his insistence that all women, even servant girls
(many of whom would have been of Ruthenian origin) should get the
vote also:

> Thereupon the ladies turned up their noses and left the chamber like
> wet hens. You see they wanted only rich women to have the vote
> and those are just the women whose support the Liberals gained.
> One of them, Mrs. McClung, personally undertook to clean out all
> the dirty corners of Manitoba, and told the people all sorts of fantas-
> tic stories about Premier Roblin.[103]

Given the highly polemical nature of newspaper reporting at the
time, such treatment of McClung was to be expected, and, indeed,
Conservative cartoonists took great pleasure in depicting her as an
angry mosquito, or as a raving battle-axe in trousers.[104] It was the triv-
ialization of her causes by Roblin and his government which inflamed
McClung, and Roblin's exercise of privilege to avoid confronting the
issues which McClung championed. One example was Roblin's treatment of the temperance issue. Candace Savage describes Roblin's
actions in this way:

> So he insisted first that the new temperance act be tested by the
> courts, and when it survived that challenge, he called a plebiscite to
> make sure that the electorate still wanted the legislation. The people
> of Manitoba had already made their views clear in two referenda
> (1893 and 1898) and in one election (1899), all of which the drys had
> won hands down. To register their disgust with Roblin's tactics,
> many prohibitionists boycotted the new tally, with the result that
> their side lost. The premier took this result as justification to repeal
> the Macdonald liquor act.[105]

Temperance advocates were thus forced to fight for the enforcement of the "local option," wherein individual municipalities could hold a referendum to "go dry" if their petitions were honoured by government. Roblin was singularly uncooperative in that regard, throwing out McClung's petitions 72 times on technicalities:

> Once we had a petition in thirty-two sheets.
> "Oh no, certainly not," we were told, "the law says a petition, not thirty-two of them."
> Next year we pasted them all together.
> "What an outrage!" said the government, "This is a mutilated petition. How can you prove to us that John Smith, five feet or so down from the top, ever saw that heading you have? Go home and forget it."[106]

The last straw for McClung was Roblin's refusal to hear another McClung-led temperance delegation in the early days of the war. On 24 September 1914, McClung published "An Open Letter to Sir Rodmond."[107] It is uncharacteristically sober, a thorough, painstaking indictment of the Roblin government, built entirely upon the disparity between Roblin's rhetoric and actual government action. As in *In Times Like These*, the war provided McClung with a "higher standard" against which to judge things, an almost irrefutable justification for challenging the status quo.

In the letter, McClung argued that the crisis created by the war demanded the closure of all outlets for the sale of alcohol. Using Roblin's own hedge about "the will of the people," McClung pointed out that, in general, "It is the voice of the people which should decide [issues like closing the bars]. Yet in time like these, times of special need, it has been done [i.e., unilateral government action taken] without this delay" ("Letter"). Replying to Roblin's oft-made claim that suffrage was unnecessary because women's political voice was already being accommodated, McClung called for him to give a "practical demonstration" of this claim by calling for a moratorium on the liquor trade:

> Ease us of this burden, until peace is declared. Let us postpone the misery, the heart-ache and the tears until a happier season, when perhaps, we can bear it. . . . You have spoken of your sympathy and admiration for the women who have been patriotic enough to let their sons and husbands go to fight the battles of the Empire, and you have condemned in the strongest terms the brutality of the German soldiers, and I am sure that you, in common with all of us, have wished that you could bring all this terrible slaughter to an end. But

> even you cannot do that! . . . But there is a stream of human misery
> here in our own province, over which you have some power. If it is
> so, that you deplore the loss of life, and sympathize with those who
> sorrow, and we believe you do, why not turn your sympathy to
> practical account, and try to mitigate the conditions here at home. . . .
> Human life and happiness, human welfare is just as precious here, as
> it is over there. This would be practical patriotism; better than tons of
> talk and reams of resolutions. ("Letter")

Argument after argument, Roblin's pronouncements are used against
him, as standards against which his government's actual actions are to
be judged. The letter's conclusion reveals the depth of McClung's
anger, and, incidentally, the rhetorical usefulness of the war in fur-
thering the feminist cause. In linking Roblin's paternalism with German autocracy, McClung's argument was driven home with a ven-
geance. She concludes:

> Somewhat after this fashion, I intended to address myself to you and
> the members of the Legislature. In your wisdom, or I should say, in
> your judgement, you saw fit to dishonor your own promise to hear
> us, and declared: "You had no time for those people." That settled it!
> Personally, you disapproved of us. Therefore, our petition to our
> representatives could not be heard. In your petty kingdom, Sir Rod-
> mond, you rule not wisely, but too well. But the world moves, and
> independence of thought is growing. Someday the people of Mani-
> toba will have democratic government. With our eyes turned toward
> Europe and its terrible conflict the majority of us realize that never
> before has autocracy been so hateful, never before has democracy
> been so sweet. ("Letter")

But even bitter protests such as this seemed, in Roblin's case, to
fall on deaf ears. Confident in his role of provincial Premier, Roblin
displayed little of the apocalypticism about women's rights which
permeated Sir Almroth's denunciations, nor is Leacock's mourning
for a lost era evident in his stance. Sir Rodmond's anti-feminism was
straightforward and practical, grounded in an uncritical acceptance of
the "cult of true womanhood" and sustained by his power, as Premier, to stifle any counter-argument to his opinion which might arise.
If, as McClung implied, he was a dictator, he was a relatively benevolent one. He made no special effort to argue against women obtaining
the vote, for such an engagement would indicate that he took the issue
seriously. Roblin operated from a position of strength — his government
could grant women the franchise, but would not — hence his argument
against McClung's suffrage petitioners could be, and was, patronizing

and banal.[108] McClung's general weapon, in response, was humour. With rational argument and moral suasion ruled out of court by the dismissive Roblin, McClung set out to make her nemesis look ridiculous. Apparently she succeeded. As the *Montreal Herald* reported:

> Last Thursday Sir Rodmond spoke here [Winnipeg] and on Monday his feminine tormentor made him look ridiculous. She has introduced into this campaign the most telling weapon with which the bombastic Premier of Manitoba could be attacked and one which no person has ever wielded against him before so poignantly and effectively. *All Manitoba has been made to laugh at Sir Rodmond Roblin by Nellie McClung.*[109]

How could McClung have turned public sentiment around so thoroughly? At least one reason might have been Roblin's own style. Bombastic and grandiloquent, it presupposed a climate of prior acceptance; his was the rhetorical flourish topping off the status quo. Once those underlying assumptions were challenged, Roblin was at a loss to generate an effective counter-argument. Instead, he resorted to a technique employed by both Stephen Leacock and Sir Almroth, that of dismissal, and appeal to self-evidence. In response to the myriad arguments put forth by McClung's suffrage delegation, for example, he flatly stated:

> I am not going to meet some of the arguments that have been submitted. That chivalry which was inspired in me by my mother bars me from making an answer to some of the arguments, arguments which I am surprised have been put forward. The answer to those arguments is so manifest that it can be seen by the most indifferent.[110]

Should the audience or readership not share in the worldview herein evoked, however, the speaker appears merely to be evading the question. McClung was able to use Roblin's evasiveness to her own political advantage, and employed the technique of "reversal" to evoke a different imaginative world from which to evaluate commonplaces such as chivalry, and love of one's mother, to which Roblin alluded.[111] This, rather than any systematic articulation of her own or another's *theory* of feminism proved, particularly given its humorous delivery, a most potent political weapon. She simply quoted her opponents against themselves.

It should not be assumed from this observation that McClung's own arguments totally lacked substance, as a brief consideration of her suffrage delegation's submission to Sir Rodmond Roblin will illustrate. When Roblin met the suffrage delegation in late January 1914, he was faced with a variety of arguments for extending the franchise to women.[112] Some, such as Rev. R. Marteinsson, speaking for the Icelandic Women's Suffrage Association, emphasized humanity's ongoing struggle to throw off oppression, and named the woman suffrage movement as "a fight for emancipation, just as the French Revolution was a struggle for the rights of the common people" (MFP). Further, government could benefit from their insight on issues like "white slavery." Alderman Rigg of Trades and Labor cited the economic changes which had forced many women into the work force, and argued that women had a right to control, through legislation, the conditions under which they sold their labour. "The hand that rocks the cradle" was to become "the hand that pulled the strings of government." Roderick McKenzie of the Grain Grower's Association affirmed women's intelligence and competence to exercise the franchise, presumably demonstrated by their contribution to building the Prairie west. Finally, Mrs. Kelly, the W.C.T.U. representative, raised two points. The first focused on the injustice of taxation without representation experienced by women, and the second on women's duties, as mothers, to act in the larger world beyond their doorstep: "Woman could not sit still when those she loved and whom she felt it her duty to guard were fighting conditions over which women had no control" (MFP).

McClung's presentation incorporated these elements and combined them into a plea for common justice. Not only had women's hard work and sacrifice shown that women had earned the vote, and not only had equal access to education proved women's competence to vote, the government needed the insights gleaned from women's particular experience to serve the cause of justice fully:

> Men had done and given of their best in the making of the laws, and in all their labors she believed they were actuated by the highest motives. But men alone could not legislate for men and women. They made the laws from the viewpoint of man alone, and in order to frame laws which would be for the benefit of all humanity, the help of women was necessary. (MFP)

Women's unique perspective obligated them to participate in the public sphere of human endeavour. As McClung put it: "Woman's place was in the home and out of it whenever she was called as a mother or a sister to guard those she loved, and to improve conditions for them" (MFP).[113] While this might prove socially expedient, benefitting all of society, ultimately the call for women's enfranchisement was not a call for "mercy, their plea was one of justice" (MFP). Women, as human beings, had suffrage as their right. Roblin's reply largely sidestepped these arguments, and focused instead on a single question — would enfranchising women improve the home? The rights of women *qua* human beings were secondary to the preservation and reinforcement of society's domestic building block. Referring to his wife, Roblin asked:

> Will anyone say she would be better as a mother and wife because she could go and talk on the streets about local or Dominion politics? I disagree. The mother that is worthy of the name, and of the affection of a good man, has a hundredfold more influence in molding and shaping public opinion round her dinner table than she would have in the market place, hurling her eloquent phrases to the multitude. It is in the home that her influence is exercised and felt. Home is the type of every national excellence. (MFP)

Moreover, suffrage agitation could precipitate a significant rise in the rate of divorce, as the American experience was proving. McClung parodied this claim in *Purple Springs*:

> We hear of women leaving home, and we hear it with the deepest sorrow. Do you know why women leave home? There is a reason. Home is not made sufficiently attractive. Would letting politics enter the house help matters. Ah no! Politics would unsettle men. Unsettled men mean unsettled bills — unsettled bills mean broken homes — broken vows — and then divorce. (PS, 273)[114]

Roblin also contended that "woman's true vocation of wife and mother" meant that she must devote herself unequivocally to those roles, in the home, for in so doing she was embodying and upholding the highest values of civilization:

> My mother, of whom Mrs. McClung· spoke, taught me to love and respect women and the home: taught me when I entered the presence of a woman to take off my hat or offer her my seat: she taught me to believe that woman had a sphere of usefulness and work that placed her above the ordinary man and that woman's place and work was to mold the heart and conscience of the child. ("Roblin Says")

In *Purple Springs* McClung transformed this "pedestal" theory, so characteristic of the cult of domesticity which Roblin upheld, into a rhapsodic — and ironical — paean to "men's true destiny":

Man has a higher destiny than politics . . . what is home without a bank account? The man who pays the grocer rules the world. Shall I call men away from the useful plow and harrow, to talk loud on street corners about things which do not concern them. Ah no, I love the farm and the hallowed associations — the dear old farm, with the drowsy tinkle of cow-bells at even-tide. There I see my father's kindly smile so full of blessing, hard-working, rough-handed man he was, maybe, but able to look the whole world in the face. . . . You ask me to change all this. (PS, 274)

As McClung's parody suggests, Roblin's romanticism led him to assume that any social change wrought by woman suffrage would be unequivocally negative, a "retrograde step" ("Roblin Says"). He dismissed, therefore, the often made claim that woman suffrage would have a "purifying influence" on politics. Indeed, he denied outright the existence of any kind of irregularity or corruption which would provide the base for that contention, indignantly calling it "the imaginings of a wicked and vile mind" (ibid.). Apparently, Roblin's alleged obliviousness to political corruption was not commonly shared. Not only did his remarks generate "incredulous laughter" from his audience (ibid.), elsewhere it was assumed that every politician in Manitoba was corrupt. As one reporter for the *Grimsby Independent* sarcastically put it, regarding McClung's "whirlwind campaign" for prohibition: "the whole campaign was run on crooked politics, crooked politicians on both sides, and there are men who stood on the platform with Nellie McClung who were so crooked they couldn't sleep straight in a bed. . . ."[115] McClung herself devoted considerable space to the realities of political corruption in *Purple Springs*.[116] Her most telling riposte, however, was made in her role as premier in the "Women's Parliament" at the Walker Theatre:

It has been charged that politics is corrupt. I don't know how this report got out, but I do most emphatically deny it. I have been in politics for a long time, and I never knew of any corruption or division of public money among the members of the house, and you may be sure if anything of that kind had been going on I should have been in on it. Ladies and gentlemen what I mean is that I would have known about it. Every time we spend a dollar on the province, we first look at it from every side to see if we could make better use of it for ourselves. . . . I ask your delegation to be of good cheer. We will try to the best of our ability to conduct the affairs of the province, and prove worthy standard-bearers of the good old flag of our grand old party which has often gone down to disgrace but never to defeat.[117]

On every count McClung turned Roblin's bombast to political advantage. Although the reality of his political power prevented the extension of the suffrage to women during his tenure as Premier, nevertheless the climate of opinion in which his anti-feminism was heard underwent a dramatic shift. By making Roblin the object of ridicule McClung undercut the power of commonplaces such as "Woman's place is in the home" to boundary political reflection, and made possible a paradigm shift wherein new roles for women could be imagined.

The anti-feminist context of McClung's political activism, as illustrated by Sir Almroth Wright, Stephen Leacock, and Sir Rodmond Roblin, assumed a dual-nature view of humanity in which the biological differences between men and women, as articulated by men from men's perspective, were understood to be normative in the social sphere as well. Whether the final court of appeal for this view was "scientific reason" (Sir Almroth), "common sense" (Leacock) or "woman's true calling" (Sir Rodmond), the political reality espoused was identical: "woman's true place" was in the home as wife and mother, as those roles were circumscribed by men in the service of male interest.

McClung's feminist response was necessarily two-fold. First, she sought to emphasize women's "common humanity" with men in the matters of human excellences, social and religious obligations, and spiritual worth.[118] As the "good" characters in her novels reveal, men and women are more alike than different; both can be noble, caring, just, merciful, wise. Likewise, both men and women can be venal, bitter, harsh, greedy and uncaring, although the circumstances within which those sins are made manifest may differ because of social roles.

However, McClung also wished to preserve for women a unique perspective and understanding which issued out of the concrete realities of women's lives. This affirmation of women's traditional experience has been misinterpreted by a number of critics who assume this alleged "maternalism" to be a defective form of feminism.[119] Normative claims for a new feminist orthodoxy aside, this reading of the material omits consideration of the anti-feminist, and often explicitly anti-woman, context within which McClung made her claims. While other feminists like Charlotte Perkins Gilman quite forthrightly argued the ineradicable thoroughgoing character of gender difference, gynocentrically articulated, McClung's stance is more nuanced. Once women's common humanity with men is affirmed, McClung allows for the possibility of significant, perspectival differences between men and women, but she refused to let male-defined, male-articulated versions of those differences stand as the human norm. This challenge from female particularity fundamentally undercut the claim to "neutral expertise" asserted by Sir Almroth, and encouraged a recognition of the problems inherent to a status quo built upon a hierarchical ordering of class, race, ethnicity, nationality and gender.[120] As this chapter has argued and attempted to show, it is only after an exploration of the features of that anti-feminist status quo that McClung's political pronouncements may be adequately assessed. To substantiate that claim further, we turn now to the text itself, McClung's famous "feminist polemic," *In Times Like These*.

Notes

1 Book review of *In Times Like These*, Los Angeles *Tribune*, 6 December 1915: McClung Papers, Add. MSS 10, Vol. 36.

2 Book review of *In Times Like These*, *Saturday Night*, 1 January 1916: McClung Papers, Add. MSS 10, Vol. 36.

3 See the Introduction, 4-6.

4 If reviews of McClung's works are any indication, the prominence which *In Times Like These* currently enjoys in the McClung corpus is a recent phenomenon, borne more out of current scholarly agendas than out of its importance for McClung's contemporaries. Reviews of McClung's works, even after the publication of *In Times Like These*, primarily identify her as the author of *Sowing Seeds in Danny*. Further, even granting the political status which McClung enjoyed in her later years, it is *Clearing in the West*, the first volume of her autobiography, which was most overwhelmingly received of all McClung's works, and it is this text which generated the bulk of her "fan mail" (see Appendix C).

5 "Woman Suffrage Book Reviewed from Two Angles," book review of *In Times Like These*, Boston *Advertiser*, 4 December 1915: McClung Papers, Add. MSS 10, Vol. 36. Subsequently referred to as Boston *Advertiser*.

6 In the absence of a truly neutral pronoun indicating "an individual of either sex," I am here employing the traditional, masculine, falsely generic form "he" to indicate the author of this piece, whose sex is not known. Given the content of the review, male authorship is not unlikely; while it is certainly possible for a woman to have expressed anti-feminist sentiments with similar vehemence, I have not encountered any in this literature. Perhaps, as with Mrs. Arthur M. Dodge's introduction to Sir Almroth Wright's *An Unexpurgated Case against Woman Suffrage* (New York: Hoeber, 1913), they were content to adopt the more "womanly" role of letting the men speak for them.

7 Boston *Advertiser*.

8 Book review of *In Times Like These*, Boston *Congregationalist*, 13 April 1916.

9 Boston *Advertiser*.

10 Ibid.

11 Book review of *Saturday Night*, 1 January 1916.

12 Ibid.

13 Boston *Advertiser*.

14 Book review of *In Times Like These*, Edmonton *Examiner*, 10 November 1915: McClung Papers, Add. MSS 10, Vol. 36.

15 Review of *In Times Like These* by "The Bookman," n.d.: McClung Papers, Add. MSS 10, n.v. See also the review of *In Times Like These* in the Los Angeles *Tribune*, 6 December 1915.

16 Book review of *In Times Like These* in "Books of the Day," Toronto *Globe*, 1 November 1915: McClung Papers, Add. MSS 10, n.v. See also the review in the *Congregationalist*: "No amount of knowledge, no literary deftness, could produce these chapters, they are primarily the utterances of character and of an exceptionally strong individuality" (Boston *Congregationalist*, 13 April 1916).

17 "Mrs. McClung's New Book": McClung Papers, Add. MSS 10, n.v.

18 Review of *In Times Like These* by "The Bookman." Although "The Bookman" does not identify these figures further, Moody is probably Dwight Moody (1837-99), an American evangelist involved in social welfare work who conducted revivals throughout the United States and Canada. Spurgeon was most likely Charles Haddon Spurgeon (1834-92), an immensely popular English Baptist preacher who opposed Higher Criticism. Alexander Grant was a major Baptist leader.

19 Review of *In Times Like These*, Boston *Congregationalist*, 13 April 1916.

20 Even the apparently progressive "Bookman" considers McClung "extremely radical concerning women and the married life," possibly because of her insistence that spouses be friends and equals.

21 McClung's dual dedication of *In Times Like These*, to "Superior Persons" and to "men and women everywhere who love a fair deal" reinforces this point.

22 Veronica Strong-Boag acknowledges this lack in her most recent article on McClung, "Ever a Crusader: Nellie McClung, First-Wave Feminist," in *Rethinking Canada: The Promise of Women's History*, ed. Veronica Strong-Boag and Anita Clair Fellman (Toronto: Copp Clark Pitman, 1986), 189, fn 12.

23 Wright, *Unexpurgated Case*.

24 McClung, *In Times Like These*, 70; the name is misspelled in the text as Sir Almoth Wright, omitting the "r." Subsequent references are given parenthetically in the text.

25 Wright, preface, 17. Subsequent references are given parenthetically in the text.

26 Sir Almroth's views on the inferiority of women's mental processes virtually guarantee that the term "he" is being used here in its specific, rather than in its falsely generic sense.

27 Sir Almroth speaks of the suffragists' "repulsion of a state or society in which more money, more personal liberty (in reality only more of the personal liberty which the possession of money confers), more power, more public recognition and happier physiological conditions fall to the share of the man" (22).

28 For an interesting discussion of John Stuart Mill and his avowed indebtedness to the intellectual prowess of his wife, Harriet Taylor, see Phyllis Rose, *Parallel Lives: Five Victorian Marriages* (New York: Vintage Books, 1983). Rose notes the disbelief with which Mill's praise of his wife was met by both his contemporaries and later critics.

29 The reality, and necessity, of women's economic dependence upon men also figures largely in the anti-feminism of Stephen Leacock, who argues that women's own inferiority necessitates their protection and seclusion in the home. See Stephen Leacock, "The Woman Question," *The Social Criticism of Stephen Leacock*, ed. Alan Bowker (Toronto: University of Toronto Press, 1973), 51-60. Feminists like McClung were well aware of the nature of the "protection" women might actually expect from men, and hence devoted considerable energy to showing, through anecdote and narrative, the painful reality of many women's lives. Moreover, McClung

acknowledged that, "Deeply rooted in almost every woman's heart is the love of home and children; but independence is sweet and when marriage means the loss of independence, there are women brave enough and strong enough to turn away from it" (ITLT, 86). She is countering the charge made by Sir Almroth and others that "independent" women were "plainly abnormal," replying instead that the rejection of conventional marriage involves courage and dignity, and could be considered in fact an act of heroism, attendant upon which comes no small loss.

30 Regarding Mill's *Subjection of Women*, for example, Sir Almroth claims: "In that skilful tractate one comes across every here and there, a *suggestio falsi*, or a *suppressio veri*, or a fallacious analogy nebulously expressed, or a mendacious metaphor, or a passage which is contrived to lead off attention from some weak point in the feminist case" (26-7). The average reader might well have been impressed by such verbiage, which certainly gives the impression of greater scholarly authority than most feminists could muster in the public mind. Modern readers who find arguments against woman suffrage absurd are invited to consider the appeal — and "scientific validity" — of sociobiology, which argues women's inherent limitations in a manner only slightly more sophisticated than Sir Almroth's. See Edward O. Wilson, *Sociobiology: The New Synthesis* (Cambridge: Belknap Press of Harvard University, 1975), 547-75. For an excellent discussion of Wilson's gender bias, see Joseph Alper et al., "Sociobiology is a Political Issue," in *The Sociobiology Debate*, ed. Arthur A. Kaplan (New York: Harper and Row, 1978), 476-88, esp. 481-5.

31 Current feminists contemptuous of McClung's alleged "maternalism" would do well to remember the powerful counter-argument her happy marriage and five children provided to this charge of feminist "abnormality." Nor has this tendency to discredit feminist argument through *ad feminem* commentary ceased — noted Canadian historian Ramsay Cook has suggested, for example, that McClung's temperance stand emerged out of her marriage to an alcoholic, even though no documentary evidence exists to support such a point (personal conversation, Learned Societies Meetings, Winnipeg, Manitoba, 3 June 1986).

32 See Thomas Kuhn, *The Structure of Scientific Revolutions*, 2nd ed., enlarged (Chicago: University of Chicago Press, 1970), esp. chs. 6-8. Thomas Kuhn's discussion of the scientific response to crisis (i.e., "paradigm breakdown") is illuminating here. He notes that the process of scientific professionalization "leads ... to an immense restriction of the scientist's vision and to a considerable resistance to paradigm change" (64). As greater and greater anomalies emerge, resistance increases correspondingly, in an attempt to keep a crumbling worldview intact. For those not so committed, these efforts to shore up the paradigm appear rather desperate and misguided. In the very intensity of their defence of the status quo, anti-feminists like Sir Almroth revealed the precariousness of their own position. Feminists were quick to exploit this weakness by identifying them with an "old order" whose days were numbered in the face of radical evolution.

33 "What is Feminism? An Absolutely Accurate Account of the Teachings of Leading Feminists, Containing Doctrines on Divorce, Attacks on the Home, the Family, the Church and Christian Marriage Made by Feminists from 1825 to 1915": McClung Papers, Add. MSS 10, Vol. 20, File 1.

34 Ibid., 1.

35 For example, see McClung's discussion of marriage, "The Sore Thought" (ITLT, 81-94).

36 Note the element of hierarchical control disguised as genteel service evident here.

37 See McClung's devastating "woman's-eye" description of such women in "Gentle Ladies" (ITLT, 60-6). Epitomized by their "anemic" and "beseeching" cry, "We are gentle ladies. Protect us. We are weak, very weak, but very loving" (ITLT, 63), it is

these women, and not the suffragists, who in McClung's view would bring the downfall of civilization. She states, "Wherever women have become parasites on the race, it has heralded the decay of that race" (ITLT, 64). For a "humorous" rendering of Sir Almroth's position, see Stephen Leacock, "The Two Sexes, in Fives or Sixes: A Dinner Party Study," *Further Foolishness: Sketches and Satires of the Follies of the Day* (New York: John Lane, 1917), 71-9.

38 In other words, because men have always *thought* women to be inferior, women are inferior. With reasoning such as this to contend with, McClung's exasperation, expressed in the following passage, is even more understandable: "After one has listened to all these arguments and has contracted clergyman's sore throat talking back, it is real relief to meet the people who say flatly and without reason: 'You can't have it — no — I won't argue — but inasmuch as I can prevent it — you will never vote! So there!' The men who meet the question like this are so easy to classify" (ITLT, 57).

39 Sir Almroth's shift is interesting here. When women want the vote, it is a dangerous thing, embodying violence and potentially destructive of human civilization. For men, it is a rather weak legislative instrument, barely capable of nudging the direction a piece of legislation might take.

40 If there is discrimination, he adds, it will be to women's benefit, for "man is more prone to discriminate in favour of woman than against her" (66). Sir Almroth would be astonished by a recent article by former Olympic runner Bruce Kidd, the central thesis of which is that "men have created sports to celebrate and buttress patriarchal (and class) power": Bruce Kidd, "Sports and Masculinity," in *Beyond Patriarchy: Essays by Men on Pleasure, Power, and Change*, ed. Michael Kaufman (Toronto: University of Toronto Press, 1987), 250.

41 This notion of the "neutrality of expertise" is also hotly challenged by feminists today, who see therein the use of authority to call premature closure on a fundamental debate about the values embodied in the paradigms the "experts" employ. The difficulty of the challenge should not be underestimated. Those with the power to establish the "rules of the game" hold a position of strength, the power of naming those who disagree as "poor sports," or worse, "poor losers," incapable of even understanding the game.

42 Hence McClung's point in *In Times Like These* about the docility of German womanhood. She points out that if the theory of women's indirect power of moral suasion were correct, the rape of Belgium could never have occurred (ITLT, 23).

43 It is interesting to consider what Sir Almroth's response to Margaret Thatcher might be.

44 Hence the counter-argument of McClung and others, that woman suffrage would be socially useful.

45 "There would after that be no electoral or parliamentary discussion which would not be open to challenge on the ground that it was impossible to tell whether the party which came out the winner had a majority which could enforce its will, or only a majority obtained by the inclusion of women" (85). McClung responded directly to this view in her speeches. In one newspaper report ("Nellie McLung [sic] Works Hard for Mothers of the West": McClung Papers, Add. MSS 10, Vol. 35) her humorous treatment of the issue is recorded: "Some said the women should not have the vote because they could not fight. 'I mean go to war,' explained Mrs. McClung, bringing renewed laughter. The time for brute force, she said, had gone by. It was no longer necessary in war to spread your enemy's features all over a vacant lot. (Much laughter and cheering.) If there was disfranchisement in the war game then every man over 45 would be debarred and so would all the smaller men. She asked the delegates, amid great laughter, how they would like that. If physical

force, she said, were the only requisite they would have to give Jack Johnson seven or eight votes." McClung's citation of a black prize-fighter is all the more provocative, given Sir Almroth's avowed opposition to granting rights to non-whites.

46 Sir Almroth's revulsion is not confined to rule by women, but extends to all who are in some way "impaired": "Every one feels that public morality is affronted when senile, infirm, and bedridden men are brought to the poll" (84-5).

47 McClung, "Dedication II" (ITLT, 4).

48 Note Sir Almroth's connection of "savages" with "wild animals."

49 That Sir Almroth considers this order to be in women's favour is clear. He states, "to break through this covenant was to abrogate a humanitarian arrangement by which the general body of non-combatants immensely benefits" (131).

50 Stephen Leacock makes similarly veiled threats to women's well-being. Calling the woman suffragist "the Awful woman with the Spectacles," he notes that in the Middle Ages she was rightly burnt at the stake as a witch. For scholars persuaded that widespread gynocide was practised under the aegis of "witchhunting," Leacock's is a particularly chilling comment (Leacock, "The Woman Question, 55).

51 Sheila Jeffreys' controversial text, *The Spinster and Her Enemies: Feminism and Sexuality, 1880-1930* (London: Pandora Press, 1985), addresses the question of the relationship between normative sexuality and feminism. She suggests that "The birth of sexology in the period from the 1890's to the First World War enabled antifeminists to mount an onslaught against feminism with all the authority of 'science'" (128). By supporting the idea of innate psychological differences between the sexes, and linking the regular active practice of heterosexual intercourse with mental, physical and emotional health, sexologists such as Havelock Ellis and Ivan Bloch were able effectively to undercut the bonds of same-sex friendships and single women's independence by deeming such lifestyles "sick" or "deficient."

52 For Sir Almroth, there is a clear connection between "sexual characters" and "racial characters," both of which are irremedial" (81).

53 Kathryn Morgan notes that Kant makes a similar point regarding women's moral capacity. See Immanuel Kant, *Observations on the Feeling of the Beautiful and the Sublime*, trans. John Goldthwait (Berkeley: University of California Press, 1960), 76-96, as cited in Morgan, "Women and Moral Madness," unpublished paper given at the Toronto Area Women's Research Colloquium, 14 November 1986.

54 Note that here Sir Almroth completely contradicts his earlier arguments that abstract principles must be superseded by consideration of "utility" and "expedience" (80).

55 There is a hierarchy in the general class of men, however: "each man's moral station and degree will be determined by the election which he makes where egoism and altruism, and where a narrower and a wider code of morality, conflict" (102).

56 "When morality takes up its abode in a man who belongs to the intellectual caste it will show itself in his becoming mindful of his public obligations" (105).

57 Carol Gilligan, *In a Different Voice: Psychological Theory and Women's Development* (Cambridge: Harvard University Press, 1982).

58 Karen McCarthy Brown, "Heretics and Pagans: Women in the Academic World," in *Private and Public Ethics: Tensions between Conscience and Institutional Responsibility*, ed. David G. Jones (New York: Edwin Mellen Press, 1978), 267.

59 Ibid., 267-8.

60 Feminists directly addressed the question of the male creation of culture in texts such as Charlotte Perkins Gilman's *Man-Made World, or Our Androcentric Culture* (New York: Charlton, 1911; rpt. Source Book Press, 1970).

61 Brown, "Heretics and Pagans," 269. See also McClung's redefinition of marriage (ITLT, 33, 84).

62 My emphasis. Given Sir Almroth's understanding of public utility, this approach to violence gives those in power considerable leeway to determine what means and ends are conformable to public advantage.

63 While McClung addressed this problem in other ways as well, one of her most powerful appeals is made in the name of religion. She states, "It is easy for bigger and stronger persons to arrogate to themselves a general superiority. Christ came to rebuke the belief that strength is the dominant force in life" ("Women and the Church," ITLT, 68).

64 "The failure to recognize that man is the master, and why he is the master, lies at the root of the suffrage movement" (159-60). He adds, rather threateningly, "woman will have to learn that when things are not offered to her, and she has not got the power to take them by force, she has got to make the best of things are they are" (162).

65 For a fascinating, if somewhat disturbing illustration of Sir Almroth's assessment of the source of this irrationality, see his posthumously published *Alethotropic Logic* (London: Heinemann, 1953). Of particular interest is chapter 21, "On Feminine Psychology," wherein he gives scientific "proof" of the validity of a number of anti-female epigrams.

66 However, upon occasion men might find such a woman "useful" for some intellectual task, in which case her disqualification is temporarily suspended. Sir Almroth describes the "naturalization" of the exceptional woman into the "country of men" as follows: "women should be admitted to masculine institutions only when real humanitarian grounds demand it; that she should — following here the analogy of what is done in learned societies with respect to foreigners — be invited to co-operate with men only when she is quite specially eminent, or beyond all question useful for the particular purpose in hand; and lastly, that when co-opted into any masculine institution woman should always be placed on a special list, to show that it was proposed to confine her co-operation within certain specified limits" (149).

67 Sheila Jeffreys discusses the issue of "surplus" women, noting that in Britain, "In the late Victorian period almost one in three of all adult women were single and one in four would never marry." In 1851, for example, the census revealed that there were 405,000 more women than men in Britain's population (Jeffreys, *The Spinster and Her Enemies*, 86). Sir Almroth estimates there were one million "excess women" in Britain as of 1912 (169).

68 Charlotte Perkins Gilman discusses at length women's "sexuo-economic" relation to men in *Women and Economics* (Boston, 1898; rpt. New York: Harper and Row, 1966). The text considers women's economic dependence upon men "abnormal," a result of men's excessively developed sexual desire, and argues that human social development has been impeded thereby.

69 Sir Almroth goes on to argue against equal pay for equal work, for two reasons. First, "even if a woman succeeds in doing the same work as man, he has behind him a much larger reserve of physical strength. As soon as a time of strain comes, a reserve of strength and freedom from periodic indisposition is worth paying extra for." (Note that the male is being rewarded for his "superiority" rather than the female being penalized for her "inferiority.") A second factor is "that woman's commercial value in many of the best fields of work is subject to a very heavy discount by reason of the fact that she cannot, like a male employee, work cheek by jowl with a male employer; nor work among men as a man with his fellow employees" (175). For a modern discussion of male reaction to a gender-integrated workplace, see Stan Gray, "Sharing the Shop Floor," in *Beyond Patriarchy*, ed. Michael Kaufman (Toronto: Oxford University Press, 1987), 216-34.

70 "The programme of this type of woman is, as a preliminary, to compel man to admit her claim to be his intellectual equal; and, that done, to compel him to divide

up everything with her to the last farthing, and so make her also his financial equal."

71 ". . . there cannot be two opinions that a virile and imperial race will not brook any attempt at forcible control by women" (82).

72 Of this attitude, Sir Almroth remarks, "It is not necessary, in connexion with a movement which proceeds on the lines set out above, any further to labour the point that there is in it an element of mental disorder. It is plain that it is there."

73 This statement is particularly ironic considering the actual conditions of life awaiting the "surplus" women who came to Canada to marry. For a fictional treatment of this problem, see McClung's *The Second Chance*, particularly chapter 25, "The Coming of Thursa," 252-67.

74 One constant point made by McClung throughout *In Times Like These* and elsewhere is that even if women accept subordinate status and concomitant domination by men, they receive no dependable protection. One particularly chilling story is that of the anti-suffragist "Mrs. B's" Polish washerwoman who "had the old world reverence for men, and obeyed [her husband] implicitly" (ITLT, 46). The washerwoman provided for their children and bought a house with her earnings. The husband then sold the house without her knowledge, leaving his wife and family penniless and homeless. Yet another anecdote relates the story of the wealthy farmer who in his will bequeathed a farm to each of his sons, but "To his daughter Martha, a woman of forty years of age, the eldest of the family, who had always stayed at home, and worked for the whole family — he left a cow and one hundred dollars." She observes, "How would you like to be left at forty years of age, with no training and very little education, facing the world with one hundred dollars and one cow, even if she were named 'Bella'?" The mother was even worse off: "To the poor old mother, sixty-five years of age, who had worked far harder than her husband, who had made butter, and baked bread, and sewed carpet rags, and was now bent and broken, and with impaired sight, he left: 'her keep' with one of the boys! How would you like to be left 'your keep' even with one of your own children? Keep! It is exactly what the humane master leaves an old horse . . ." (ITLT, 91). The point McClung is making is that not only is this economic dependence demeaning, it is an unjust and inaccurate assessment of the worth of women's actual labour. Furthermore, men cannot necessarily be depended upon to take care of "their womankind" (Wright, 186), a fact which makes feminism necessary. For a current treatment of this issue, see Barbara Ehrenreich, *The Hearts of Men: American Dreams and the Flight from Commitment* (Garden City, N.Y.: Anchor Press, 1983).

75 See Alan Bowker's Introduction to *The Social Criticism of Stephen Leacock*, xii-xiii. Leacock produced one famous speech as a pamphlet, entitled "Greater Canada," which is included in this collection. Leacock's tour lasted from April 1907 to March 1908, and covered eastern Canada, England, Australia, New Zealand, South America, and the Canadian west.

76 Bowker, Introduction, *Social Criticism of Stephen Leacock*, xxi. McClung staunchly opposed this kind of imperialist racism, proclaiming in *In Times Like These*, "In our blind egoism we class our foreign people as ignorant people, if they do not know our ways and our language. They may know many other languages, but if they have not yet mastered ours they are poor, ignorant foreigners. We Anglo-Saxon people have a decided sense of our own superiority, and we feel sure that our skin is exactly the right color, and we people from Huron and Bruce feel sure that we were born in the right place, too. So we naturally look down upon those who happen to be of a different race and tongue than our own" (ITLT, 53). McClung was also particularly aware of prejudice against Orientals. See *In Times Like These*, 90: "Similarly Chinamen are always severely dealt with. Give it to him! He has no

friends!''; see also *Painted Fires*, where McClung has her heroine work for a sympathetically portrayed restaurant owner named Sam Lee—although to have a "white girl" work for a "Chinaman" was at that time completely against the law.

77 Some examples are: "The Two Sexes, in Fives or Sixes: A Dinner Party Study" and "The Grass Bachelor's Guide," both from *Further Foolishness*, 162-73 and 174-84 respectively; "The Perfect Lover's Guide," *The Garden of Folly* (New York: Dodd, Mead, 1924), 171-204; "An Appeal to the Average Man," Preface to *Winnowed Wisdom* (Toronto: MacMillan, 1926), vii-xii, wherein he claims, "The average woman cannot think. But she can argue. The average woman . . . only got as far in arithmetic as proper fractions. Those stopped her" (xi); and "Are Witty Women Attractive to Men?" *The Leacock Roundabout* (New York: Dodd, Mead, 1965), 379-84, wherein he urges women to be sweet, not witty, and to breed, for "Without our own children, the wave of outside brutes from an unredeemed world will kill us all . . . we must save ourselves first" (383).

78 Leacock, "Apology of a Professor," *Social Criticism*, 27-39.

79 Leacock, "The Devil and the Deep Sea," *Social Criticism*, 41-50.

80 Leacock, "The Woman Question," *Social Criticism*, 51-60. This piece, reprinted from *Maclean's* magazine, 28, 12 (October 1915), 7-9, was also reissued with "Apology of a Professor" and "The Devil and the Deep Sea" in Stephen Leacock, *Essays and Literary Studies* (Toronto: Gundy, 1916), which suggests that the reading public had ample opportunity to become aware of his anti-feminist perspective.

81 He goes on to observe: "Women who embody, so St. Augustine has told us, the very principle of evil, can only really feel attracted toward bad men. The professor is too good for them" (36).

82 "In past ages there was the authoritative moral code as a guide—thou shalt and thou shalt not—and behind it the pains, and the penalties, and the three-pronged oyster fork. Under that influence, humanity, or a large part of it, slowly and painfully acquired the moral habit" ("Devil," 45-6).

83 Gilman, *Man-Made World*, 139.

84 See McClung, "Bells at Evening," *All We Like Sheep* (Toronto: Allen, 1926), 235-61. McClung tells the story of an old woman who dies and goes to heaven, where she meets her husband and soldier son. Heaven appears like an improved version of her old home in Brandon, and when she asks what she will do now, she is told by her husband that they have work to do saving souls. There is no hell for McClung. Those who have lived a good life on earth have the responsibility of helping those who have sinned help themselves. As the old woman's husband, who was formerly a minister, says of the work: "Much the same as we did on earth. I have charge of the people who come over unprepared, and who have terrible remorse over their wasted lives, and all sorts of bad habits to overcome. They are not so different from the poor souls I used to have in this very room" (259).

85 "We were hoping that the Awful Woman would explain how war would be eradicated. She didn't. She went on to explain instead that when women have the vote there will be no more poverty, no disease, no germs, no cigarette smoking and nothing to drink but water. It seemed a gloomy world" ("Woman Question," 52).

86 Note Leacock's appeal to what he assumes is pre-existent agreement with his view of women's incapacity. He continues this appeal in speaking of the necessity of mothers being always "in the home": "Sensible people understand it as soon as it is said. With fools it is not worth while to argue" (58). This repeated appeal to common conviction and refusal to account for this conviction in any detailed way on the grounds that it would not be "worth while" to talk to "fools" must have proved tremendously frustrating to feminists attempting to argue their point rationally and systematically.

87 "But after the women have obtained the vote the question is, what are they going
to do with it? The answer is, nothing, or at any rate, nothing men would not do
without them" (56). Leacock changed his opinion on this point once voting women
showed sufficient political power to bring in prohibition. See "The Tyranny of Prohibition," *Social Criticism*, 61-69.

88 Here Leacock seems to be implying that if men had not "lost something"—i.e., a
certain animality, or manliness—they would have succeeded in keeping the
"Awful Woman" in her place. Sir Almroth's discussion of the feminist abrogation
of the laws of civilization makes a similar point in reverse, i.e., that these women
have not been dealt with more severely because men are too civilized. However, Sir
Almroth implies this veneer can easily be broken through should women's outra-
geous behaviour continue.

89 Nellie L. McClung, "Speaking of Women," *Maclean's*, 29 (May 1916), 25-6, 96-7.
Subsequently referred to as "Speaking."

90 Neither Leacock nor McClung mentions the other anywhere in print, nor does
Leacock's name appear in McClung's personal papers. Given the high profile
enjoyed by both, and the opposition of their viewpoints, it is intriguing that they
(apparently) never found themselves in open debate. Possibly neither was willing
to risk his/her reputation in that sort of "popularity contest."

91 ". . . we might with equal foolishness declare that because a man (as a rule) cannot
thread a needle, or 'turn a heel,' therefore he should not ever be allowed to vote.
Life is more than laying of bricks or threading of needles, for we have diverse gifts
given to us by an all-wise Creator!" ("Speaking," 26). McClung's appeal to "God's
wisdom" over "male opinion" is a fairly standard practice of hers in this debate.

92 McClung makes this point somewhat more trenchantly in "Should Women
Think?": "That seems to be the haunting fear of mankind—that the advancement
of women will sometime, someway, someplace, interfere with some man's comfort" (ITLT, 32).

93 McClung goes on: "I remember once hearing an eloquent speaker cry out in alarm,
'If women ever get the vote, who will teach us to say our prayers?' Surely his experience of the franchised class had been an unfortunate one when he could not
believe that anyone could both vote and pray!" ("Speaking," 25). This latter is a
direct, though camouflaged reference to Leacock's article, where he laments, "No
man ever said his prayers at the knees of a vacuum cleaner, or drew his first lessons in manliness and worth from the sweet old-fashioned stories the vacuum
cleaner told" ("Woman Question," 58).

94 McClung makes this point far more sharply in *In Times Like These*: "The tender-
hearted and chivalrous gentlemen who tell you of their adoration for women, cannot bear to think of women occupying public positions. . . . They cannot bear, they
say, to see women leaving the sacred precincts of the home—and yet their offices
are scrubbed by women who do their work while other people sleep—poor
women who leave the sacred precincts of home to earn enough to keep the breath
of life in them, who carry their scrub-pails home, through the deserted streets, long
after the cars have stopped running. They are exposed to cold, to hunger, to
insult—poor souls—is there any pity felt for them? Not that we have heard of.
The tender-hearted ones can bear this with equanimity. It is the thought of women
getting into comfortable and well-paid positions which wrings their manly hearts"
(ITLT, 52).

95 My emphasis. In saying this, McClung is challenging the traditional point that "the
exception proves the rule." The reference to "figures" is a direct swipe at Leacock
("Woman Question," 53).

96 The vitality and usefulness of older women becomes an important theme in her later articles and short stories.

97 A despot can always blame error on others who lack the power to defend themselves. In a democracy, in contrast, everyone (theoretically) has an equal voice. Here McClung is rather cleverly applying an argument regarding the despotic rule of the husband in the traditional family in such a way that readers familiar with her work would catch the subtext, and those new to her perspective would read her simply as praising Western democracy over German autocracy.

98 McClung is here also implying that having to pay for their own mistakes rather than having the power to blame their errors on women would prove educative for men.

99 Catherine Cleverdon suggests, to the contrary, that winning the suffrage battle in the Prairie provinces was a relatively painless process. She states: "Only in Manitoba was there any considerable activity prior to 1910, or a struggle with an unfriendly government. In Saskatchewan and Alberta it was only necessary to arouse enough general interest in the issues to ask for and receive the franchise from governments that never denied the justice of their requests": Cleverdon, *The Women Suffrage Movement in Canada* (Toronto: University of Toronto Press, 1974), 46. Cleverdon's analysis omits a larger consideration of the issues of feminism and anti-feminism, and reads the historical record back through the rosy lens of achieved political victory. A less "liberal," more systemically oriented feminist analysis might consider other factors, such as Roblin's anti-feminism, of greater ongoing significance, even though it did not, in the end, prevent women from obtaining the vote. In any case, it is worth noting that when Roblin was finally removed from office, it was not over the issue of woman suffrage, but over a scandal which broke out regarding his financial handling of the construction of the new Legislative Buildings. Roblin was replaced by Liberal T.C. Norris, allegedly a supporter of the woman suffrage movement. Even so, the bill which he prepared to present in the Legislature was framed in such a way as to prevent women from being able to run for office, although they would be allowed to vote for male candidates. It took Lillian Beynon Thomas' organization of an "eleventh hour" protest to generate sufficient pressure on the government to force Norris to make the requisite changes to the bill. Cleverdon's reading of government behaviour in this is generous, to say the least (Cleverdon, 62-4).

100 "The Chief" attains peace in the novel, but only after he has suffered to the extent of the suffering he inflicted upon others.

101 See Savage, *Our Nell*, 232, n. 28.

102 "Orange Jingoes and Presbyterian Bull-dogs": McClung Papers, Add. MSS 10, Vol. 35. (Subsequently referred to as "Orange.") The Manitoba Free Press describes the paper as follows: " 'Canada' was established last fall as a Conservative Ruthenian organ by the Roblin forces. The first issue appeared on 1 September 1913, and across two columns of the first page was a picture of the Premier of Manitoba, Sir Rodmond Roblin. . . . The editorial offices of 'Canada' were located, and still are located, in the Charles H. Forrester Block on Fort Street. In the same building are the Provincial Police Department, the Provincial Police Court, the Provincial Liquor License Department, and several other departments of the Manitoba government.

"The president of the company which publishes 'Canada' is Theo. Stefanik. . . . Suffice it to say that Stefanik has been the chief intermediary between the Roblin Government and its undertaking to the Ruthenian population that if the Ruthenian population voted 'Roblin' they would be undisturbed in the conduct of their schools, compulsory education would not be enforced amongst them, efficient teaching of English would not be required, and teachers possessing no adequate knowledge of the English language would not be interfered with."

103 Persons who assume McClung's "bourgeois" or "Anglo" values undercut her support amongst non-English-speaking working girls and women ought to consider the powerful propaganda levelled at her to create precisely that impression. McClung herself argued the plight of these women against the strongly patriarchal nature of their traditions. In that sense, the concern of Ruthenian males for the loss of tradition was well placed, inasmuch as McClung's call for the equal valuation of women with men strongly challenged eastern European assumptions. Moreover, girls and women working as servants would need to learn English. Their employment in English-speaking homes would provide opportunities for acculturation and adaptation to mainstream Canadian culture, resulting in further erosion of "pure" Ruthenian tradition. Nevertheless, McClung considered it not inappropriate to challenge any tradition which held that women were to be kept uneducated, ignorant, inarticulate and subservient to men.

104 For example, the Liberal paper the *Manitoba Free Press*, in which "Orange Jingoes and Presbyterian Bull-dogs" appeared, described the vice-president of the company which published "Canada" as follows: "Paul Gigejczuk, second only to Stefanik as a tool of the Roblin Government in debauching and degrading the Ruthenian population . . ." ("Orange").

105 Savage, *Our Nell*, 77.

106 McClung, as quoted in ibid., 77.

107 "An Open Letter to Sir Rodmond": McClung Papers, Add. MSS 10, Vol. 17. Subsequently referred to as "Letter."

108 In *Purple Springs* the Premier's attitude, as parodied by Pearl, is described as follows: "She was in the Premier's most playful, God-bless-you mood, and simply radiated favors and goodwill. The delegation was flattered, complimented, patted on the head, as she dilated on their manly beauty and charm" (PS, 272).

109 "Manitoba Tories Worried over Lady Orator's Campaign," *Montreal Herald*, 9 July 1914: McClung Papers, Add. MSS 10, Vol. 35; my emphasis.

110 "Premier Roblin Says Home Will Be Ruined by Votes for Women," *Manitoba Free Press*, 20 January 1914. Subsequently referred to as "Roblin Says."

111 Other feminists have adopted this strategy to drive home their point regarding the nature of prejudice against women. See, for example, Dorothy L. Sayers, *Are Women Human?* (1947; rpt. Grand Rapids: Eerdmans, 1971), and Mary Daly, *Gyn/Ecology: The Metaethics of Radical Feminism* (Boston: Beacon Press, 1978). Daly raises the technique to a point of high theoretical significance, charging that the male-created world is so distorted that only by reversing every assumption undergirding the status quo can truth for women be known.

112 Accounts of this meeting may be found in the *Manitoba Free Press*, 28 January 1914 (subsequently referred to as MFP), and the *Grain Growers Guide*, 14 February 1914.

113 Note McClung's use of the terms "mother" and "sister," echoed also in Mrs. Kelly's presentation for the W.C.T.U. Here women's identity and social responsibility are constituted independent of their relationship, if any, with men, which suggests a fundamental redefinition of the patriarchal home.

114 See also "Women Score in Drama and Debate," *Manitoba Free Press*, 28 January 1914, which reported McClung, as Premier, pronouncing, "Down to the south, where men had the vote, it had been shown that seven-eighths of police court offenders were men and only one-third of church members were women."

115 "A Hot One for Miss Nellie McClung": McClung Papers, Add. MSS 10, Vol. 36.

116 See particularly chapter 7, "The Innocent Disturber," and chapter 12, "The Machine."

117 "Women Score in Drama and Debate."

118 Dedication II to *In Times Like These* begins, "Believing that the women's claim to a common humanity is not an unreasonable one . . ." (ITLT, 4). Elsewhere she states, "Women are not angels or glorified beings of any kind; they are just human beings, seeking only fair play and common justice": McClung, "The Awakening of Women," 258.

119 Carol Bacchi's *Liberation Deferred? Ideas of the English Canadian Suffragists* (Toronto: University of Toronto Press, 1983) is a recent example of this approach to feminism.

120 This simultaneous emphasis upon common humanity and particularity of vision is characteristic of many current theologies of liberation which are generated out of a recognition and experience of injustice (i.e., being treated as *less* than equals, as deviations from "normative humanity"), and which move to redress this imbalance through speaking out from that particular experience in order to transform the structures which create and maintain oppression. See, for example, Beverly Harrison, *Making the Connections* (Boston: Beacon Press, 1985).

IV

In Times Like Hers: An Analysis of *In Times Like These*

> True statesmanship is the art of finding out which way Almighty God is going then getting things out of his road.[1]

In her 1972 Introduction to *In Times Like These*, Veronica Strong-Boag makes the claim that Nellie McClung's feminism "reflects the evangelical social reformer's perception of a civilization in need of redemption."[2] Her feminism was secondary, a result of the belief that "only women can be the redeeming agents" (ITLT, xix). This characterization of McClung is not unique. Scholars as diverse as Ramsay Cook,[3] Thomas Socknat,[4] and Carol Bacchi[5] all assume McClung's feminist commitment to be subsequent to her "evangelical zeal," although they vary in their evaluation of the worth of that Christian conviction. Usually, this relationship is simply assumed. Socknat, for example, asserts: "At the core of McClung's feminism, a product of the Social Gospel, was the faith in women as redeeming agents in a militaristic civilization. Peace would not arrive until women were allowed to say what they thought of war" (84). He offers no evidence in support of this position, presumably because the "larger" aims and goals of the Social Gospel are self-evident. Cook is similarly off-hand in his treatment, although he sees McClung's religion as an impediment to her radicalism rather than as a larger ground for it.[6]

Notes to Chapter IV are on pages 176-83.

As neither of these scholars' primary agenda is feminist activism, their absorption of McClung into their own operative categories is perhaps understandable. Yet even scholars with an avowed feminist interest, like Carol Bacchi and Veronica Strong-Boag, tend to depict McClung in this way. I am convinced this reading of McClung needs to be revised.

This chapter will attempt to offer an alternative interpretation of McClung, and will illustrate its contentions in relation to two main issues. The first is the charge of "maternalism"[7] often levied at McClung by her detractors, who take it as evidence of the religiously based limitation of her feminism. As I shall suggest, this evaluation rests upon current assumptions about what constitutes normative feminism, and upon the failure to consider the context of *In Times Like These* and its location within the larger body of McClung's work. A second concern is the religious ground of McClung's feminist social activism. I shall here argue the thorough integration of McClung's religion and feminism, manifest both in the content and structure of *In Times Like These*. As a collection of sermons which were also political speeches, *In Times Like These* approaches the genre of practical theology wherein divine intention and specific social actions are understood to function in concert. McClung's statement, cited at the opening of this chapter, that "true statesmanship is the art of finding out which way Almighty God is going then getting things out of his road" stands in support of this claim, which will be further substantiated by closer examination of the text of *In Times Like These* itself.

To begin, then, let us turn to the question of McClung's alleged "maternalism" and the consequent judgment of her deficient feminist analysis. Three documents will be considered in this regard: Carol Bacchi's *Liberation Deferred? Ideas of the English Canadian Suffragists, 1877-1918*, Veronica Strong-Boag's Introduction to the University of Toronto Press's 1972 reissue of *In Times Like These*, and Strong-Boag's recent reevaluation of McClung, "Ever a Crusader: Nellie McClung, First-Wave Feminist."[8] Each has been influential in determining how McClung has been read, Strong-Boag through her Introduction, and Bacchi as author of the most recent full-length treatment, after Catherine Cleverdon, of the woman suffrage movement in Canada. The assumptions underlying their interpretive schema must therefore be explored in some detail, with Bacchi's *Liberation Deferred?* to be considered first.

As its title suggests, *Liberation Deferred?* is dubious about the feminism of the English-Canadian suffrage movement. The text concludes that first-wave feminism "failed" in Canada because bourgeois reformers, many of them religious, took over the movement and turned it to their own ends. Fearing a loss of social power, the reformers attempted to reinforce their own class interests through control of those not of the "educated Anglo-Saxon, Protestant elite" (8). Bacchi states:

> The types of reforms advocated suggest the nature of their fears. Temperance, the Canadianizing of the foreigner, the battle against prostitution, the campaign for compulsory education, the desire to rescue delinquents — all reveal a common desire to restore a degree of control over society and chiefly over its deviants. (9)

The church was a prime agent in exercising this control, both as a mainstream institution and in its activist manifestation, the Social Gospel.[9]

Assuming "the Church's fundamental conservatism" (66), Bacchi is unnuanced in her understanding of women's religious social activism. She is particularly critical of what she sees as the Church's positive evaluation of women's traditional role of mother and caregiver in the home, and holds this affirmation of women's traditional experience to be so constraining that religious women had to be "instructed" to become socially active.[10] Being a religious woman, McClung becomes subject to this model in Bacchi's analysis. Even though she acknowledges McClung to be one of the feminists who "chafed under the restrictions imposed by the Churches" (67), Bacchi is guided by the presuppositions of her model to adjudge McClung's social activism insufficiently radical in relation to "true" feminism, which Bacchi considers "the call to enter and compete with men in the male sphere" (147). She states: "Even a suffragist as prominent as Nellie McClung, a temperance woman and a good representative of the social reform wave, could recommend careers only to women with grownup children, women who had already fulfilled their maternal responsibility" (32-3).

In fact, this interpretation is contradicted by McClung herself. In 1928 she wrote an article for Maclean's Magazine entitled, "Can a Woman Raise a Family and Have a Career?" in which she states: "In reply to the question: 'Can a woman raise a family and have a career?' then, I say, whole-heartedly, YES!"[11] But, she notes, this goal can only be achieved if she has the "love and loyalty" of her family, and their willingness to contribute their share to the maintenance of family life.[12] Further, regarding maternal responsibility, McClung states outright:

> I have never suffered from the obsession that no one can care for a child but its mother. . . . The women who helped me to raise my children loved them sincerely and were loved in return. Four of them named their children for mine, which shows, I believe, that their memories of the family are not unpleasant. (71)

This Position is supported in *In Times Like These* as well. In "Women and the Church" McClung challenges the church's view of a woman's proper role "as helpmate for man, with no life of her own" (ITLT, 75). She goes on to point out that

> Children do not need their mother's care always, and the mother who has given up every hope and ambition in the care of her children will find herself left all alone, when her children no longer need her—a woman without a job. But, dear me, how the church has exalted the selfsacrificing mother, who never had a thought apart from her children, and who became a willing slave to her family. (71)

Bacchi's misreading of McClung is due in part to her understanding of what feminism is. Bacchi's normative feminism is characteristically "liberal" in its assumption that the public sphere is the proper locus for truly "human" activity.[13] Women's traditional experience, and the values and perspectives arising out of experiences like mothering are considered of less value than competing with men on men's terms. The redefinition of the public sphere in women's terms and from women's perspective, as advanced by organizations such as the W.C.T.U. (to which McClung belonged) is seen as necessarily confirming rather than as potentially challenging the patriarchal order. Accepting patriarchal culture's devaluing of women's experience as an objective assessment, Bacchi does not consider the potential significance of a mutual redefinition of public and private spheres.[14]

Too, her definition of any "broader awareness of social conditions" as "secular" (61) assures her negative evaluation of religious feminists, and contributes to her misreading of the textual evidence. The quotation which she cites from McClung to support her charge of maternalism, for example, is taken out of context to mean, in Bacchi's view, that social involvement for women is possible only after their domestic duties have been discharged. In fact, in "Speaking of Women," from which Bacchi quotes, McClung was responding to Stephen Leacock's virtually total limitation of all women to the maternal role. (See his "The Woman Question," discussed in Chapter III above.) McClung's point throughout is that women, as full human beings, can do many things, but even if a woman should choose the maternal path for a time, this does not exhaust her usefulness to society.

Bacchi's devaluation of women's traditional experience, and of McClung's attempts to speak from and to it, is characteristic of a certain phase of feminist scholarship.[15] However, this move obscures important subtleties of first-wave feminist activism, and underestimates entirely the powerful challenge to the status quo which women's speaking "in a different voice" posed. Bacchi's characterization of McClung's "maternalism" is therefore suspect, requiring considerable further substantiation before it can be accepted.

Veronica Strong-Boag is another who sees McClung as a maternal feminist par excellence. Like Bacchi, she considers McClung to be "ultimately conservative," at least in part because of her religious faith (ITLT, xv). She states categorically: "A mind formed by a Victorian belief system and a Methodist social gospel both of which emphasized the special attributes of women was limited in its freedom to develop" (ITLT, xx). The inherent limitations upon free thought thus imposed rendered McClung's positions on the issues of her day "naive," although understandably so:

> If McClung was naive in her reactions to drink, the city, and industrialism, and in her expectations for Canada and its women, it was a naiveté born of the liberal's belief in human perfectibility and a social Christian's confidence in the force of good. In all these assumptions she was a creature of her time and place. (ITLT, xx)

More generous in her treatment of McClung's religion than Bacchi, Strong-Boag is nevertheless concerned about McClung's failure to develop a more "radical" feminist analysis. Two issues in particular draw her focus: McClung's "petit bourgeois" sympathies and her apparent "special nature" view of women. Regarding the first, Strong-Boag repeatedly emphasizes McClung's "middle-class rural upbringing" (ITLT, xx), and argues that this "agrarian bias" made McClung incapable of understanding the problems facing the urban working class. Her chastisement of McClung for failing to support the Winnipeg General Strike illustrates this view:

> Her agrarian bias made it difficult for McClung to appraise industrial problems realistically. . . . Her reliance on Christian stewardship as an all-encompassing solution to the hard issues of urban-industrial society exemplified that strain of Social Gospel thought which was turning radicals of her generation away from the churches. (ITLT, xv)

Moreover, McClung's affiliation with "a generation which customarily thought in terms of moral absolutes and was ignorant of more subtle theories of social pathology" (ITLT, xvii) rendered her position on social issues like prostitution unsophisticated and ultimately unworkable. In the end, "McClung's rural sympathies made her analysis appear ever more irrelevant in an urban age" (ITLT, xix).

Strong-Boag's second concern is McClung's support of the "mothering ideal":

> The mothering ideal was central to McClung's feminism. As traditionally as any of her opponents she regarded motherhood as the highest achievement of her sex. She believed that "every normal woman desires children." *In Times Like These* contains no radical reinterpretation of the feminine [*sic*] personality. Instead, McClung's demand for women's rights is presented as a logical extension of traditional views of female moral superiority and maternal responsibility. Women must at last emerge from the home and use their special talents to serve and save the race. (ITLT, viii)

For Strong-Boag, this belief in women's inherent moral superiority had dire consequences, not least of which was its characterization of men:

> Despite her close social and political relationships with a number of men, McClung's arguments often have anti-masculine overtones. Men were frequently portrayed as aggressive, selfish, and uncontrollable. Women were their victims. This myopia is often an unfortunate corollary to the claim of female moral superiority. It leads to a type of reverse sexual discrimination that is one of the most serious flaws of the feminist argument. (ITLT, xx)[16]

Another difficulty inherent in the maternalist view was its failure "to provide modern women with satisfactory role models. . . . Instead, in a newly secular world and an increasingly permissive society, [McClung] left women with a missionary role which emphasized the centrality of the maternal experience" (ITLT, xix). Feminists like McClung were unable to understand what would become the reality of many modern women's lives, and to analyze adequately its causes and solutions.[17] Strong-Boag notes, too, the "contradictions" of first-wave feminist argumentation, i.e., the egalitarian demand for rights pertaining to women, as human, and the inegalitarian assertion that "only women had the spiritual and moral resources to reform society" (ITLT, ix).[18] This theoretical inconsistency resulted in first-wave feminism's "failure." Nevertheless, Strong-Boag concedes that first-wave feminism is not entirely to blame for women's current situation: "The failure of feminism was not in McClung's particular shortcomings, but in her successors' failure to reappraise the situation and avoid the same pitfalls" (ITLT, xx).

In the 14 years intervening between the Introduction to *In Times Like These* and "Ever a Crusader," Strong-Boag's position has shifted considerably. She attributes the move to Ellen DuBois' ground-breaking article, "The Radicalism of the Woman Suffrage Movement: Notes toward the Reconstruction of Nineteenth-Century Feminism."[19] DuBois' thesis is that

> the significance of the woman suffrage movement rested precisely on the fact that it bypassed women's oppression within the family, or private sphere, and demanded instead her admission to citizenship, and through it admission to the public arena. By focusing on the public sphere, and particularly on citizenship, suffragists demanded for women a kind of power and a connection with the social order not based on the institution of the family and their subordination within it. (63-4)

Strong-Boag follows this analysis closely in "Ever a Crusader," a piece which is substantially an expansion and revision of her 1972 Introduction to *In Times Like These*. While still contending that McClung "regarded successful motherhood as the fulfilment of her sex" (182), she does note, in contrast to her earlier piece, the challenges posed to the status quo by the argument from women's "special nature." More importantly, in "Ever a Crusader" Strong-Boag distances herself from the 1972 Introduction's call for theoretical consistency. She acknowledges: "For this hard-pressed generation, politics was a pragmatic exercise: the niceties of theory dissolved before the need to win supporters" (182).

"Ever a Crusader" represents an important development in the way first-wave feminism is understood. Present-day political agendas are not so readily imposed upon the material, as with Bacchi and in Strong-Boag's earlier work. Rather, McClung is discussed in the context of the real limitations and possibilities which shaped her life in a given historical moment. Allowance is also rightly made for the fact that McClung could not, in fact, anticipate all the features of the future we now inhabit. Strong-Boag's reinterpretation of McClung reflects "stage three" feminist scholarship's sensitivity to historical realities. Its reluctance to make sweeping generalizations on the basis of current theoretical or political assumptions offers an important corrective to the presentist approach which tends to characterize earlier work.

Nevertheless, problems remain. Of particular importance is the near-universal tendency to take *In Times Like These* as exhaustively representative of McClung's feminist understanding, and the standard against which all her other work, if considered at all, ought to be judged. As reviews of *In Times Like These* and her other books demonstrate, contemporaneous opinion did not accord *In Times Like These* this status, nor, in fact, did McClung herself. McClung's stories, articles, novels and speeches must be considered equally reflective of her world view if an accurate understanding of her perspective is to be obtained.

Too, the effect of context in shaping the political content of *In Times Like These* needs fuller attention. Some effort has been made, above, to illustrate the features of the anti-feminist opposition to women's equal rights, and the variety of strategies and arguments which needed to be employed to win the public to the feminist cause.[20] Moreover, the fact that *In Times Like These* was, by and large, a collection of speeches,[21] written with a specific and practical political purpose, needs to be taken into fuller account. So doing would serve to offset the tendency to reify McClung's rhetoric into some kind of over-arching "feminist theory." While McClung did indeed borrow catchphrases and even ideas from other feminists, her own agenda was not primarily informed by speculative reflection and systematically arrived at conclusions.[22] Effectiveness was her main rationale in this political fight, leading her to adopt an elegant turn of phrase or a particularly provocative argument with apparently little thought to their further philosophical implications. Much of what is perceived to be McClung's "maternalism" in *In Times Like These*, it will be shown, in fact derives from this practice.

One central source for McClung's borrowing was American sociologist and theorist Charlotte Perkins Gilman (1860-1935), specifically her 1911 publication *The Man-Made World; or, Our Androcentric Culture*.[23] Although knowledge of Gilman has been lost for several scholarly generations, in her day Gilman was a social theorist of considerable importance. Historian Carl Degler comments:

> in the first two decades of the twentieth century her books ran through numerous editions and were translated into half a dozen foreign languages. Her views on the place and future of women were sought, commented upon, and avidly discussed in this country and in Europe. Her dozens of articles appeared in popular and scholarly journals alike, and as a lecturer she was in great demand in the United States, England, and on the continent.[24]

Ann Lane concurs:

> Gilman had an enormous reputation in her lifetime, but she is almost unknown to ours. A serious critic of history and society whose intriguing ideas have never been adequately examined, she tried to create a cohesive, integrated body of thought that combined feminism and socialism. She struggled to define a humane social order built upon the values she identified most closely as female values, life-giving and nurturing. She constructed a theoretical world view to explain human behaviour, past and present, and to project the outlines of her vision for the future. It was a theoretical structure that encompassed anthropology, history, philosophy, sociology, and ethics. Her cosmic efforts were not always successful, but she did create a social analysis that is largely coherent and awesome in its proportions.[25]

Gilman's thought was broadly Social Darwinist in scope, significantly influenced by sociologist Lester Ward, to whom *Man-Made World* is dedicated. Adopting Ward's "Gynaecocentric Theory of Life,"[26] Gilman asserted that "women, as a collective entity, could, if they so chose, be the moving force in the reorganization of society" (*Herland*, x). The motive for social reorganization was neither "justice" nor the "divine intention" which McClung would identify; rather, Gilman saw racial evolution as a communal responsibility, one which existing social structures around gender roles prevented women from effectively exercising.

These barriers to social evolution have arisen, argued Gilman, because our current society has been built on androcentric values. The world has been "named" by men, and reflects the masculine characteristics of "desire," "combat" and "self-expression" (131). While essential for acts of mating, as a basis for civilization these qualities obscure and override the more general human qualities common to both men and women (e.g., compassion, intelligence, industry), as well as specifically female qualities like nurturance, upon which the survival of the whole race depends.[27]

In saying this, Gilman is quick to point out that she has no intention of substituting female domination for male domination, nor has she any intention of denigrating men by considering them specifically as "males" rather than as the prototype of normative humanity:

> the effort of this book is by no means to attribute a wholly evil influence to men, and a wholly good one to women; it is not even claimed that a purely feminine culture would have advanced the world more successfully. It does claim that the influence of the two together is better than that of either one alone; and in special to point out what

special injury is due to the exclusive influence of one sex heretofore. (132)

In any case, she says,

> Men have written copiously about women, treating them always as females, with an offensiveness and falsity patent to modern minds. This book treats of men as males in contradistinction to their qualities as human beings, but never approaches for a moment the abusiveness and contempt that has been shown to women as females. (6)

(Note that Gilman is here subjecting men to precisely the same kind of "objective," "scientific" analysis undertaken by Sir Almroth with regard to women.) While specific elements in Gilman's thought might prove problematic for modern readers (her emphasis upon chastity, for example, or her racism), her feminist analysis is sophisticated and witty. On the "double standard," for example, she argues acerbically:

> It is essential to the best growth of humanity that we practice the virtue of chastity; it is a human virtue, not a feminine one. But in the masculine hands this virtue was enforced upon women under penalties of hideous cruelty, and quite ignored by men. Masculine ethics, colored by masculine instincts, always dominated by sex, has at once recognized the value of chastity in the woman, which is right; punished its absence unfairly, which is wrong; and then reversed the whole matter when applied to men, which is ridiculous. . . . Under the limitations of a too masculine ethics, we have developed on this one line social conditions which would be absurdly funny if they were not so horrible. (133-4)

Man-Made World illustrates the adverse effects of male dominance in chapters ranging from "The Man-Made Family" to "Masculine Literature" to "Games and Sports" through "Politics and Warfare" to "Industry and Economics." Her concern, in showing "maleness" in contradistinction to a truly human norm, is likewise to lift up what might be considered a specifically "female" sensibility. (Gilman's later works probe this question in great detail.)[28] In this regard, it is important to be clear about Gilman's understanding of motherhood. While she states, "Here is woman. Let us grant that Motherhood is her chief purpose," she also adds "(As a female it is. As a human being she has others!)" (168). Her feminist utopian novel *Herland* amply illustrates that the physical act of childbearing is not in and of itself exhaustive of motherhood. Rather, it is the nurturant, educative attention which is constitutive of "conscious human motherhood"

(162), not simply a physical function of sex difference. Motherhood for Gilman was a social act, not a biological inevitability.

However, it may be argued that, despite her concern for men's and women's "common humanity," Charlotte Perkins Gilman's emphasis on the distinctiveness of male and female characteristics, based on sex, ultimately implies a dual nature view of humanity. Certainly, many of her statements would lend themselves to this interpretation, particularly if quoted without regard for her larger theoretical framework. McClung's use of Gilman in this way makes it important to examine more closely the similarities and differences of their perspectives.

As we have seen, *Man-Made World* addresses a range of topics, most of which also emerge in *In Times Like These*. However, it is in the chapter "Ethics and Religion" that McClung's indebtedness to Gilman becomes most apparent. In a passage concerning the influence of men upon religion, Gilman states that "religion is partly explanation — a theory of life; it is partly emotion — an attitude of mind; it is partly action — a system of morals" (137). This formula reappears in McClung, in an article entitled "What Religion Means to Me":

> And so it is that religion is an explanation, and an emotion, and a code of ethics. It tells us something of how we come to be here, and where we are going. It is a code of ethics, inasmuch as it holds us to a certain standard of conduct.... And it is an emotion, inasmuch as we find our hearts strangely warmed when we see the woods ablaze with autumn or hear church bells ringing, because we know God loves us, and has not left us comfortless.[29]

(This transformation of analysis into sermon is typical of McClung.)

Similar parallels exist between *Man-Made World* and *In Times Like These*. Gilman's chapter, "Masculine Literature" argues that history has been written from the point of view of men, reflecting male interest:

> Men, being the sole arbiters of what should be done and said and written, have given us not only a social growth scarred and thwarted from the beginning by continual destruction; but a history which is one unbroken record of courage and red cruelty, of triumph and black shame. (92)

McClung echoes her concern: "history, romance, legend and tradition have been written by men, have shown the masculine aspect of war and have surrounded it with a false glory and sought to throw the veil of glamour over its hideous face" (ITLT, 15). On marriage, McClung's call for mutuality, cited previously, finds its ground in Gilman. McClung talks about "the pleasant glowing embers of comradeship

and friendship"; Gilman cites "love, high pure enduring love, combined with the broad deep-rooted friendliness and comradeship of
equals" (43).

Following this theme, with a critical eye to her culture, Gilman
argues that male preference for dainty little women, and the corresponding necessity for women to accentuate their ineffectuality
through restrictive and unhealthy clothing, has brought the race to its
present decadent state (54-6). McClung notes the same phenomenon
in the chapter, "The New Chivalry," in *In Times Like These* (41), adding
in a subsequent chapter: "the physical disabilities of women which
have been augmented and exaggerated by our insane way of dressing
has had much to do with women's thought" (ITLT, 62).

Both Gilman and McClung saw Christianity as emphasizing the
human over the masculine. Gilman tells us:

> As a male he fought, as a male human being he fought more, and
> deified fighting; and in a culture based on desire and combat . . .
> there could be but slow acceptance of the more human methods
> urged by Christianity. "It is a religion for slaves and women!" said
> the warrior of old. (Slaves and women were largely the same thing.)
> (200)

In McClung it is rendered: "the nobility of loving service freely
given . . . did not appeal to the military masculine mind. It declared
Christianity was fit only for women and slaves, whose duty it was to
lovingly serve men" (ITLT, 69). There are numerous other sections
which might likewise be profitably compared.[30]

McClung's indebtedness to Gilman's text is significant, in that it
locates her within a larger tradition of feminist reflection. Dolores
Hayden's ground-breaking work, *The Grand Domestic Revolution: A
History of Feminist Designs for American Homes, Neighborhoods, and Cities*, names this "material feminism."[31] Hayden's work is invaluable in
reassessing the social agendas of women like Gilman, to whom Hayden devotes an entire chapter. In Hayden's opinion:

> The overarching theme of the late nineteenth and early twentieth
> century feminist movement was to overcome the split between
> domestic life and public life created by industrial capitalism, as it
> affected women. Every feminist campaign for women's autonomy
> must be seen in this light. (4)

Contrary to the limiting stereotype of maternal feminism promoted by
Bacchi and the early Strong-Boag, Hayden asserts:

> Most feminists wished to increase women's rights in the home and simultaneously bring homelike nurturing into public life.... Whether feminists sought control over property, child custody, divorce, "voluntary motherhood," temperance, prostitution, housing, refuse disposal, water supplies, schools, or workplaces, their aims were those summarized by the historian Aileen Kraditor: "women's sphere must be defined by women." (4-5)

This demand was a radical one, both in terms of women's autonomy, and in terms of the actual structural economic changes such a redefinition would necessitate. Far from projecting a sentimentalized, bourgeois notion of Victorian "true womanhood" upon the public sphere, these women "defined women's control over women's sphere as women's control over the reproduction of society" (Hayden, 5). Antifeminists were well aware of the depth of feminism's challenge to the base of their power — hence what seem now to be the rather hysterical assertion of Sir Almroth Wright and others that feminism would bring about the end of civilization.[32] They knew that a "grand domestic revolution" which deprivatized women's reproductive and domestic labour would shatter their control irrevocably.[33]

It is important to note, too, the differences between the challenges to the established social order posed by material feminists and those attributed to the Social Gospel. Because of McClung's Christianity and her social concern there has been a tendency, as we have seen, simply to subsume her work within a Social Gospel framework. However, this is both inappropriate and misleading. As Gilman herself astutely noted, "Two great movements convulse the world today, the women's movement and the labor movement. Each regards the other as of less moment than itself. Both are parts of the same world process" (190). Social Gospel scholarship has focused its attention almost exclusively upon the labour movement, and has generated its interpretive categories from that base. The women's movement, if noted at all, is generally reduced to the question of woman suffrage, and perhaps the temperance crusade.[34]

In so doing, current scholars reflect the emphasis upon men's experience which was characteristic of those figures identified as the movement's leaders. While radical on working men's rights in the public sphere, these men tended to leave gender roles, and the economic structures which such roles assumed, intact.[35] Walter Rauschenbusch, for example, did not even consider the possibility of women leaving the home; others, like Salem Bland, saw women becoming workers in the public sphere with men, but had no notion of the mutual redefinition of home and workplace, based on women's experience, which material feminism required. This one-sided focus upon men and men's concerns is further highlighted by what was arguably the movement's most potent symbol and rallying cry — that of "Brotherhood."[36]

A similar perspective has been sustained in scholarship on the Social Gospel novel.[37] Overwhelmingly, the narratives investigated feature a central dynamic involving labour/management struggles, usually in an urban environment. Moreover, the protagonist is virtually always male, even in those novels authored by women.[38] While noting some exceptions, Susan Lindley is forced to conclude:

> This study of women and the Social Gospel novel suggests that for most authors, particularly men, any radicalism that the Social Gospel inspired did not extend to the home, the family, and traditional sex roles. For the most part, women are victims, inspirations to men, or responsibilities to men, not significant thinkers, actors, or initiators.[39]

The precise nature and character of the Canadian Social Gospel movement is a complicated issue, raising far more questions than can be addressed adequately here. However, one observation may be made. It may not be necessary to assume this androcentric reading of the Social Gospel to be normative, and the standard against which all facets of turn-of-the-century reformism, feminism included, ought to be judged. If, indeed, as Allen claims, "The social gospel rested on the premise that Christianity was a social religion, concerned . . . with the quality of human relations here on earth" (4), an interpretation of the movement which also includes an application of that understanding grounded in women's experience would seem possible, and perhaps even necessary. Gilman's observation likewise suggests a more pluralistic approach might allow several strands of the Social Gospel to emerge, but one of which was composed primarily of Protestant male ministers concerned with working men's rights adjudicated in the public sphere.

However this question is resolved, it must still be stated that the economic critique mounted by material feminism, while differing in focus from labour's class analysis, was no less sweeping and no less important. McClung has been labelled "naive" and "bourgeois" because she did not undertake a critique of capitalist society along the lines of the Marxist-inspired labour movement. Nevertheless, through Gilman, she is connected with an equally important challenge to the structural inequities perpetuated by an androcentric, competitive economic system. Frances Willard's W.C.T.U. dictum, to "make the whole world home-like," takes on a completely different meaning when understood as a demand that the public sphere become accountable to women and women's lives, as defined by women themselves.

Yet while McClung's debt to Gilman is great, there exist nevertheless significant differences between *In Times Like These* and *Man-Made World* which illustrate the importance of McClung's religion for her social activism. It is true that in *In Times Like These* McClung adopts much of Gilman's Social Darwinist language, to the extent that she seems to be affirming a view of humanity which sharply demarcates male and female behaviour at more than a merely phenomenological level. For Gilman, biological gender difference had an irreducible significance, although she held that basing the organization of all human society upon the perspective of one sex, the male, is both unwarranted and destructive. That gender difference existed for McClung at the phenomenological but not the ontological level will be illustrated in relation to two issues, "the law of life," i.e., religion, and the disruption of that law, through warfare.

Gilman opens *Man-Made World* as follows: "Let us begin, inoffensively, with sheep . . ." (9). She lists various "sheeply" activities, grazing, gambolling, jumping, in short, all the behaviours pertaining to genus ovis. Her concern, however, is to do more than to distinguish what is "ovine or bovine, canine, feline or equine" (11). She wants to determine "ramishness" and "eweishness," i.e., the fundamental differences between males and females of any species. This introductory chapter, "As to Humanness," pursues the question in some detail, with particular attention being paid to male behaviour. She concludes: "To butt—to strut—to make a noise—all for love's sake; these are acts common to the male" (13). The female creature, in contrast, "exhibits love and care for her little ones, gives them milk and tries to guard them" (11-12). Although human nature is not limited to these differences, they remain ineradicable, a necessary part of the evolutionary process.[40] The "law of life" for Gilman is determined by this process, with the ultimate goal of "race improvement" inevitably given, short of human tampering. The dominance of the male (sex-type) over the female (race-type) is evidence of such tampering, and must be eradicated to allow nature to take its proper course. Hers is not a completely deterministic universe, for humans can consciously direct the course of evolution through their social actions; nevertheless, the fundamental structure of the evolutionary process, based on sex difference, remains intact.

Gilman's religion emerges out of this biologistic base, a result of humans trying to express their deepest understanding of life. When males create religion, it is adversarial, otherworldly and punitive, filled with an egocentrism Gilman considers totally unworthy:

> It is this purely masculine spirit which has given to our early con-
> cepts of deity the unadmirable qualities of boundless pride and a
> thirst for constant praise and prostrate admiration, characteristics
> certainly unbefitting any noble idea of God. Desire, combat and self-
> expression all have had their unavoidable influence on masculine
> religions. (140)

Women's religion, grounded in the primary experience of nurturance, takes an entirely different form. This description is found in Gilman's tales of an all-female utopia, *Herland*:

> They developed their central theory of a Loving Power, and
> assumed that its relation to them was motherly — that it desired their
> welfare and especially their development. Their relation to it, simi-
> larly, was filial, a loving appreciation and a glad fulfilment of its
> high purposes. Then, being nothing if not practical, they set their
> keen and active minds to discover the kind of conduct expected of
> them. This worked out in a most admirable system of ethics. The
> principle of Love was universally recognized — and used. . . . They
> had no ritual, no little set of performances called "divine service,"
> save those glorious pageants I have spoken of, and those were as
> much educational as religious, and as much social as either. But they
> had a clear established connection between everything they
> did — and God. Their cleanliness, their health, their exquisite order,
> the rich peaceful beauty of the whole land, the happiness of the chil-
> dren, and above all the constant progress that they made — all this
> was their religion.[41]

A properly ordered world would absorb the dynamism of male religion within the more fundamental nurturant power of female religion, to its improvement. Throughout, Gilman's definition remains a
functionalist one, as confirmed in the concluding chapter of *His Religion and Hers*. "Hope and Power":

> We need to see and use the power to carry on this racial task, this
> natural task, this task which is no struggle against our own impulses
> and desires but the fulfilment of those essentially distinctive of our
> race. . . . Each of us, once grasping the full sense of a God that works,
> of our natural relationship to that power being simply fulfilment, the
> carrying out of our natural race-development, may draw a long

breath and take hold in earnest. Such power is not "angry." One does not have to apologize to God for every foolishness, any more than a tree apologizes to the sun for worm-eaten apples.[42]

Seen in this light, warfare, strictly speaking, is more of a bending than a breaking of the law of life, for, as she states in *Man-Made World*, "Maleness means war" (*M-MW*, 92). Nature is constructed on the principle of complementarity, according to gender. Gilman states: "The basic feminine impulse is to gather, to put together, to construct; the basic masculine impulse to scatter, to disseminate, to destroy" (*M-MW*, 114). When held in check by a larger humanity, this masculine impulse serves as a "leaven" in human progress. In an androcentric world, however, male destructiveness is not only tolerated, but celebrated. Gilman remarks, with some disgust, "In warfare, per se, we find maleness in its absurdest extremes. Here is to be studied the whole gamut of basic masculinity, from the initial instinct of combat, through every form of glorious ostentation, with the loudest possible accompaniment of noise" (*M-MW*, 211). A human world would channel this energy to more useful ends; nonetheless, the inherent destructiveness of the male remains essential to Gilman's whole schema.

Contrast this with McClung's meditation upon the same matter. Her earlier paragraphs echo Gilman's on the social celebration of the warrior, but when she comes to the question of war's inevitability, her argument takes a significant turning. She states: "But although men like to fight, war is not inevitable. War is not of God's making. War is a crime committed by men and, therefore, when enough people say it shall not be, it cannot be" (ITLT, 15). The point that "war is not of God's making," i.e., not intrinsic to Creation, is an essential point of difference between McClung and Gilman. What for Gilman is an "instinct," bound by nature and inevitable in its expression, is for McClung merely a "predilection," a habit of being which can be changed. (It should be noted that McClung's perspective leaves men with a far greater responsibility for changing their behaviour than Gilman's more biologistic analysis allows. Indeed, it was this faith that men could change which was at the heart of McClung's activism.) War, for McClung, was men's wilful breaking of the "law of life," to everyone's loss. Conversion, however, was always a possibility, and it was to this end that McClung preached her text against war.

In Times Like These is infused with the spirit of McClung's religion. Note her transformation of Gilman in chapter 1 of the text: "We will begin peaceably by contemplating the world of nature, trees and plants and flowers, common green things against which there is no law — for surely there is no corruption in carrots, no tricks in turnips, no mixed motive in marigolds" (8). Yet while "The whole world of nature seems to present a perfect picture of obedience and peaceful meditation," there is an inherent dynamism, an energy which is neither male nor female, which spurs young plants "to grow — to spread — to travel — to get away from home" (8). Growth is the law of nature, but it is not limited, as with Gilman, to the specialized interrelated functions of maleness and femaleness. In her reflection upon this point, McClung transforms theory into a sermon — and a mandate for social action:

> There is no resignation in Nature, no quiet folding of the hands, no hypocritical saying, "Thy will be done!" and giving in without a struggle.... Resignation is a cheap and indolent human virtue, which has served as an excuse for much spiritual slothfulness. It is still highly revered and commended. It is so much easier sometimes to sit down and be resigned than to rise up and be indignant. (9)

Social activism has divine sanction, whatever a more traditional Christian sensibility might suggest to the contrary:

> "Thy will be done," they said, and now we know that it is not God's will at all. It is never God's will that any should perish! People were resigned when they should have been cleaning up! "Thy will be done!" should ever be the prayer of our hearts, but it does not let us out of any responsibility. It is not a weak acceptance of misfortune, or sickness, or injustice or wrong, for these things are not God's will.
>   "Thy will be done" is a call to fight — to fight for better conditions, for moral and physical health, for sweeter manners, cleaner laws, for a fair chance for everyone, even women! (9)

Though a brief four pages, "The War That Never Ends" is a passionate, powerful rallying cry for social justice. It establishes at the very outset that change is natural and good, part of God's plan for Creation. Further, human resistance to change, i.e., "indifference and slothfulness," is the "sin of the world ... more than real active wickedness" (10). Injustice and inequity have come about both because of this laziness, and because "some ... have reached out and taken more than their share, and try to excuse their 'hoggishness' by declaring that God did not intend all to travel on the same terms ..." (11). To reestablish a proper balance, "the even chance for everyone — is the plain and simple meaning of life" (11). She rousingly concludes:

> To this end let us declare war on all meanness, snob bishness, petty
> or great jealousies, all forms of injustice, all forms of special privi-
> lege, all selfishness and all greed. Let us drop bombs on our preju-
> dices! Let us send submarines to blow up all our poor little petty
> vanities, subterfuges and conceits, with which we have endeavored
> to veil the face of Truth. Let us make a frontal attack on ignorance,
> laziness, doubt, despondence, despair, and unbelief!
>
> The banner over us is "Love," and our watchword "A Fair
> Deal." (11)

Although many of the 12 chapters of *In Times Like These* were
given as speeches, it is not unreasonable to assume that their editing
and ordering here had some inner logic. Each chapter will now be
considered briefly in turn, with an eye to its central theme and issues
raised. A final reflection upon the text as a whole will draw together
the various points made in this and the previous chapter, bearing in
mind the limitations of earlier readings of McClung. It will likewise
suggest that a fuller, more accurate reading of *In Times Like These*
demands a fresh approach to McClung's feminism, which must be
seen at the same time as within the material feminist tradition and
profoundly religious at its core.

McClung follows "The War That Never Ends" with "The War
That Ends in Exhaustion Sometimes Mistaken for Peace." This meditation on male-made war is deeply indebted to Charlotte Perkins Gilman, and reflects Gilman's negative assessment of masculine aggression. Yet, as shown above, McClung rejects war's inevitability,
because male character is not a "given," but a habit of mind. This
habit of mind has been strongly reinforced, in McClung's view, by an
androcentric reading of history, which emphasizes political conflict
and glorifies battle. Like Gilman, McClung too calls for "new histories" to be written from the standpoint of "the people," such that
"the hero will not be any red-handed assassin who goes through
peaceful country places leaving behind him dead men looking sight-
lessly up to the sky. The hero will be the man or woman who knows
and loves and serves" (16). At this point, however, McClung takes a
turning. She rejects Gilman's evolutionary schema which places the
white race at the helm of history, and challenges the self-satisfied
complacency of British imperialism. There was no divine sanction for
Britain's behaviour. She informs the reader:

> England did not draw her policy from the open Bible when in 1840
> she forced the opium traffic on the Chinese. England does not draw
> her policy from the open Bible when she takes revenues from the

> liquor traffic, which works such irreparable ruin to countless thou-
> sands of her people. England does not draw her policy from the
> open Bible when she denies her women the rights of citizens, when
> women are refused degrees after passing examinations, when lower
> pay is given women for the same work than if it were done by men.
> Would this be tolerated if it were really so that we were a Christian
> nation? God abominates a false balance, and delights in a just
> weight. (18-19)

These inequities were due (McClung once again returning to Gilman's language) to "male statecraft" which encouraged a disparity between individual and national ideals.[43] So-called "Christian nations" were the worst culprits here, wreaking havoc not only on their own citizens, but on the world at large:

> Take the case of the heathen—the people who we in our large-
> handed, superior way call the heathen. Individually we believe it is
> our duty to send missionaries to them to convert them into Chris-
> tians. Nationally we send armies upon them (if necessary) and con-
> vert them into customers! Individually we say: "We will send you
> our religion." Nationally: "We will send you goods, and we'll make
> you take them—we need the money!" Think of the bitter irony of a
> boat leaving a port loaded with missionaries upstairs and rum
> below, both bound for the same place and for the same
> people—both for the heathen "with our comp'ts." (19)

Racism, imperialism and injustice to women are linked in this chapter to a national egoism grounded in male aggression. (Considering McClung was writing in wartime, this attack upon the Empire took some courage.) She leaves her readers with a Scriptural justification for her case, found in the image of Christ weeping over Jerusalem. The quotation is a telling indictment of men's intransigence: "O Jerusalem, Jerusalem, how often would have gathered you, as a hen gathereth her chickens under her wings, but you would not" (19).

In "What Do Women Think of War? (Not That It Matters)," McClung suggests that a possible antidote to the male perspective may be found in women's experience. Gilman's influence is once again evident, in McClung's claim that "Women are naturally guardians of the race" (22) and "The woman's outlook on life is to save, to care for, to help" (23). McClung rejects, however, the sentimentalized stereotype of maternal domesticity which romantic anti-feminists argued would produce peaceful, loving, moral men. She asserts:

> According to the theories of the world, the gentle sons of gentle
> mothers will respect and reverence womankind everywhere. Yet, we
> know that in the invasion of Belgium, the German soldiers made a
> shield of Belgian women and children. . . . What, then, is the matter
> with the theory? Nothing, except that there is nothing in it—it will
> not work. Women who set a low value on themselves make life hard
> for all women. The German woman's ways have been ways of pleas-
> antness, but her paths have not been paths of peace; and now,
> women everywhere are thinking of her, rather bitterly. Her peaceful,
> humble, patient ways have suddenly ceased to appear virtuous in
> our eyes and we see now. It is not so much a woman's duty to bring
> children into the world, as to see what sort of world she is bringing
> them into, and what their contribution will be to it. (24)

The war was proof to McClung that women's activism was absolutely
essential, and she launches into a firm defence of the militant suffra-
gettes on this ground:

> The knitting women know now why the militant suffragettes broke
> windows and destroyed property, and went to jail for it joyously,
> and without a murmur—it was the protest of brave women against
> the world's estimate of woman's position . . . now they know that
> these brave women in England, maligned, ridiculed, persecuted, as
> they were, have been fighting every woman's battle, fighting for the
> recognition of human life, and the mother's point of view. (25)

Tragically, ironically, it is "the woman who knits" who "was so sure
it was her duty to bring children into the world" (26) who has had to
suffer most among women for her compliance, for it has been her children who have been sacrificed by the very system she supported. Nor
can there be Biblical comfort in this bleak picture, for even Abraham's
sacrifice does not apply. McClung concludes: ". . . now she knows it
was not so hard on Abraham, for he knew it was God who asked it,
and he had God's voice to guide him! Abraham was sure, but about
this—who knows?" (26). The sense of loss conveyed here, not only
over the death of a child, but of loss of faith in life's coherency, is profound. In her onslaught against the ideology of "true womanhood,"
McClung is gathering steam.

"Should Women Think?" continues this theme, and broadens its
development. McClung begins with the story of Mary and Martha,
highlighting its significance by remarking, "Trivial little incident, is it
not? Strange that it should find a place in the sacred record" (30). The
purpose of the tale, however, is to show "the spiritual is greater than
the temporal," i.e., "Mary had learned the great truth that it is not the
house you live in or the food you eat, or the clothes you wear that

make you rich, but it is the thoughts you think" (31). McClung affirms Martha in all her "truly feminine" virtues of caring for the physical needs of her family. However, this is only a "good." As she points out: "Every day we choose between the best and the second best, if we are choosing wisely. It is not generally a choice between good and bad — that is too easy. The choice in life is more subtle than that, and not so easily decided. The good is the greatest rival of the best" (31). The "best" for McClung, is right thinking, which she connects with the spiritual life. But for women, is it worth it? She inquires of her readers:

> in all seriousness, and in no spirit of flippancy, "Should women think?" They gain in power perhaps, but do they not lose in happiness by thinking? If women must always labor under unjust economic conditions, receiving less pay for the same work than men, if women must always submit to the unjust social laws, based on the barbaric mosaic decree that the woman is to be stoned, and the man allowed to go free; if women must always see the children they have brought into the world with infinite pain and weariness, taken away from them to fight man-made battles over which no woman has any power; if women must always see their sons degraded by man-made legislation and man-protected evil — then I ask, Is it not a great mistake for women to think? (31-2)

The women who do not think, the "Martha women," are comfortable and confident in the world's good opinion of them. Their labour is even useful labour — as far as it goes. Scripture offers a better model, however, which McClung reinforces with a theological observation of her own:

> We must think because we were given something to think with, ages ago, at the time of our creation. If God had not intended us to think, he would not have given us our intelligence. It would be a shabby trick, too, to give women brains to think, with no hope of results, for thinking is just an aggravation if nothing comes of it. (32)

Women have not only the ability but also the responsibility to think, even though the world punishes them for it and claims it will destroy the home. McClung objects: "Intelligence on the wife's part does not destroy connubial bliss, neither does ignorance nor apathy ever make for it . . . the happiest marriage is the one where the husband and wife come to regard each other as the dearest friend, the most congenial companion" (33). While the conventional woman, typified by the "young wife, daintily frilled in pink" (33), may be initially satisfied in her role, ultimately she loses out on the most important gift of marriage — true comradeship in a fellowship of equals. Her unwillingness to think hurts others as well, as the world glorifies her selfish, indolent behaviour as "true womanhood." McClung concludes her indictment with a prayer:

> From plague, pestilence and famine,
> from battle, murder, sudden death,
> and all forms of cowlike contentment,
>   Good Lord, deliver us! (35)

"The New Chivalry" continues McClung's attack on the romantic, sentimental view of women to which traditionalists subscribed. The old chivalry is unworkable, she claims, calling instead for a new chivalry of "brave women and fair men."[44] Despite its high-sounding phrases, the old chivalry failed to protect women in general. As McClung remarks,

> Chivalry is like a line of credit. You can get plenty of it when you do not need it . . . the young and pretty woman, well dressed and attractive, can get all the chivalry she wants . . . but the poor old woman, beaten in the battle of life . . . can go her weary way uncomforted and unattended. (41)

In fact, chivalry is based, not on men's "natural" desire to protect "the fair sex,"[45] but upon the enforced dependency of women upon men. Consequently, women are forced to gear their energies toward gaining men's positive attention by enhancing their appearance. Further,

> Women cannot be blamed for this. All our civilization has been made to the end that women make themselves attractive to men. The attractive woman has hitherto been the successful woman. . . . Is it any wonder that women capitalize their good looks, even at the expense of their intelligence? The economic dependence of women is perhaps the greatest injustice that has been done to us, and has worked the greatest injury to the race. (ITLT, 40)[46]

The pretty woman is rewarded, and is married regardless of any deficiencies of character or intelligence which might obtain. Homely women are punished, in past ages by being called "witches, dreadful witches, and . . . drowned . . . on public holidays, in the mill pond!" (ITLT, 39), and currently by being denied the companionship of marriage and family. She asks, in despair,

> Oh, why do some of our best men marry such odd little sticks of pin-head women, with a brain similar in caliber to a second-rate butter-fly, while the most intelligent, unselfish, and womanly women are left unmated? I am going to ask about this the first morning I am in heaven, if so be we are allowed to ask about the things which troubled us while on our mortal journey. I have never been able to find out about it here. (ITLT, 41)[47]

The weapon of "necessary beauty" is even wielded at those for whom marriage is not the issue:

> When a newspaper wishes to disprove a woman's contention, or demolish her theories, it draws ugly pictures of her. If it can show that she has big feet or red hands, or wears unbecoming clothes, that certainly settles the case—and puts her where she belongs. (ITLT, 40)[48]

Hence, while men's chivalry claims to revere women and to place them on a pedestal, it is in fact only extended to those women whom men find attractive, and of whose behaviour they approve. A true chivalry, for McClung, would have to be based not on any coinciden-tal attributes of youth, or beauty, or artificial allure, but on justice. Truly chivalrous men, like Dr. Clay of the Pearlie Watson trilogy, rec-ognize that "women are often outraged insulted, ill-treated" (ITLT, 42), and that the best help they could be given is the means by which to fight their own battles, i.e., the vote. Those opposed to women's advancement on "chivalrous" grounds in fact want nothing more than the maintenance of their own power. As she remarks in one oft-quoted passage, "That seems to be the haunting fear of man-kind—that the advancement of women will sometime, someway, someplace, interfere with some man's comfort" (ITLT, 32).

"Hardy Perennials!" continues the theme of justice, and bears all the marks of McClung's long-standing battle with Sir Rodmond Rob-lin for women's enfranchisement. Its topic is the persistence of preju-dice, and as the reader is led systematically through the varieties of argument against woman suffrage, and McClung's often humorous but always incisive refutations of them, a new understanding of the problem begins to emerge. Once again, McClung links women's activ-ism and "divine discontent" (ITLT, 44), and asserts that it is neither wicked nor new:

> In the old days when a woman's hours were from 5 A.M. to 5 A.M., we did not hear much of discontent among women, because they had not time to talk, and certainly could not get together. The horse

on the treadmill may be very discontented, but he is not disposed to
tell his troubles, because he cannot stop to talk. (ITLT, 44-5)

McClung's continuing discussion reflects Dolores Hayden's point
regarding feminist response to changing economic conditions. With
the advent of machinery and factory-made articles, women have more
leisure than in the past, and a revolution in women's thinking is the
result: "For generations women have been thinking and thought without expression is dynamic, and gathers volume by repression. Evolution when blocked and suppressed becomes revolution" (ITLT, 45).

One step in this revolution is the structural analysis of social evils,
in material feminist terms, the deprivatizing of women's traditional
experience. McClung asserts:

> If women would only be content to snip away at the symp toms of
> poverty and distress, feeding the hungry and clothing the naked, all
> would be well and they would be much commended for their kind-
> ness of heart; but when they begin to inquire into causes, they find
> themselves in the sacred realm of politics where prejudice says no
> women must enter. (ITLT, 47)

McClung goes on to make her familiar argument that "the taint of corruption" is no basis for excluding women from full participation in
the nation's political life: "Any man who is actively engaged in politics, and declares that politics are too corrupt for women, admits one
of two things, either that he is a party to this corruption, or that he is
unable to prevent it—and in either case something should be done"
(ITLT, 48). However, she does not make the argument, contra Strong-
Boag, that only women can be the "purifiers." She says instead: "If
politics are too corrupt for women, they are too corrupt for men, for
men and women are one—indissoluble joined together for good or
ill" (ITLT, 48). McClung is responding to the prejudice which would
prevent women from exercising full responsibility in the public
sphere, not constructing a reverse prejudice of her own. All persons,
she argues, deserve a chance to participate in public life: "It does not
matter whether it is the best, or second best, or the worst who is asking for a share in citizenship; voting is not based on morality, but on
humanity" (ITLT, 56).

Whether or not individuals are intelligent, ignorant, "foreign-
born" or British, all share a common humanity which carries with it
responsibility for the shape of public life. This observation gives her
the opportunity to strike another blow against British chauvinism,
what she calls "this old drivel of the 'folds of the flag'" (ITLT, 55). In

fact, as *Painted Fires* illustrates, it is often the immigrant who sees and experiences flaws in the social fabric most acutely. She assures her readers: "We have no reason to be afraid of the foreign woman's vote. I wish we were as sure of the ladies who live on the Avenue" (ITLT, 55).

Concluding with a rather nasty swipe at Sir Rodmond Roblin, who is compared to a selfish old ox with "both feet in the trough" (ITLT, 57-8), "Hardy Perennials" demonstrates the power of prejudice to thwart reasoned argument, and illustrates the usefulness of humour in sparking understanding. Persons who have evaluated McClung's arguments independent of the highly prejudiced context within which she was forced to function often unwittingly misrepresent her position by emphasizing and taking as theory what in the context of the speech/essay is primarily a rhetorical ploy, or a line of argument pre-determined by her anti-feminist opposition. (Her discussion of women's ability to clean up political corruption, and Strong-Boag's misreading of that assertion, is one illustration of the problem.)

Having attended to men's role in creating and sustaining gender injustice, McClung turns in "Gentle Lady" to consider women's responsibility in the matter. Returning to a theme introduced in "Should Women Think?" i.e., that non-activist women make life hard for other women (ITLT, 34), in "Gentle Lady" McClung excoriates women who live up to the feminine stereotype and support the status quo. While the domestic martyrdom the "gentle lady" espouses is not entirely her fault, having come "from long bitter years of repression and tyranny" (ITLT, 61), nevertheless, her "very personal and local point of view ... the whole world as related to herself" must be rejected as socially irresponsible (ITLT, 63).

The "gentle lady" was a favourite weapon of antisuffragists like Sir Almroth and Stephen Leacock, and for that reason McClung found women of that type doubly dangerous. While acknowledging the basis of the "gentle lady's" opposition to women's rights,[49] she is nevertheless disgusted by their attitude. She illustrates her point:

> The anti-suffrage attitude of mind is not so much a belief as a disease. I read a series of anti-suffrage articles not long ago in the New York Times. They were all written in the same strain: "We are gentle ladies. Protect us. We are weak, very weak, but very loving." There was not one strong nourishing sentence that would inspire anyone to fight the good fight. It was all anemic and bloodless, and beseeching, and had the indefinable, sick-headache, kimona, breakfast-in-bed

> quality in it, that repels the strong and healthy. They talked a great deal of the care and burden of motherhood. They had no gleam of humor — not one. (ITLT, 62-3)

These women were "parasites" to McClung (ITLT, 64). Their refusal to accept responsibility for full adult humanity harmed everyone, and contributed to the "race's decay" (ITLT, 64). In Gilman's terms, they were denying women's true purpose in life, i.e., "to guide and sustain life, to care for the race; not feed on it" (ITLT, 64). Moreover, their selfishness and indolence were the very essence of sin, as defined by McClung in "The War That Never Ends," and it was this sinful self-absorption which prevented them from seeing that "the new movement among women is a spiritual movement" (ITLT, 64).

Whatever McClung has said about male perfidy pales beside this critique. Concerned totally with their status as "the sex" and their effectiveness at conveying sex appeal (ITLT, 62), these "male-identified" women undercut every attempt by self-identified women to improve the lot of all. In so doing, they are traitors to both God and humanity. Nevertheless, McClung does not despair of their eventual conversion. She concludes the piece with this appeal:

> Too long have the gentle ladies sat in their boudoirs looking at life in a mirror like the Lady of Shalott, while down below, in the street, the fight rages, and other women, and defenseless children, are getting the worst of it. But the cry is going up to the boudoir ladies to come down and help us, for the battle goes sorely; and many there are who are throwing aside the mirror and coming out where the real things are. The world needs the work and the help of the women, and the women must work, if the race will survive. (ITLT, 66)[50]

Continuing her appeal to religion in support of her cause, McClung next turns her attentions to the institution of the church, and finds it sadly wanting. "Women and the Church" is an important essay, not only for what it tells the reader about McClung's own religious understanding, but because so many of her arguments are being reproduced in current feminist theology.[51] This suggests that the conditions which McClung addressed in 1915 have altered less than might be expected; moreover, a fuller understanding of past activists like McClung might help provide a better basis for building toward change. In any case, "Women and the Church" is valuable in itself, both for its specific insights regarding the church, and for its illustration of McClung's transformation of Charlotte Perkins Gilman's thought.

"Women and the Church" opens with a clear statement of the equality of men and women established at Creation. Genesis affirms this: " 'God created man in his own image . . . male and female created he them.' That is to say, He created male man and female man. Further on in the story of the creation it says: 'He gave them dominion, etc.' " (ITLT, 68).[52] She continues: "It would seem from this, that men and women got away to a fair start. There was no inequality to begin with. God gave them dominion over everything; there were no favours, no special privileges. Whatever inequality has crept in since, has come without God's sanction" (ITLT, 68). Discrimination on the basis of sex is established as contrary to God's intention, an analogous point to that made in Rosemary Ruether's 1975 publication *New Woman/New Earth*.[53]

McClung locates the source of sex discrimination not in "male character," but in a biological accident made culturally normative. Men are, by and large, bigger than women. This superior physical strength "is an insidious thing," says McClung, "and has biased the judgement of even good men."[54] Unlike Gilman, who would attribute male dominance to the inherent aggression of the male character, McClung makes a more general point. She observes: "It is easy for bigger and stronger people to arrogate to themselves a general superiority. Christ came to rebuke the belief that brute strength is the dominant force in life" (ITLT, 68).

Further, Christ's teachings were truly "democratic." McClung explains: "He made no discrimination between men and women. They were all human beings to Him, with souls to save and lives to live, and He applied to men and women the same rule of conduct" (ITLT, 68). This application of "the same rule of conduct" is significant, in that it argues against the dual-nature view of humanity implicit in Gilman and sometimes attributed to McClung. She is willing to admit perspectival variance based upon biological differences — for example, linking male strength to the creation of the "military masculine mind" (ITLT, 69) — these differences are subject to a single ethical norm which affirms men's and women's "common humanity."

Yet while Christ might have been a "true democrat" (ITLT, 68), the church as an institution is not, having "departed in some places from Christ's teaching — noticeably in its treatment of women" (ITLT, 69). This has been due to the dominance of the male perspective in the church's institutional establishment, and has resulted in a situation where women are the chief church attenders, doing much to support the life of the institution, but are excluded from decision-making. She observes caustically: "The women may lift mortgages, or build churches, or any other light work, but the real heavy work of the church, such as moving resolutions in the general conference or assemblies, must be done by strong, hardy men!" (ITLT, 72). Appeal to Scripture as the basis for women's exclusion from church courts carries no weight for McClung. She comments, with a subtle gibe at male egotism:

> Christ's scribes were all men, and in writing down the sacred story, they would naturally ignore the woman's part of it. It is not more than twenty years ago that in a well-known church paper appeared this sentence, speaking of a series of revival meetings: "The converted numbered over a hundred souls, exclusive of women and children." If after nineteen centuries of Christian civilization the scribe ignores women, even in the matter of conversion, we have every reason to believe that Matthew, Mark, Luke or John might easily fail to give women a place "among those present" or the "also rans." (ITLT, 69)

McClung pursues this theme, drawing heavily upon Gilman's chapter in *Man-Made World* entitled "Masculine Literature." She points out that "Almost all the books written about women have been written by men" (ITLT, 70). The result has been that "religion has been given a masculine interpretation" (ITLT, 70), which has distorted the teachings of Christ and contributed to women's subjugation.[55] This "masculine interpretation" is evident in at least two areas, the images and stories told by the church to illustrate the faith, and the exclusion of women from the ministry. Regarding the first, McClung makes another point which re-emerges in feminist theology: "The tragedy of the 'willing slave, the living sacrifice,' naturally does not strike a man as it does a woman."[56] Where Christ's stories were addressed to men and woman equally, the church has chosen to emphasize those elements which reinforce women's subordination. In concert with this, women have been denied ordination, but this is the church's position, not God's. She cannily enlists Scripture to make her point:

> if a woman should feel that she is divinely called of God to deliver a message, I wonder how the church can be so sure that she isn't. Wouldn't it be perfectly safe to let her have her fling? There was a rule given long ago which might be used yet to solve such a problem: "And now I say unto you, Refrain from these men, and let them

alone, for if this council, or this work, be of men, it will come to
naught, but if it be of God you cannot overthrow it, lest haply ye be
found even to fight against God." (ITLT, 73-4)

The refusal to let women preach is based not on tradition, but on
arrogance. As she notes somewhat bitingly, "It must be great to feel that
you are on the private wire from heaven and qualified to settle a matter
which concerns the spiritual destiny of other people" (ITLT, 74).

This usurpation of God's authority, based on male dominance and
"sex jealousy," has crippled the church's effectiveness in combatting
the very social evils it claims to oppose. For example,

> The church has deliberately set its face against the emancipation of
> women, and in that respect it has been a perfect joy to the liquor traf-
> fic, who recognize their deadliest foe to be the woman with a ballot
> in her hand. The liquor traffic rather enjoys temperance sermons,
> and conventions and resolutions. They furnish an outlet for a great
> deal of hot talk which hurts nobody. (ITLT, 74)

The church, as an institution, has become the unwitting perpetrator of
abuse, and its unwillingness to challenge convention and follow
Christ's "plain teaching" will have a serious price: "But when it is all
over, the battle fought and won, and women are regarded everywhere
as human beings and citizens, many women will remember with bitterness that in the day of our struggle, the church stood off, aloof and
dignified, and let us fight alone" (ITLT, 73).[57]

McClung retained her affiliation with the church, although she
remained actively critical of many of its actions. What emerges in
"Women and the Church," however, is a sense of her profound faith,
which transcended any particular institutional affiliation and which
manifested itself in healing social action. Gilman's version of religion
grounded in women's experience resonated strongly with McClung's
Methodist tradition of "loving service freely given," allowing her to
borrow freely Gilman's insights and analysis to strengthen her case
here. Her concern for primary structures of injustice, as illustrated by
her retelling of the Good Samaritan story at the end of "Women and
the Church," reflects both these traditions.[58] McClung's claim that
"the demand for votes is a spiritual movement" is inseparable from
her need "to demonstrate God to the world" (ITLT, 78). As "Women
and the Church" attests, feminist social activism was McClung's religious vocation.

In "The Sore Thought" McClung returns to the theme of marriage,
another male-defined institution. Once again, Gilman's influence is

evident, as McClung reproduces many of the arguments put forward in *Women and Economics*. While McClung does not go so far as Gilman to suggest that man-made marriage is little more than legalized prostitution,[59] she does describe at length the acute dependency of women upon male favour. Women must always wait to be courted, wait to be asked out, wait while the man makes up his mind whether to marry, or not, and onoe married, wait for her husband to decide when he will come home, for freedom of movement is a male prerogative (ITLT, 83). Complicating this dependency is the cultural insistence that women remain "innocent," i.e., ignorant of the biological facts regarding sexual relations. To combat this, McClung boldly calls for publicly funded sex education, so that young girls might have some defence against "male chivalry and protection": "I would like to see this work done by trained motherly and tactful women, in the department of social welfare, paid by the school board. I know the mothers should do it, but many mothers are ignorant, foolish, lax, and certainly untrained" (ITLT, 84). Such education is doubly necessary because "fallen" women not only lose their value in the man-made marriage market, but they must also support the consequences of their "fall," i.e., children.[60]

The injustice of this situation demands two things: a change in the nature of marriage, and a change in the laws which governed men and women in the public sphere. In fact the "new" marriage which she envisioned has been in part realized in contemporary society, although perhaps more in relation to sexual than economic matters:

> The time will come, we hope, when women will be economically free, and mentally and spiritually independent enough to refuse to have their food paid for by men; when women will receive equal pay for equal work, and have all avenues of activity open to them; and will be free to choose their own mates, without shame, or indelicacy; when men will not be afraid of marriage because of the financial burden, but free men and women will marry for love, and together work for the sustenance of their families. It is not too ideal a thought. It is coming, and the new movement of women who are crying out for a larger humanity, is going to bring it about. (ITLT, 85-6)

Further, she challenges critics like Sir Almroth who (quite revealingly) say that if women were economically independent of men, they would not marry. McClung's response to this point has been criticized by current feminists who hear her saying that women must be married to be fulfilled. True, she did not anticipate current lesbian separatist analyses which see all marriage as "enforced heterosexism." Her single-nature view of humanity required her acceptance of men as equally human, although her feminism prohibited her from tolerating patriarchal dominance. As the quotation above reveals, McClung hoped for an equal partnership of men and women in marriage, a kind of "mutuality." However, should this prove impossible in either an economic or an emotional sense, McClung felt that marriage should be rejected. As she says:

> Deeply rooted in almost every woman's heart is the love of home and children; but independence is sweet and when marriage means the loss of independence, there are women brave enough and strong enough to turn away from it. "I will not marry for a living," many a brave woman has said. (ITLT, 86)

Contra Sir Almroth Wright, women desire the love and companionship which marriage and family life can provide—but not at the price of male dominance. In any case, as stated in *In Times Like These* and developed in her later stories, McClung did not believe that even non-patriarchal marriage was the answer for every woman. Rather, the issue was freedom of choice, and the mutual responsibilities of men and women in marriage. She predicts: "When women are free to marry or not as they will, and the financial burden of making a home is equally shared by husband and wife, the world will enter upon an era of happiness undreamed of now" (ITLT, 86).

The chapter concludes with a consideration of the laws currently governing women, particularly those with regard to the welfare of children. Her criticism of "the Bishop" who always calls for "more children" is a subtle support of birth control, and the necessity of women's reproductive freedom:

> "By all means let us have more babies," says the Bishop. Even if they are anemic and rickety, ill-nourished and deformed, and even if the mothers, already overburdened and underfed, die in giving them birth? To the average thinking woman, this wail for large families, coming as it always does from men, is rather nauseating. (ITLT, 87)

If men were truly concerned about children, McClung suggests, they would spend less time calling for more of them, and more time taking care of the ones already in existence. As it stands, however, "legislators are more willing to pass laws for the protection of cattle than for the protection of children, for cattle have a real value and children have only a sentimental value" (ITLT, 88). That such should be the case is a result of "male statecraft" (ITLT, 89). Were women to have a hand in the legislation of human welfare, a far higher value would be set on human life.

In the end, however, both men and women have responsibility for the situation. Calling on all persons to work for change, she says, "in reality the individual has not been to blame. The whole race is suffering from masculinity; and men and women are alike to blame for tolerating it" (ITLT, 90). It is this mutual responsibility which demands woman suffrage, which men had the power to grant, but which women also had to use intelligently.

"The Land of the Fair Deal" moves McClung's discussion from general social critique to her specific hopes for Canada's future. In its expansiveness, richness of resources, and "newness," Canada embodied all the values of McClung's pioneer spirit. For McClung, Canada was to be the "Land of the Second Chance," the "Land of Beginning Again," a land, ultimately, of the "Fair Deal":

> we ask for no greater heritage for our country than to be known as the land of the Fair Deal, where every race, color and creed will be given exactly the same chance; where no person can "exert influence" to bring about his personal ends; where no man's or woman's past can ever rise up to defeat them; where no crime goes unpunished; where every debt is paid; where no prejudice is allowed to masquerade as a reason; where honest toil will insure an honest living; where the man who works receives the reward of his labor. (ITLT, 97)

Building this egalitarian society is possible in McClung's view because "We have no precedents to guide us, and that is a glorious thing, for precedents, like other guides, are disposed to grow tyrannical, and refuse to let us do anything on our own initiative" (ITLT, 96). Clearly, McClung was casting her gaze westward, and underestimating and/or ignoring the worth and influence of Quebec, and of the bourgeois Anglo-Ontario culture with which she is sometimes identified.

The piece is thoroughly inspirational, as McClung for the moment abandons analysis of "what is" in her eagerness to show what "could be." Nevertheless, she does identify one major stumbling block to the implementation of her vision. The liquor traffic, she argues, must be abolished if Canada is ever to achieve its ideal. Appeal to convention did not sway McClung on this matter. In keeping with her emphasis on new beginnings, she says: "Social customs may change. They have changed. They will change when enough people want them to change. There is nothing sacred about a social custom, anyway, that it

should be preserved when we have decided it is of no use to us"
(ITLT, 101). Those who persist in upholding a destructive custom like
drinking show no more intelligence than lizards, who follow their fellows, one after another, into a campfire (ITLT, 101-2).

Neither is liquor drinking solely an individual matter. McClung
likens the situation to a war waged upon women and children (ITLT,
99) who have no choice in becoming the victims of alcohol abuse by
men. There are many casualties in this war; as she points out, "Three
thousand women were killed in the United States in one year by their
own husbands who were under the influence of liquor" (ITLT, 99).
Those who assert men should have the right to exercise "individual
liberty" regardless of concern for others are no better than the Kaiser
(ITLT, 102). Support of this sort of individual liberty is not "democracy," as some would insist, but totalitarianism, the rule of the strong
over those with no power to oppose them.

McClung is firm in her support for a truly democratic Canada, one
based on "equality of chance, equality of opportunity" (ITLT, 100). In
its violation of women and children, and its destruction of men's lives,
the liquor traffic subverts democracy at its core. It was necessary
therefore that laws be enacted to prevent the sale of liquor in Canada,
if the Land of the Fair deal was ever to come about.

McClung's position on temperance is commonly ridiculed for its
"prudishness" and "naiveté." While the issue will not be debated at
length here, two suggestions will be made. First, the use of alcohol
had, and continues to have, serious social costs: health care of alcoholics and persons with alcohol-related illnesses, accidents caused by
drunk driving, child abuse, wife-beating, ruined marriages, and loss
of employment resulting in poverty is but a partial list. Canadian society has decided to tolerate these costs, for whatever benefits alcohol
use might provide. McClung's position was that the costs were simply
too great. Secondly, important parallels may be seen between the temperance issue as raised by McClung, and the current debate about
pornography. The issues of individual liberty, the "private" nature of
its consumption, its deleterious effect upon women and children, ille-
gal revenues and the dangers of state legislation of the matter are
raised in both instances. Canadian society's response to pornography
is still being debated, as alcohol use is not. It should be acknowledged, however, that opinion is divided across the political spectrum,
and not only conservatives support the prohibitive platform. Nellie
McClung's opposition to the liquor traffic might be seen as having

more in common with radical feminist Susan G. Cole's opposition to pornography: than as representative of a desire to "control the masses," as Carol Bacchi would suggest. For both McClung and Cole, the price paid by others for male "liberty" is far too great to be borne.

Legislation was also necessary, for McClung, because the law had moral value, and a role in instructing a humanity which could always be improved. Moreover, this educational function was a religious responsibility. Her essay concludes on a fine sermonic note:

> It is the moral impact of a law that changes public sentiment, and to say that you cannot make men sober by law is as foolish as to say you cannot keep cattle from destroying the wheat by building a fence between them and it, or to claim you cannot make a crooked twig grow straight by tying it straight. Humanity can do anything it wants to do. There is no limit to human achievement. Whoever declares that things cannot be done which are for the betterment of the race, insults the Creator of us all, who is not willing that any should perish, but that all should live, and live abundantly. (ITLT, 105)

Throughout *In Times Like These*, McClung has been attending to the importance of perspective in human understanding, and the need to reassess priorities to create a more humane world for all. As she moves towards the text's conclusion, she offers the reader one final viewpoint to be considered, namely, the superiority of country life. The argument put forth in "As a Man Thinketh" has been criticized, as in Strong-Boag's introduction to *In Times Like These*, as naive, and even "irrelevant in an urban age" (xix). However, McClung's love of country life may be understood in a different light. It is true that she claims:

> We need the unaffected honesty and sterling qualities which the country teaches her children in the hard, but successful, school of experience, to offset the flashy supercilious lessons which the city teaches hers; for the city is a careless nurse and teacher, who thinks more of the cut of a coat than a habit of mind . . . who dazzles their eyes with bright lights and commercial signs, and fills their ears with blatant music, until their eyes are too dull to see the pastel beauty of common things, and their ears are holden to the still small voices of God; who lures her children on with many glittering promises of ease and wealth, which she never intends to keep, and all the time whispers to them that this is life. (ITLT, 119)

However, this viewpoint is not unique to McClung, or even particularly unusual. Throughout history there have been many religious viewpoints and secular philosophies which have valued the world of nature over the products of human artifice. McClung is reflecting a religious understanding in which God is perceived directly through the world of nature. Whatever its other values, the city interrupts this connection, and overwhelms "the still small voices of God" in its deafening commercial roar.

Further, country life has a special value for women, in that here they are valued for their labour and not merely their sexual attractiveness.[62] Country life contributed to women's self-reliance and sense of autonomy. McClung says, "When the city woman wants a shelf put up she 'phones to the City Relief, and gets a man to do it for her; the farmer's wife hunts up the hammer and a soap box and puts up her own shelf, and gains the independence of character which only comes from achievement" (ITLT, 109). At its best, country life provides women with a freedom and sense of accomplishment which city life disallows.[63]

Nevertheless, McClung recognizes that this is an ideal. Actual country life was in the main no less determined by male priorities than life in the city, with the result that the farm wife was often overworked to the point of misery, and even death. McClung's novels depict graphically the misery of such women. "As a Man Thinketh" raises the point again, and urges farmers to value their wives as more than pieces of farm machinery to be replaced once they break down.

To "Brother Bones," whose mother did all the work on the farm, raised seven children and buried seven more, McClung says:

> That's just the point, Brother Bones. It is a great thing to have the memory of such a self-sacrificing mother, but it would be a greater thing to have your mother live out her days; and then, too, we are thinking of the 'seven' she buried. That seems like a wicked and unnecessary waste of young life, of which we should feel profoundly ashamed. (ITLT, 118)[64]

"As a Man Thinketh" is more than merely a paean to country life, although that intent would not be unworthy in and of itself. In its affirmation of the values which nourished McClung herself, it was a challenge to rural men not to take female labour for granted. Even in her most inspirational mode, McClung's feminist agenda remained intact.

"The War against Gloom" brings In Times Like These full circle. McClung began the text with "The War That Never Ends," her understanding of the nature of creation and affirmation of God's support of those who fight injustice. "The War against Gloom" acknowledges that the fight is often a long and discouraging one, and that persons might falter and lose heart despite the sincerity of their convictions. In fine sermonic form, McClung offers her readers an antidote to despair, to encourage and empower them in the battle.

Her first step is to remind them of the power of thought. No matter how oppressive external conditions might be, one's mental attitude is a primary resource for providing the energy to combat them: "Life is a great struggle against gloom, and we could fight it better if we always remembered that happiness is a condition of heart and is not dependent on outward conditions. The kingdom of heaven is within you" (ITLT, 125). Although "men try to define themselves by houses and lands and manners and social position (123), this is contrary to God's intent to value each individual equally; moreover, it does not make people happy, or good. In fact, so essential is the proper mental attitude that "The respectable man who keeps within the law and does no outward harm, but who thinks sordidly, meanly, or impurely, is the man of all others who is farthest from the kingdom of God . . ." (123). Everyone has the potential to think rightly, and this is a tremendous power.

McClung recognized, however, that having the "right mental attitude" might be "easier said than done," particularly when one's opposition seemed overwhelming. In response, she makes two points. First, one has to keep oneself in perspective. She reminds her readers:

> It is a great mistake for us to mistake ourselves for the President of the company. Let us do our little bit with cheerfulness and not take the responsibility that belongs to God. None of us can turn the earth around; all we can ever hope to do is to hit it a few whacks on the right side. (ITLT, 124)[65]

That is, persons have genuine responsibility to determine "the right side" and to make their contribution to the struggle, but they are not ultimately responsible for more than their own efforts. Her second point is that, while we might not see it, God has the power to bring good out of evil; even "the war has . . . brought many by-products which are wholly good" (ITLT, 125).

She then combines these points, to say that while misfortunes in life are inevitable, we can choose to meet them bravely, confident of God's support. Furthermore, there is scriptural affirmation for this:

> "Thou shalt not be afraid of the terror by day, nor of the arrow that flieth by night, nor for the pestilence that walketh in darkness, nor for the destruction that wasteth at noonday."

> You will notice here that the promise is that you will not be
> afraid of these things. They may come to you, but they will not over-
> power you, or destroy you utterly, for you will not be afraid of them.
> It is fear that kills. (ITLT, 128)

Trust in God provides the antidote for that fear. McClung offers the
analogy of a young child left at home with responsibility to keep
house while its mother is away. She describes the child's anxiety at
performing all the required tasks, the fear that something might go
wrong, that some disaster might occur. Then the mother finally
returns, and "the awful burden of responsibility is lifted" (ITLT, 128).
McClung instructs her readers:

> That is what it feels like when you "get religion." The worry and
> burden of life is gone. Somebody else has the responsibility and you
> work with a light heart. It is the responsibility of life that kills us, the
> worry, fear, uncertainty, and anxiety. How we envy the man who
> works by the day, just does his little bit, and has no care! This immu-
> nity from care may be ours if we link ourselves with God. (ITLT, 128)

The nature of McClung's religion, and its centrality for her social
activism, now become clear. As *In Times Like These* demonstrates,
McClung was not informed by any dogmatic appropriation of "Christian principles" or "Protestant theology" in her work. Rather, her
faith emerged out of, and was articulated through her experience of a
loving family who did the hard work of building a new life in a new
land. The mandate to build a better world was the very essence of her
religion, and was its own reward. She says:

> That's the way it is in religion—by which we mean the service of
> God and man. It takes you—all the time; and the reward is work,
> and peace, and a satisfaction in your work that passeth all under-
> standing. No more grinding fear, no more "bad days," no more
> wishing to die, no more nervous prostration. Just work and peace!
> (ITLT, 127)

She continues: "In 'walking humbly, doing justly, and loving mercy,'
there is no place for worry and gloom; there is great possibility of love
and much serving, and God in His goodness breaks up our reward
into a thousand little things which attend us every step of the
way . . ." (ITLT, 128). This "work and peace," not worldly success, nor
any "glorious afterlife," was faith's true reward. Moreover, it was
extended to all. McClung's religion was thoroughly ecumenical, as
her concluding poem shows.[66]

Read as a whole, *In Times Like These* emerges as a text with specific religious dimension and intent. McClung's faith permeates every aspect of it, from its structure to the particular issues addressed within. The rhythm of the text discloses this most fully. *In Times Like These* opens with a sermon on the nature of creation, defined as growth and change, and an "altar call" for social activism to end injustice. Specific instances of injustice, the "facts of the case," are then brought forth: war, prejudice, and the man-made institutions of marriage and the church are all brought under scrutiny. Men and women alike are challenged as to their responsibility in maintaining an unjust status quo, and an alternative vision of peace and equality is offered, achieved by hard work and sustained by faith. It then ends with a benediction and an assurance of God's continuing presence and support.

Throughout McClung has woven a thread of Scriptural allusion and religious observation which intricately links her political analyses with her religious vision. This vision was a simple one: all are equal in the sight of God; therefore, all should have an equal chance — a "fair deal" in God's created order. The structural inequalities which developed as a result of male dominance (Gilman's "androcentric culture") need to be expunged, and social priorities rearranged so that those least able to impress their will upon the world (children, women, the aged, immigrants) were given the greatest attention and care, until such time that true equality of opportunity was achieved.

McClung grounded all this in her own — in women's experience, and as a result she has been challenged for being a "maternalist." As has been shown, however, the active care which defined her religious feminism was a possibility for all, male and female, Christian and non-Christian alike. Speaking from the position of women's specificity highlighted the particular features of injustice generated by an androcentric world. The position taken here affirms Miles' contention that this affirmation of human equality, combined with a social critique firmly rooted in concrete, particular female experience, was absolutely necessary for a truly transformative feminist praxis to emerge.

McClung did not end all the ills set forth in *In Times Like These*. However, she did much more than her "little bit" to end injustice. In preaching her message of religious affirmation, as mediated by and through feminist social activism, she indeed succeeded in her goal of hitting the earth "a few whacks on the right side."

Notes

1 Notebook, McClung papers, Add. MSS 10, Vol. 26.

2 Strong-Boag, Introduction, *In Times Like These*, xiv. Subsequent references will be given parenthetically in the text.

3 Cook, *The Regenerators*; see esp. chapter 7, "Toward a Christian Political Economy," 105-22.

4 Thomas P. Socknat, *Witness against War: Pacifism in Canada, 1900-1945* (Toronto: University of Toronto Press, 1987).

5 Carol Bacchi, *Liberation Deferred? Ideas of the English Canadian Suffragists, 1877-1918* (Toronto: University of Toronto Press, 1983); see esp. chapter 4, "In Defense of the Church," 58-68. Subsequent references will be given parenthetically in the text.

6 Cook, 122. As I have discussed elsewhere, there are significant problems in Cook's treatment of religious social activism in general, and feminism in particular. See my book review of *The Regenerators, Toronto Journal of Theology*, 3, No. 1 (Spring 1987), 163-5.

7 "Maternal feminism" is generally understood to refer to the patriarchal conservative view of a dual-natured humanity, as articulated by women. Fundamental biological and ontological differences between the sexes are assumed, but the value of those traditional qualities shifts so that in "maternal feminism" traditional female virtues are accorded higher status than their male counterparts. ("Feeling" is considered more important than "reason," for example.) In the social realm, however, "women's special nature" was understood to demand women's full participation, as purifiers and transformers of an overly masculine culture. Opposition to maternal feminism usually centres on two points: (1) its dual-nature view of humanity, and (2) its failure to mount a class-conscious political and economic critique. Historian Wayne Roberts is typical in his conclusion that "the lack of a consciously anti-capitalist perspective subjected the suffrage movement to certain basic imperatives of capitalism, which, in turn, maternal feminism expressed. The denial of women's rationality, self-interest and autonomy was bound up with the sexual economics of the capitalist production cycle": see Wayne Roberts, " 'Rocking the Cradle for the World': The New Woman and Maternal Feminism, Toronto, 1877-1914," in *A Not Unreasonable Claim: Women and Reform in Canada, 1880's-1920's*, ed. Linda Kealey (Toronto: Women's Press, 1979), 46. Religious conviction is assumed to reinforce this cultural blindness, both with regard to class issues and to the "contradictions" of women's role as mothers and keepers of the home.

8 Strong-Boag, "Ever a Crusader," 178-90. This list is hardly exhaustive; the stereotype of maternal feminism informs much of the scholarship on first-wave social activism in Canada. Once again, Wayne Roberts is typical in his conclusion that "The contradictory nature of maternal feminist aspirations . . . accounts for the ultimately disappointing and limited ideological and political gains made by the first self-conscious generation of women activists in Canadian history" (" 'Rocking the Cradle,' " 45).

9 Bacchi sees the Social Gospel movement as "defensive" and "preservative" by nature (64). However, her recognition that "Even the more radical social gospel ministers advocated a conventional distribution of sexual functions" (64), raises an extremely important point regarding the masculine focus of Social Gospel analysis. Bacchi interprets this to mean that religious, activist women must have been constrained by the limits of their brothers' theories, rather than considering the possibility that Christian feminism activism might have entertained a critique of sex roles on its own.

10 ". . . the social gospel awakened Christian women to their social duty. Women were instructed that, like the men, they had an obligation to earn their salvation through

good works. They were told that they, as individuals, had an 'individual responsibility' to spread the faith and reform the world" (6).

11 Nellie L. McClung, "Can a Woman Raise a Family and Have a Career?" *Maclean's Magazine*, 41 (15 February 1928), 71.

12 Ibid. Current awareness of the difficulties facing families where the single parent, or both parents, work outside of the home substantiates McClung's claim in this regard. In her own case, as this article indicates, she was inestimably aided by her mother-in-law, Annie McClung.

13 For an overview of various feminist political philosophies, see Alison Jaggar, "Political Philosophies of Women's Liberation," in *Feminism and Philosophy*, ed. M. Veterling-Braggin, *et al.* (Totowa: Littlefield, Adams, 1977), 5-21.

14 For a provocative exploration of the differences between male and female perspectives on matriarchy, see Rosemary Radford Ruether, "Radical Victorians: The Quest for an Alternative Culture," in *Women and Religion in America: A Documentary History*, Vol. 3: *1900-1968*, ed. Rosemary Radford Ruether and Rosemary Skinner Keller (San Francisco: Harper and Row, 1988), 1-10.

15 The introduction to Veronica Strong-Boag's article, "Ever a Crusader" names three stages of scholarship on first-wave feminism, as follows: "The pioneering historians tended to see the suffragists as heroines, organizing lobbying campaigns and overcoming the prejudices of their day to win the vote. The next group of historians, however, either dismissed suffragism as a superficial reform based on an inadequate analysis of the economic and social order, or saw late nineteenth and early twentieth-century suffragists as middle-class reformers seeking the vote so as to impose social controls on immigrants and the working class. They pointed out that these first-wave feminists tended to see their maternal role as the justification for their empowerment, not questioning women's 'natural' responsibility for home maintenance and childcare." The third stage of scholarship "perceives women's demand for the vote as potentially radical, offering ... the unconventional prospect of women seeking a direct connection with the state rather than allowing male family members to act as mediators for them" (178). The interpretation offered in this chapter likewise considers woman suffrage as "potentially radical," but would give greater weight to attempts by McClung and others to make the public sphere accountable to women's experience.

16 Strong-Boag's concern regarding McClung's depiction of men is curious, in that she seems to be implying that to describe male behaviour as "aggressive, selfish, and uncontrollable" (xx) is always illegitimate. Novelist and poet Margaret Atwood comments on the problem of portraying men in fiction: "one must conclude that the less than commendable behaviour of male characters in certain novels is not necessarily due to a warped view of the opposite sex on behalf of the authors. Could it be ... I say it hesitantly, in a whisper, since like most women I cringe at the very thought of being called — how can I even say it — a man-hater ... could it be that the behaviour of some men in what we are fond of considering real life ... could it be that not every man always behaves well? Could it be that some emperors have no clothes on?": Margaret Atwood, "Writing the Male Character," *This Magazine*, 16, 4 (September 1982), 6. Strong-Boag's sensitivity on this point is even more curious, considering the political realities McClung was attempting to address in her text.

17 "McClung never really came to terms with women whose major function would not be motherhood, nor did her analysis of working women make much allowance for the disadvantaged who had little but exhaustion to offer their families" (ITLT, xix). Strong-Boag's contention is significantly undercut once McClung's narratives are taken into account, as this work attempts to demonstrate through a close study of her novels.

18 A different analysis of this dimension of feminist activism is offered in Angela R. Miles, "Ideological Hegemony in Political Discourse: Women's Specificity and Equality," in *Feminism in Canada: From Pressure to Politics*, ed. Angela Miles and Geraldine Finn (Montreal: Black Rose Books, 1982), 213-27. In contrast to Strong-Boag, Miles argues that "feminism's progressive power lies essentially in its ability to affirm both women's specificity and equality in a transcendent and revolutionary synthesis of these two apparently contradictory conditions. If women's politics as women attempts to bypass, ignore or deny women's specificity, its expression of women's interests will necessarily remain merely the expression of sectional interest. In this case it will be incapable of challenging current male ideological hegemony which is enforced and protected by both right-wing and liberal definitions of political discourse. Paradoxically, it is only if we manage to build a new politics on the basis of our specificity as women that the militant expression of our sectional interest can represent a major new definition of this discourse and a new departure for humanity as a whole" (214). Operating out of the assumptions of liberal political discourse, both Bacchi and Strong-Boag see first-wave feminism's emphasis upon women's specificity as illegitimate and politically debilitating. The approach undertaken here finds Miles' analysis far more satisfying, particularly in its use of "a historical and material analysis which treats women activists and their movement as both products and producers of social change" (Miles, 214). This focus upon women as historical actors within a specific social context allows for a fuller, more accurate description of their work to emerge than a primarily "ideas" based approach.

19 Ellen DuBois, "The Radicalism of the Woman Suffrage Movement: Notes toward the Reconstruction of Nineteenth-Century Feminism," *Feminist Studies*, 3, Nos. 1/2 (Fall 1975), 63-72, cited in Strong-Boag, "Ever a Crusader," 189, n. 7.

20 Strong-Boag briefly acknowledges the lack of attention paid to the anti-feminist context of first-wave social activism in "Ever a Crusader," 189, n. 12.

21 For example, "The New Chivalry" was given at All Souls' Church (Unitarian) in Winnipeg on 15 February 1914; "The War That Never Ends" on 2 February 1914, at the First Presbyterian Church (Winnipeg?); and "Should Women Think?" at Deer Park Church (n.d., n.p.): McClung Papers, Add. MSS 10, Vol. 26.

22 McClung's notebooks for *In Times Like These* reveal long sections written with very little correction, interspersed with phrases, McClung's and others', apparently for later development. The text of the speeches themselves, when given, consisted of little more than key phrases jotted down in pencil on old envelopes.

23 Charlotte Perkins Gilman, *The Man-Made World; or, Our Androcentric Culture* (New York: Charlton, 1911). Subsequent references will be given parenthetically in the text. Specific reference is made to Gilman in Vol. 28 of McClung's Papers, where the note "C.P. Gilman's book 209. M-M World" appears at the top of a draft of what appears to be "Women and the Church."

24 Carl Degler, Introduction to Charlotte Perkins Gilman's *Women and Economics: A Study of the Economic Relation between Men and Women as a Factor in Social Evolution* (1898), ed. Carl N. Degler (New York: Harper and Row, 1966), vi. Other of Gilman's works included *The Home: Its Work and Influence* (New York: McClure, Phillips, 1903) and *His Religion and Hers: A Study of the Faith of Our Fathers and the Work of Our Mothers* (New York: Century, 1923).

25 Ann J. Lane, Introduction to Charlotte Perkins Gilman's *Herland* (1915; New York: Pantheon Press, 1979), ix.

26 Gilman describes the Gynaecocentric Theory of Life as follows: "the female is the race type, and the male, originally but a sex type, reaching a later equality with the female, and, in the human race, becoming her master for a considerable historic period," to the race's detriment (*M-MW*, 5).

27 "Woman's natural work as a female is that of the mother; man's natural work as a male is that of the father; their mutual relation to this end being a source of joy and well-being when rightly held: but human work covers all our life outside of these specialities. Every handicraft, every profession, every science, every art, all normal amusements and recreations, all government, education, religion; the whole living world of human achievement: all this is human. That one sex should have monopolized all human activities, called them 'man's work,' and managed them as such, is what is meant by the phrase 'Androcentric Culture' " (*M-MW*, 25).

28 For example, *Herland* is a utopian novel which envisages a country populated only by women. Reproduction is achieved through parthenogenesis, but only a few women are actually chosen for this task. Motherhood is understood far more broadly as the desire to care for and serve the race the country's highest ideal. Gilman's *His Religion and Hers* offers a sophisticated exploration of the generation of religious understanding as grounded in male and female experience. Far in anticipation of current feminist theologians like Rosemary Radford Ruether, Gilman characterizes "his religion" as other-worldly, dogmatic, hierarchical and adversarial. "Her religion," by contrast, is educative, nurturant, and this-worldly. In a most moving passage, Gilman describes religion, as created by women, "the thought of God aroused by birth": " 'Here is Life. It comes in instalments, not all at once. The old ones die, the new ones come. They do not come ready-made; they are not finished, they have to be taken care of. It is a pleasure to take care of them, to make new people. . . . The seed which I planted and took care of is better than what grew without help. I can make things better by taking care of them. . . . Teaching is a help in living. Care and teaching makes things better. . . . I can make things! and to make them beautiful! I will teach my daughter. . . . Life, always coming, through motherhood, always growing, always improving through care and teaching! . . . What does it all? What is behind it all? Who is the first Mother, Teacher, Server, Maker? What power under all this pouring flood of Life? What Love behind this ceaseless mother-love? What goodness to make Life so good, so full of growing joy?' . . . Thus would the woman's mind have reached the thought of God" (249-51).

29 Nellie L. McClung, "My Religion," *Be Good to Yourself* (Toronto: Thomas Allen, 1930), 125-32, 132; rpt. as "What Religion Means to Me," *The Quest*, 5, No. 13 (29 March 1942), 194, 197, 206.

30 For example, see, the following (first page reference is to *Man-Made World*, the second to *In Times Like These*): on the effect of proprietary ownership of women in marriage, 42 and 75; on men and history, 90ff. and 15ff.; on Christianity's opposition to brute force, 138 and 68; on growth as the major process in life, 139 and 8ff.; on women and work, 148 and 82; on male statecraft vs. human statecraft, 189 and 89; on "crimes with no name," i.e., economic crimes against humanity, 204 and 90; on "new histories," 213 and 16; on "the God of Battles" vs. "the God of Workshops," 213 and 15. Other themes which are pursued throughout both texts include the debilitating effects of women's economic dependence upon men and a concern for the underlying causes of poverty and crime.

31 Cambridge: M.I.T. Press, 1981.

32 Gilman was evidently familiar with anti-feminists like Sir Almroth Wright, and responded to their arguments in *Man-Made World*. For example, in "Politics and Warfare" she comments: "The inextricable confusion of politics and warfare is part of the stumbling block in the minds of men. As they see it, a nation is primarily a fighting organization; and its principal business is offensive and defensive warfare; therefore the ultimatum with which they oppose the demand for political equality — 'women cannot fight, therefore they cannot vote' " (224). See Wright, 83, cited above, Chapter III.

33 Typical reforms promoted by material feminists included the establishment of socialist villages, collective child-rearing, cooperative housekeeping, community kitchens and cooked food services and wages for housework. McClung reflects this concern for cooperative labour in *In Times Like These*. Speaking of the overwork of women on the farm, she remarks somewhat tongue-in-cheek: "Now, if men, with their good organizing ability and their love of comfort and their sense of their own importance, were to set down to do the work that women have done all down the centuries, they would evolve a scheme something like this in each of the country neighborhoods. There would be a central station, municipally owned and operated, one large building fitted out with machinery that would be run by gasoline, electricity, or natural gas. This building would contain in addition to the schoolrooms, a laundry room, a bake-shop, a creamery, a dressmaking establishment, and perhaps a butcher shop" (ITLT, 118). She also adds, "No woman can bake, wash, scrub, cook meals and raise children and still be happy. To do all these things would make an archangel irritable, and no home can be happy when the poor mother is too tired to smile!" (116-17).

34 An examination of the two main Canadian works on this issue illustrates this point. Richard Allen's *The Social Passion* lists no entries for feminism, or even for woman suffrage, although the W.C.T.U. is cited in relation to prohibition. Ramsay Cook's *The Regenerators* is somewhat more generous in the number of its references to women (17), although here, too, feminism is omitted as an interpretive category. Their treatment of McClung is similarly limited: Allen cites her three times, by name only (43, 162, 204); Cook names her once, in relation to the Single Tax (122).

35 For an excellent analysis of male Social Gospel leaders' reactions to the "Woman Question," see Ronald Huff, "Social Christian Clergymen and Feminism during the Progressive Era, 1890-1920," unpublished Ph.D. thesis, Union Theological Seminary, 1987. Huff concludes: "the reaction of these clergymen to feminism was decidedly mixed. Not only did they disagree with each other over feminist issues, but as individuals they often experienced internal conflict. . . . The most active support for or opposition to women was sometimes taken back by the undertow of the perhaps unstated contradiction, even within a sentence or phrase. The incongruities were between the ideals inherent within the 'new social theology,' which in theory wholeheartedly supported women's gains toward equality, and the innate proclivities of the writer's heart" (193-4). Huff's last point is particularly important, in that it confirms the necessity of moving beyond mere theory in analyses of gender politics.

36 For a discussion of the Brotherhood movement in Canada, see Allen, *Social Passion*, 231-8.

37 See, for example, Susan Lindley, "Women and the Social Gospel Novel," *American Society of Church History*, March 1985, 56-73; Grier Nicholl, "The Christian Social Novel and Social Gospel Evangelism," *Religion in Life*, 34 (1965), 548-61; M. Vipond, "Blessed Are the Peacemakers: The Labour Question in Canadian Social Gospel Fiction," *Journal of Canadian Studies*, 10 (1975), 32-43.

38 See, for example, Agnes Maule Machar, *Roland Graeme: Knight* (Montreal: Drysdale, 1892).

39 Lindley, "Women and the Social Gospel Novel," 71. As Chapters I and II of this work demonstrate, McClung completely rejects this stereotype.

40 "One of the most uplifting forces of nature is that of sex selection. The males, numerous, varied, pouring a flood of energy into wide modifications, compete for the female, and she selects the victor; thus securing to the race the new improvements" (*M-MW*, 29-30).

41 Gilman, *Herland*, 114. Gilman's description of the differences between women's and men's religion (111-7) is both humorous and extremely telling.

42 Gilman, *His Religion and Hers*, 297.

43 "Individually we know it is wrong to rob anyone. Yet the state robs freely, openly, and unashamed, by unjust taxation, by the legalized liquor traffic, by imposing unjust laws upon at least one half of the people" (ITLT, 19).

44 McClung, introductory quotation to "The New Chivalry" (ITLT, 37). Note the shift in meaning of "fair" in this reversal, from "comely" to "just."

45 McClung is scathing on this term. She warns, "Keep your eye on the man who refers to women as the 'fair sex' — he is a dealer in dope!" (ITLT, 38).

46 McClung is drawing here on Gilman (M-MW, 26-43) and, in all likelihood, upon *Women and Economics* as well.

47 It should be noted here that McClung is not saying that all women need be married, for either economic or psychological reasons, simply that physical beauty is a poor basis upon which to build a life-long partnership.

48 McClung addresses the theme of "necessary beauty" at length in *The Second Chance* and briefly in *Purple Springs*.

49 "The ultra feminine felt they were going to lose something in this agitation for equality. They do not want rights — they want privileges — like servants who prefer tips to wages. This is not surprising. Keepers of wild animals tell us that when an animal has been a long time in captivity it prefers captivity to freedom, and even when the door of the cage is opened it will not come out — but that is no argument against freedom" (ITLT, 62).

50 McClung's concern for women's "racial responsibility" has sometimes been read as a "special nature" view of women. The interpretation offered here, however, would place greater emphasis on McClung's use of Gilman for rhetorical purposes, and further acknowledge the significant political threat posed by anti-suffrage women to McClung's feminist cause. A direct appeal to conservative women to become political radicals would be unlikely to win their support; however, by redefining the traditional role of "mother" not only to include but to necessitate political activism, McClung could both confirm women's traditional experience and mobilize women who might otherwise reject her views outright. For an intriguing discussion of the way in which conventional perceptions of women were transformed to unconventional ends, see Ann D. Braude's important article, "Spirits Defend the Rights of Women: Spiritualism and Changing Sex Roles in Nineteenth-century America," in *Women, Religion and Social Change*, ed. Yvonne Yazbeck Haddad and Ellison Banks Findly (Albany: SUNY Press, 1985), 419-32.

51 For example,see Rosemary Radford Ruether, *New Woman/New Earth: Sexist Ideologies and Human Liberation* (New York: Seabury Press, 1975).

52 McClung's use of "man" is here interpreted inclusively, as per her reference to "male man and female man." Had McClung intended to affirm a dual-nature view of humanity, she might have appealed to the alternate account of creation in Genesis 2:4-24, or have talked of the creation of Man and Woman.

53 Ruether, 66.

54 It is important to consider the emphasis on women's physical fitness given by groups like the W.C.T.U. in relation to this point.

55 "The church has contributed a share, too, in the subjection of women, in spite of the plain teaching of our Lord . . ." (ITLT, 71).

56 For current discussions of this point, see Valerie Saiving Goldstein, "The Human Situation: A Feminine View," *Journal of Religion*, 40 (April 1960), 100-12, and Judith Plaskow, *Sex, Sin and Grace: Women's Experience and the Theologies of Reinhold Niebuhr and Paul Tillich* (Washington: University Press of America, 1980), particularly chapter 4, "Theology and Women's Experience," 149-75.

57 In *In Times Like These*, McClung is still optimistic enough to say, "Women are not discouraged or cast down. Neither have they any intention of going on strike, or withdrawing their support from the church. They will still go on patiently, and earnestly and hopefully" (73). By 1921, however, her views had changed. Her address to the 5th Ecumenical Methodist Conference held in London, England, affirms her own continued support of the church ("The Awakening of Women"). However, she challenges the Conference: "But many of the bravest, cleverest, most patriotic women who serve their fellow men in sincerity of soul are outside the Church, and not concerned with it at all. And maybe you wonder why? I can tell you, if you are quite sure you would like to hear. The Church of Christ should have championed the woman's cause; is [sic] should have led all the reform forces in bringing liberty of soul and freedom of action to women. It has not done so. I mean officially. Individual members and ministers have done so, and to them we are very grateful, but the Church has been slow to move, still, and cold. It preached resignation when it should have sounded the note of rebellion. Many of the brightest women grew impatient and indignant, and went out of the Church figuratively slamming the door" (258). While McClung herself remained "to interview the preacher," she nevertheless is firm in stating she fully understood why these women were leaving.

58 "The road from Jerusalem to Jericho is here, and now. Women have played the good Samaritan for a long time, and they have found many a one beaten and robbed on the road of life. They are still doing it, but the conviction is growing on them that it would be much better to go out and clean up the road!" (ITLT, 79).

59 ". . . woman's economic profit comes through the power of sex-attraction. When we confront this fact boldly and plainly in the common market, we are sick with horror. When we see the same economic relation made permanent, established by law, sanctioned and sanctified by religion, covered with flowers and incense and all accumulated sentiment, we think it innocent, lovely, and right" (Gilman, *Women and Economics*, 63).

60 Canadian law governing the guardianship of children worsened this "double-bind." Married women had no legal right to their children, to the extent that a man could will away his unborn child. Bastards, however, were fully the woman's responsibility, leaving men entirely free of the consequences of their actions. McClung was appalled at this situation, and made the guardianship of children one of the themes of *Purple Springs*.

61 See Susan G. Cole's review of *Women against Censorship*. ed. Varda Burstyn (Vancouver: Douglas and McIntyre, 1985) in *Canadian Journal of Women and the Law*, 1, No. 1 (1985), 226-39. McClung would concur with Cole's observation that "Most of the violence against women takes place in private — in the family — where men's liberties, including their right to abuse women, remain, for all practical purposes, protected against any threat from state authority" (236). Government intervention is therefore necessary to protect women from men's "freedom."

62 McClung develops this theme at length in *The Second Chance*, where young Arthur Wemyss comes to see "the beauty of Martha," the hard-working farm girl, after his flashy fiancée has rejected him for an equally flashy city storekeeper.

63 The character who best expresses this ideal for McClung is Helmi Milander, the heroine of *Painted Fires*.

64 To alleviate some of this suffering, McClung was a staunch supporter of travelling public-health nurses, and made one the heroine of her spirited novella, *When Christmas Crossed "The Peace"* (Toronto: Thomas Allen, 1923).

65 McClung here astutely notes the problem of "burn out" which afflicts many participants in movements for social reform.

66 God knew that some would never look
       Inside a book
       To know His will,
   And so He threw a varied hue
       On dale and hill.
   He knew that some would read words wrong,
   And so He gave the birds their song.
       He put the gold in the sunset sky
       To show us that a day may die
       With greater glory than it's born,
           And so may we
       Move calmly forward to our West
           Serene and blest! (ITLT, 129)

Conclusion

Writing in 1930, McClung summed up what religion meant to her. She tells her readers:

> I have never been much of a theologian. Doctrinal discussions have a mouldy taste and are dusty to the palate. I believe we all know enough to live by. It is not so much spiritual food we need as spiritual exercise. But I love the Bible for its stately music and the beauty of its diction, and the words of Christ have the power to set all the bells in my heart ringing. I long to know the mind of the Lord. I would like to know just what was in His mind when He cut short Peter's protestation of love by saying, "Feed My Lambs." That was a slogan for all of us to take from His lips. He tells us in these three words how to show our love. It is not, "Chant my praises," "Defend my theories," "Kill my enemies." No, no—but a greater, better, lovelier task: "Feed my lambs."[1]

In saying this, she is repeating the point made throughout her work, that it is active care, not doctrinal purity nor "the church militant" which appropriately mediates God's love to the world. As she instructed the Fifth Ecumenical Methodist Conference, reflecting on her own and others' experience of nation-building in the Canadian west,

> In our preachers and workers we are not so strong on fine points of doctrine as we are on the spirit of service. Our W.M.S. women try to interpret the love of God to our people from distant lands; our new Canadians by building hospitals and boarding-schools for the children in the far distant districts. Linen sheets, loving and skilful hands, seem to be a good way to interpret God's love. It is effective. It works. It gets the message over. The people come to us so strange,

---

Notes to the Conclusion are on pages 191-2.

so lonely, so homesick. It gives the opportunity for showing the
spirit of love. Our workers are not so intent on making Methodists
out of these people as they are on interpreting God's love to them.
Indeed, our Methodists working here forget that they are Methodists, so intent are they on their big work. Their theology might not
get by the Ecumenical Conference, but it has vitality; it brings joy in
heaven.[2]

McClung sought to "bring joy in heaven" in all that she did. This
mediation of God's love took many forms for her, from stories and
novels to political campaigns for temperance and women's rights, but
whatever its manifestation, her religious conviction remained her
mobilizing force.

This dissertation has attempted to demonstrate the centrality of
religion for McClung's social and political activism through an examination of her novels, and the text and context of *In Times Like These*. It
shifted attention from those elements of McClung which had hitherto
served as the primary focus of scholarship, namely, the "feminist
ideas" of *In Times Like These*, to the larger worldview embodied in her
narratives. Further, bearing in mind that McClung's purpose in writing was didactic, it examined the context of each of her works to lift
up those elements in her environment which influenced the means by
which her message was conveyed. The historical, political and personal realities of McClung's world were thereby disclosed. It is hoped
that a richer, more vibrant, more accurate portrait of McClung has
been the result.

The course of the study demanded that virtually all the dominant
stereotypes of McClung be challenged, more particularly assertions of
her "naive bourgeois maternalism" and her allegedly deficient analyses of class and gender. These criticisms tend to be inter-related,
reflecting a larger set of assumptions about religion, feminism and
social activism. To illustrate these, and to clarify the conclusions of
this inquiry, these criticisms will be considered briefly in turn. One
preliminary comment is in order, however.

This dissertation has attempted to show that "theory" is not a particularly useful category for investigating McClung's religious social
activism. As this section's opening quotations indicate, practical
action was far more important to McClung than abstract systematiza-
tion; certainly, she was always willing to sacrifice consistency for
expediency in her political battles. Some of the reasons for this stance
may have been unique to McClung, but others reflect the ongoing
political reality that prejudice distorts discourse and thwarts straight-

forward political action. A variety of strategies are therefore required to equalize the balance of power, only one of which is the generation of theory. Indeed, as examination of McClung's anti-feminist context has shown, coherence of argument may be less effective against prejudice than a more eclectic, humorous mode of combat. Arising as they do out of theoretical presupposition, the criticisms of McClung addressed here are already suspect, as they fail to account for the external realities which determined discourse. It is precisely for this reason that McClung's novels are an essential component for assessing her work, for it is here she exercised the fullest control over the means and mode of her expression.

Characteristically, the writers who identify McClung as a "maternalist" derive their position from examination of *In Times Like These*, and omit any larger consideration of McClung's work. They tend to assume, if not always to articulate, a normative view of feminism which sees any affirmation of women's traditional experience as necessarily confirming a patriarchal status quo. In contrast, this study takes the position that the argument from women's specificity provided a powerful challenge to the androcentric imagination, particularly in its demand that the public sphere become accountable to women's experience, as defined by women. Hayden's category of "material feminism" is far more useful than that of "maternal feminism" in disclosing this dimension of McClung's perspective.

Too, McClung's appeals to home and motherhood provided her with a political link to more conservative women who might otherwise be reluctant to enter the public fray. By addressing their traditional concerns, and recasting them from a feminist perspective, she was able to mobilize many in the service of her cause. In doing this, McClung effectively employed Charlotte Perkins Gilman to strengthen her political arguments, although comparison of *In Times Like These* and *The Man-Made World* reveals important differences in the bases of their perspectives. Further comparison of *In Times Like These* with McClung's novels reveals what were long-standing beliefs and what were merely rhetorical flourishes employed in the heat of political battle. Neither Pearlie Watson nor Helmi Milander is the sentimental "do-gooder" the stereotype of maternalism would seem to require. Rather, they are strong, independent, courageous women who defy convention and fight for their beliefs. Once McClung's fiction is taken into consideration, the stereotype of maternalism is difficult to sustain.

As examination of the McClung corpus bears out, McClung believed in the fundamental equality of all persons, regardless of race, religion, or gender.[3] Indeed, it was this conviction which demanded political activism in the service of justice. While McClung was quick to acknowledge perspectival differences emerging out of specific experience (for example, her claim that women value human life more than men, because they are more intimately aware of the costs of bringing that life into the world), she rejected a dual-nature view of humanity which assumed destructive male behaviour to be "natural," and therefore to be expected.[4] In McClung's moral economy, gender in no way removed the obligation to extend to all the active care which her religion required.

Calling McClung "bourgeois" raises another set of problems, not the least of which is that the term is rarely defined, and its ideological underpinnings are therefore left unexamined. In this literature, however, it seems to be connected with McClung's ethnicity, and with the fact that she did not mount a Marxist-inspired critique of industrial capitalism. As indicated at the outset, this study has undertaken a pluralistic approach to social activism, with no single cause or analytical perspective assumed to be normative. However, it is worth repeating that McClung was well aware of working conditions in general, but that she chose to focus upon women's experience in her criticism of them.[5] In so doing she made an important contribution to increasing the public's awareness of the realities of many women's lives.

A similar problem arises when McClung's relation to the Social Gospel movement is considered. As Chapter IV of this dissertation suggests, however the character of McClung's activism is defined, it is illegitimate to generate evaluative categories out of male experience and concerns, apply them to McClung whose interest was women's experience, and because she does not reproduce the male-defined agenda judge her approach therefore "deficient." Here, too, her novels stand as an important corrective to the stereotype, as Chapters I and II of this dissertation demonstrate.

Finally, there is the issue of McClung's "naiveté." In one sense, this judgement is not totally inaccurate, inasmuch as the McClung of *Sowing Seeds in Danny* and *The Second Chance* lacked the worldly experience she would later gain. However, there is a more pejorative dimension to this charge, in its implication that, faced with the evidence, McClung somehow failed to see more, or differently, than she did. This study has tried to engage on her own terms, and to assess her work in relation to the possibilities afforded her in her historical context, thereby reflecting the "stage three" approach to women's history. In this light, charges of naiveté may be seen as reflecting "stage two" scholarship's negative normativism. However, there is an additional point to be made. McClung wrote to inspire and empower. She was necessarily optimistic as she "preached her text" of social transformation, for only in this way could she enlist others to her cause. Her religion provided ongoing support, but as all the texts we examined show, McClung was well aware of life's painful realities, and the destruction lack of active care could cause. As the last chapter of *In Times Like These* takes care to point out, faith does not promise that there will be no suffering, but that pain and sorrow can be survived. In that sense, McClung's optimism was justified, for she believed everyone had the possibility of a "second chance." Evaluations of McClung which consider her "naive" need to take into much fuller account this dimension of her faith, as well as the fact that she was preaching a text of personal and political empowerment which demanded the generation of positive energy to get others to enter the fray.

In meeting the criticisms cited above, this study has attempted to demonstrate the usefulness of shifting attention from theory to narrative and from abstract ideas to cultural systems in the study of religion and gender. Recognizing the embodied political reality of human life, it has suggested that particularly in situations where communication is distorted by prejudice and inequities of power, more than argument needs to be examined for a full and accurate analysis. The advantages of the "thick description" approach advocated by Geertz[6] and employed here are many. First, the subject matter emerges in much greater dimension than more narrowly focused theoretical approaches permit, opening out directions for further study. This capacity to generate questions may be one of its greatest strengths. Further, this mode of scholarship is uniquely suited to the study of complex social realities like religion and gender which are highly sensitive politically. The interdisciplinary approach demanded by the methodological shift from theory to narrative is particularly useful in undercutting the tendency to polemic which often characterizes engagement of these issues. Finally, new possibilities emerge for making connections between apparently diverse elements — a crucial contribution, as the introductory overview of the disparate strands of McClung scholarship illustrates.

Theologian George Lindbeck has discussed at length the view of religion which this methodology implies.[7] Lindbeck rejects both the propositional model of religion, which emphasizes beliefs (i.e., "theory," "ideas"), and the more "experiential-expressive" model which assumes the particular features of religious systems to be ultimately insignificant. He offers instead "a cultural-linguistic alternative" (33) which understands religion as "a kind of cultural and/or linguistic framework or medium that shapes the entirety of life and thought ... an idiom that makes possible the description of realities, the formulation of beliefs, and the experience of inner attitudes, feelings, and sentiments" (33). Moreover, it is "a communal phenomenon," a shared language, with its own vocabulary of symbols and "a distinctive logic or grammar in terms of which this vocabulary can be meaningfully deployed" (33). Lindbeck's model is extremely useful for understanding McClung, and in illuminating her use of literature as pulpit. The cultural-linguistic model emphasizes the importance of narrative in conveying religious understanding.[8] Not every story is religious, however: "It must be used ... with a view to identifying and describing what is taken to be 'more important than everything else in the universe' and to organize all life, including both behaviour and beliefs, in relation to this" (32-3). Clearly, this was McClung's intent.

Yet as noted above, McClung became decreasingly successful in this task. The early narratives of *Sowing Seeds in Danny* and *The Second Chance* are harmonious and seamless, with resolution easily achieved through a little human effort. By *Purple Springs* and *Painted Fires*, the narrative structure has been fractured. *Purple Springs* attempts to combine melodramatic subtext (Pearl's conflicted romance with Dr. Clay) with political reportage, while *Painted Fires* is a jumble of causes, each important but strung together rather than woven into a single whole. A number of factors may be held responsible.

First, McClung's own political experience rendered her somewhat more sceptical about the easy resolution of human problems through changed "mental attitudes" and a little political "elbow grease." Both *Purple Springs* and *Painted Fires* register this change, but it is only in *Painted Fires* that McClung's failure to imagine a coherent socio-political alternative becomes fully apparent. A second factor, noted in Chapter I, was a shift in literary tastes such that McClung's "Sunday School stories" (read here in Lindbeck's terms as narratives "with a view to identifying and describing what is taken to be 'more important than everything else in the universe'") were dismissed as embarrassingly moralistic. She retained her readership, but primarily with *Clearing in the West*, her autobiographical re-creation of the world which informed *Sowing Seeds in Danny* and *The Second Chance*.

Finally, there is the question of McClung's feminism. Lindbeck has said that religion is a "linguistic framework ... that shapes the entirety of life and thought." As this dissertation has demonstrated throughout, McClung's religion, feminism and social activism were inextricably intertwined in a common language articulating social change in the service of God's intended justice. Like her religion and her literary style, McClung's feminism came to be seen as old-fashioned[9] and irrelevant, to the extent that the term is not even mentioned in the introductory description to her first syndicated newspaper column for the *Edmonton Bulletin*.[10]

McClung had lost her voice. Her language — religious, feminist, activist — was no longer the language of common parlance. Later scholars (to continue the metaphor) came to recognize a few words here and there, but overall her speech remained disjointed and distorted. However, through renewed scholarly interest in religion and in gender, fresh resources are emerging. By returning to the narratives, by investigating the whole context of McClung's life and work, it is possible to learn to hear McClung's voice clearly once again. To do so is essential, for only then can the full significance of this vital, courageous and fascinating Canadian be articulated. It is hoped that this dissertation has made some contribution toward that important task.

Notes

1 McClung, "My Religion," 30.
2 McClung, "The Awakening of Women," 260.
3 This point is also made in "The Awakening of Women," where McClung states unequivocally: "Women are not angels or glorified beings of any kind; they are just human beings, seeking only fair play and common justice" (259).
4 As McClung remarks on a similar point in *In Times Like These*, "I am glad I never said anything as hard as that about men" (39).
5 McClung engaged the experiences of women working in the public sphere when she dragged Sir Rodmond Roblin into the sweatshops of Winnipeg's garment district. Her concern for women's traditional labour is demonstrated in her opening salvo in "The Awakening of Women": " 'The Awakening of Women' is a rather misleading title. Women have always been awake. The woman of fifty years ago who carded the wool, spun it, wove the cloth to clothe her family, made the clothes without any help from Mr. Butterick or the *Ladies Pictorial*, brewed her own cordials, baked her own bread, washed, ironed, scrubbed, without any labour-saving devices, and besides this always had the meals on time, and incidentally raised a family, and a few

chickens and vegetables in her spare time, may be excused if she did not take much interest in politics, or even know who was likely to be the next Prime Minister. But her lack of interest was not any proof that she was asleep — she was only busy!" (257-8).

6 Geertz, "Thick Description: Toward an Interpretive Theory of Culture," in his *Interpretation of Cultures*, 3-30.

7 George A. Lindbeck, *The Nature of Doctrine: Religion and Theology in a Postliberal Age* (Philadelphia: Westminster Press, 1984). Subsequent references will be given parenthetically in the text.

8 "Religions are seen as comprehensive interpretive schemes, usually embodied in myths or narratives and heavily ritualized, which structure human experience and understanding of self and world" (Lindbeck, 32).

9 Dorothy Sayers notes this tendency to think of feminism as "old-fashioned" in her 1938 address given to a Women's Society, reprinted as *Are Women Human?* (Grand Rapids, Mich.: William B. Eerdmans Publishing, 1971).

10 "Mrs. Nellie McClung, author, stateswoman, lecturer, prairie school teacher, former member of the Alberta legislature, and friend and comforter of many a woman pioneer who braved the hardships of western homesteads and distant farms, is now on the staff of The Bulletin" (*Edmonton Bulletin*, 30 May 1936).

Appendices

Appendix A

Nellie McClung Papers,*
Provincial Archives of
British Columbia,
Victoria, British Columbia

---

*   Duplicate of finding Aid No. 4

Originals.   10 feet, 10 inches.

1894-1950

Nellie Lititia [*sic*] (Mooney) McClung was born in Chatsworth, Ontario on 20 October 1873. Her family moved to Wawanesa, Manitoba in 1880 and upon graduation from the Winnipeg Normal School, Miss Mooney began her teaching career at Manitou, Manitoba at the age of 16. In 1896 she married Robert Wesley McClung, a pharmacist in Manitou. In 1908, her first novel, *Sowing Seeds in Danny*, was published. Other novels, essays, short stories, and sketches soon followed and continued to appear into her seventieth year. The McClung's moved to Winnipeg in 1911 when Mr. McClung took up work with an insurance company. Nellie became active in various organizations, including the Canadian Women's Press Club and the Winnipeg Political Equality League. Her activities in temperance and women's suffrage leagues continued when they moved to Edmonton in 1914 where she campaigned vigorously for social reform and women's rights. She served in the Alberta legislature with the Liberals from 1921 to 1926. After her political defeat she fought to establish Canadian women's rights to seats in the Senate. In 1933 the McClung family moved to Victoria. From 1936 to 1942 she served as the first woman member of the CBC Board of Governors. In 1938 she represented Canada as a delegate to the League of Nations. She died in 1951 at the age of 77.

The collection consists of correspondence, newspaper clippings, handwritten and typescript copies of published and unpublished works, notes for speeches and scrapbooks.

A photograph album has been deposited with Visual Records. 98307-1.

The unit was presented to the Provincial Archives by Mr. R.W. McClung in November 1953.

1. Original Manuscripts

The original manuscripts (the first rough drafts) of the McClung collection are contained in nine grey boxes. The articles and novels are written in scribblers. Where a title has been placed at the start of a composition, this has been noted in the list below. Each scribbler has been examined but the list of titles is not necessarily comprehensive.

Volume
1/1:   July 29, 1936, miscellaneous
1/2:   "The Last Reserves"
1/3:   "The Believing Church"
1/4:   "Land of Heroes"; "The Old Year Passes" (Dec. 30/39)

1/5:   The Black Curtain (Book No. 1)

1/6:   On the Trail (Book No. 2, chapter 7)

1/7:   The Ordination Debate in Calgary; Thanksgiving

1/8:   No. 4 Book (1933)

1/9:   Chpt. 18: My first sight of Brandon

1/10:   Synopsis

1/11:   The Day Before Xmas

1/12:   One Hundred Years Ago!

Volume

2/1:   The Reprieve

2/2:   Winds of the World; We played for keeps

2/3:   Monotony . . . ; Dear Listener; The scent of Water; Leisure . . .

2/4:   On the Opening of the new Transmitter at CFTR, Victoria, Jan. 10/39; The first lap of winter; Long Road; The Spirit of B.C.

2/5:   The End of the Circle; Consider the Ant

2/6:   Letters outward, 1934; Religion into our time; All in one day; Food is a factor in the war

2/7:   This is an age of doubt! . . . ; The Roads of Nova Scotia; Cooperation in Nova Scotia; Community Housing in Nova Scotia

2/8:   The Woman Who Rode Away; Current Events, Sept. 22/37; Over CHAB, Moose Jaw, 1939; We Are on the spot!; Case for the Newspaper

2/9:   Martha Jones the Orphan; Freewheeling; Let The School Bells Ring

2/10:   Feb. 20; The Minor Poet (1940-1941); Hardly on Speaking Terms

2/11:   A Year From Now; Mary Bell Andrews . . .

2/12:   Nov. 8/41; Gordon Head, Month of Memories

2/13:   Mean People Are News

2/14:   Coming Home; You have to face it now (Nov. 22/41)

2/15:   The Moving Finger Writes

2/16:   The Canadian Family; Mothers' Day; the Threat to Democracy; A Plea For A [sic] Our Old Books; Down In the Human Heart

2/17:   Our Frozen Assets; We Are all in This Race; W.M. Davidson; There are Still Many Causes For Gladness; Spring Thinking

2/18:   Chpt. XVI . . . to Chpt. XX

2/19:   The first day of spring

2/20:   Have Women Failed; Women and Fashion: St. Aiden's of Victoria

2/21:   Neighbours on the Left

2/22:   Bob Steele (10) . . . [?]

2/23:   A Day of Reckoning; Bad Blood; The Development of the Novel, CNCP June 29/32

Volume

3/1:   The last Sunday in 1940

3/2:   When Tom came over from Milford . . .
3/3:   More About Food (Feb. 24/41); Women Can Solve This One
3/4:   Manners
3/5:   What Have We to Say to Our Youth; Graduation Address; Empire Day; The Battle of Ideas
3/6:   This Century for Canada: Summary of Broadcast Business and Professional Club, Nov. 16/39
3/7:   Scrip Commission
3/8:   The storm had choked . . .
3/9:   Maidie Martin
3/10:   Bob Steele (9) . . . [see 2/22]
3/11:   Alberta's Outcroppings of Literature
3/12:   Winds of the World
3/13:   Do We Want Women At The Peace Conference
3/14:   Do We Want Women At The Peace Conference
3/15:   Chpt. IV Should Women Think?
3/16:   The Signing of The Charter
3/17:   If prejudices belong to the vegetable world
3/18:   Synopsis of Sowing Seeds in Danny
3/19:   Manitoba Lacrosse Country
3/20:   Shall Women Preach
3/21:   Nellie McClung's Expense Account, meeting of the Board of Governors, April 5th and 16th, 1940
3/22:   Notes on Calgary Speech; Let Us Look at Ourselves
3/23:   Political Talks, March 1940
3/24:   CBC Trouble; The Challenge of Christmas; Another Year is Ending
3/25:   March 14, 1931, CKLC
3/26:   How It feels to be a defeated candidate
3/27:   Goodbye Summer!; A Day at the Fair
3/28:   Will you help?; The Shadow of Ladyhood
3/29:   The Way to Peace; Good Speech
3/30:   The Ordination of Women, To the Ministry of the Church; Satan Has Entered the Garden
3/31:   May 16, 1910
3/32:   The Old Prejudices
3/33:   Thanksgiving Day
3/34:   The Dividends of Life (May 17/36)
3/35:   June 1918, Who Speaks for Canada
3/36:   Theodore . . . [?]
3/37:   Picnics . . . [?]
3/38:   Chapter X to XI [?]
3/39:   The Making of a Teacup Reader; Grounds for Hope
3/40:   We Make Our Own Luck (Jan. 25/30)

3/41:   What is wrong with Women's Organizations?; Russia, the Kulaks; Bootlegging to the U.S.

Volume

4/1:   The Age of Romance; Seven Cents; Nellie McClung Says There Are No Idle Words; Work Among Girls!
4/2:   Thirty Years; Senate Decision
4/3:   [Story?]
4/4:   Mrs. Coulter . . . 4
4/5:   Poems (1927)
4/6:   The Dramateurs
4/7:   Jan. 1931; The Step-Mother; The Black Curse
4/8:   Conservatives belittle Liberal Women
4/9:   Prying Open The Future
4/10:   The Fortune Teller
4/11:   A Time To Weep
4/12:   Clem's Wife . . .
4/13:   The Fortune Teller; Lady Josephine's Pearls
4/14:   The Day of the Funeral Everything Stopped
4/15:   Current Events, May 1930
4/16:   Background
4/17:   April 24, 1933
4/18:   Women and People Grace Church, Sept. 9/28
4/19:   The Muirheads Farm
4/20:   Sept. 17, 1919, The young doctor
4/21:   Conservation
4/22:   The Glorious First [of July]; The Wind; The Macdonald's Gathering
4/23:   This Is The Victory; September, Labour Day; Message to the children of democracies
4/24:   More About Medicinal Plants; By strangers told
4/25:   What Have We to Write About?
4/26:   Dunant — The Forgotten Man
4/27:   The Dustman's Daughter
4/28:   The Art of Conversation
4/29:   [Story]

Volume

5/1:   A Day in Vancouver; Confessions of a Onion Grower
5/2:   Next Monday is Labor Day! Find the Scapegoat — the Japanese Canadians
5/3:   The Romance of Religion; Then and Now; New Frontiers; The Gift of the Desert; They come to us; What Does the Church Think of Home Missions; No Holiday
5/4:   Winter Gardening; Gardening by Catalogue
5/5:   Girls Conference, April 25/37

5/6:   The Verdict of History II; Rain in the Night
5/7:   Will religion survive?; Fashion in Flowers
5/8:   Young Master; Does reading really matter?; Jews in Canada
5/9:   Coming Home; The Coronation
5/10:   Holiday on the Highway
5/11:   Perfection; The Informal Garden
5/12:   The Empire Builders; Higher Education
5/13:   This is a war of ideas!; Hail to the hardy ants
5/14:   [Story?]
5/15:   The Value of a Handicraft Festival
5/16:   The Romance, in Everyday Life; Nothing to do but work (poem)
5/17:   Something pleasant may happen today!
5/18:   The Development of Personality
5/19:   Over the Rainbow (Speech to Vancouver Board of Trade); The
        Writer's Creed and other essays
5/20:   A Time for Everything; One Thing is Certain
5/21:   "Come ye thankful People come!"
5/22:   Six Weeks Vacation — "Truth is Stranger Than Fiction"
5/23:   Chapter I . . .
5/24:   What is real life (May 29, 1937)
5/25:   The Christmas Gift; The Christmas Letter
5/27:   Chapter IX The First Winter
5/28:   Family reminiscences; Well people should pay
5/29:i The call of The Wild; The Dividends of Life
5/30:   Minerva Jones Reporting
5/31:   Words; Have an Apple/ Must We Have Fears; Canada
5/32:   Current Events
5/33:   Goodwill (May 18/01); Current Events
5/34:   What is Wrong With Women's Organizations [or]
5/35:   Debate: Women representatives; Sowing Seeds in Danny
5/36:   Sowing Seeds in Danny
5/37:   Sowing Seeds in Danny
5/38:   Synopsis of the "Second Chance"
5/39:   The Calling of the Spring; The Callow Lily
5/40:   Thrums
5/41:   Sowing Seeds in Danny

Volume
6/1:   In Praise of Green Peas; When the Dr. retired; End of The Summer;
        Let Us Go To The Flower Show; Going To Town (Vancouver Pan-
        Pacific Conference)
6/2:   The Humour of Everyday Life: Letter to the editor (Oct. 19/23)
6/3:   Women Will Talk
6/4:   Expense Book, May 1935; Defensive Commo Sense; Beach Talk; The

Homemakers; On Leaving Home; In Praise of Green Peas; The Day of Mouring [*sic*]; An Onion Scrapbook

6/5:   Easter Adventure; Easter Morning

6/6:   This Is It

6/7:   Mother Has Her Innings!

6/8:   Women

6/9:   A Christmas Story; The Scent of Water

6/10:   The Last Picnic; Going To Town

6/11:   The Voice of Canada; What Can We Do

6/12:   Dickensians; A Day At the Fair

6/13:   The Depression in Saskatchewan; Travelling

6/14:   Teacher says: Hidden Treasure; The Canadian Scene

6/15:   Current Events, Jan. 20/36; Magic

6/16:   Miscellaneous Essays

6/17:   Uneasy Women

6/18:   A Child Remembers

6/19:   Music in The Air

6/20:   Books For Xmas Presents; re: Pacifists are Traitors; Second Blooming

6/21:   Canadian Club (Mar. 31/ 37); Rain In The Night

6/22:   Danae . . .

6/23:   The Child's First Years — Their Significance

6/24:   What Have We Learned in 1937?; What Is News; We Are At War; The Last Day of The War

6/25:   The New Deal — Observations of a Visitor; North Hill United Church, May 28/34

6/26:   South of the Rio Grande: Pretty As Paint; Mexican Pictures

6/27:   As The Year Ends; Don't Break The Chain!

6/28:   Dominion Day; A Message To The Women's Institutes!; The Things That Remain; Setting The Captive Free; Ukrainians in Canada

6/29:   Autobiographical sketch; The Broken Body

6/30:   The Long Fall Drizzle and other stories

6/31:   The Place of Religion in the Modern World and Why; James Burwash, General Merchant

6/32:   Women Talking

6/33:   Current Events, Sept. 18/39; One Day Off; Frances Willard

Volume

7/1:   Sowing Seeds in Danny

7/2:   Margaret Kenny

7/3:   School Book

7/4:   Eva St. John . . .

7/5:   Helmi . . .

7/6:   Helmi . . .

7/7:   Amia was born on Christmas Eve

7/8:   The House of Hope
7/9:   Second Spring; The First Woman; Onions and Twitch Grass
7/10:   Easter Message (April 21/35)
7/11:   A fine day in Vancouver; one good Sleep; one of the Least; This Changing World
7/12:   The Day I Went To Chilliwack; The Wealth in Words
7/13:   Commencement; Victoria City; Odds and Ends (Aug/34)
7/14:   Cats I have Known
7/15:   Mother's Day Reform; Light and Leading; Prohibition
7/16:   The Spirit of The Garden
7/17:   Conversations; Farming
7/18:   Miscellaneous writings (Oct. 10/35)
7/19:   The Premier's Announcement on Woman Suffrage
7/20:   The Fellowship of Booklovers; The Little Church Under the Hill
7/21:   "Prince of the House of Clay"
7/22:   The Unafraid Woman!; Sowing Seeds in Danny
7/23:   Sowing Seeds in Danny
7/24:   Sowing Seeds in Danny
7/25:   Sowing Seeds in Danny
7/26:   Sowing Seeds in Danny
7/27:   Sowing Seeds in Danny
7/28:   Is This Then All?; After Twenty Years
7/29:   Sowing Seeds in Danny
7/30:   Women and Politics
7/31:   Book Six of a continuing story
7/32:   Royal Templar Social
7/33:   Up to Scotland
7/34:   Poetry For The Common Day
7/35:   Speak For Canada; New Year Thoughts; Good Gossip; Will The Church Survive
7/36:   How It Feels To Be A Defeated Candidate
7/37:   Miscellaneous Writings
7/38:   Sowing Seeds in Danny
7/39:   Sowing Seeds in Danny
7/40:   Chinese Dummies
7/41:   Sowing Seeds in Danny

Volume
8/1:   Rain; The One-Way Road
8/2:   A Cure For Blues
8/3:   Working for our desires
8/4:   The Country School; A plea for Parents; The Snobbery of Childhood
8/5:   Manners
8/6:   Current Events

8/7:   Scribbles
8/8:   How Should We Celebrate July 1?
8/9:   Short Story
8/10:   Little Minnie Morrison
8/11:   Miscellaneous Writings
8/12:   Prohibition
8/13:   Travelling With Friends; The Alibi
8/14:   Notes
8/15:   Poison
8/16:   For The Life Is More Than Meat
8/17:   Flowers For The Living
8/18:   Chapter 10: The Marchesal
8/19:   Why Women Do Not Vote; Will Christmas Survive
8/20:   Life has a way of going on . . . (Part II of a novel [?])
8/21:   Canadian Manners; The One Way Road; The Journeying God
8/22:   Bells At Evening
8/23:   Seven Cents; Keeping Friends With The Family
8/24:   Short Story
8/25:   Mrs. Clearmont . . .
8/26:   Personality
8/27:   Current Events
8/38:   Every cloud has a silver lining
8/29:   Current Events (1930; 1931)
8/30:   Current Events (Feb. 20/29; 1928)
8/31:   Current Events (1929-1930)
8/32:   Current Events 1930
8/33:   Current Events
8/34:   Are You A Good Listener (Oct. 17/42)

Volume
9/1:   Poor Fish!; The Angel of the Frost
9/2:   Current Events; Presenting Mrs. Ferne; Radio Talk; The Last Night;
         New Years Resolution
9/3:   Home Missions
9/4:   McDougall Church (Aug. 15/16)
9/5:   Elizar Ann — A Study in Paints
9/6:   Winds of the World
9/7:   Millford Band of Hope; Incidents; Sowing Seeds in Danny
9/8:   Sowing Seeds in Danny
9/9:   Sowing Seeds in Danny
9/10:   From A Train Window; Rainy Sunday; Think On The Things
9/11:   Sowing Seeds in Danny
9/12:   Can A Woman Have A Career and Raise a Family
9/13:   Out Our Way; The Beaver Speaks; With a Scotch Flavour

9/14:   Women in Literature; Our Present Discontents; The National Idea
9/15:   Thanksgiving
9/16:   Planting Time; The Threat of Thrips
9/17:   The Party at the Slaters; Sowing Seeds in Danny
9/18:   The House of the Good Neighbour
9/19:   Rain Before Seven
9/20:   The House of Bread
9/21:   The House of Bread
9/22:   The House of Bread
9/23:   The House of Bread
9/24:   Shall Women Think?
9/25:   Sowing Seeds in Danny
9/26:   Sowing Seeds in Danny
9/27:   Blue Lily of the Nile
9/28:   Come Fall, Let us be Reconciled; A plea For Old Books; The Common Touch
9/29:   Great Things Are Happening; The Mood of the Country
9/30:   Canadian Fiesta!; Let Us Pass On!
9/31:   The Small Town
9/32:   Essay
9/33:   Going South; Closing the House
9/34:   Current Events
9/35:   Let Us Keep The First; Danger, Men At Work; The World of Tomorrow; Speak Up, Canada
9/36:   Minerva Jones Reporting
9/37:   A Day on the Train; Good Old Ontario; Sudbury
9/38:   Chapter 12: Back To Camp; Chapter 8 — Off to Switzerland

2. Correspondence

Volume 10:   Folder 1 — 1894, 1905, 1906, 1907.
              Folder 2 — 1908.
              Folder 3 — 1910, 1911, 1913, 1914, 1915.
Volume 11:   Folder 4 — 1916, 1917, 1918, 1919, 1920, 1921, 1923.
              Folder 5 — 1924, 1925, 1926.
              Folder 6 — 1927, 1928, 1929, 1930.
              Folder 7 — 1931, 1932, 1933, 1934, 1935.
Volume 12:   Folder 8 — 1936.
              Folder 9 — 1937, 1938, 1939.
              Folder 10 — 1941 to 1950.
              Folder 11 — undated.

3. Miscellaneous Manuscripts

Volume 19:   Original Manuscript of "Painted Fires" and published
              version in a newspaper serial. Galley proofs of
              "Flowers for the Living."

Volume 20:   Folders 1 to 3 — Miscellaneous material;
              Folder 4: Galley proofs of "The Stream Runs Fast."

Volume 21:   Originals of "The Stream Runs Fast" written 1943-1944
              Galley proofs of "The Stream Runs Fast."

Volume 22:   Folder 1 — Miscellaneous Articles (MSS)
              Folder 2 — Miscellaneous Articles (MSS)
              Folder 3 — Poems
              Folder 4 — Miscellaneous Articles (MSS)
              Folder 5 — Book Reviews
              Folder 6 — "The Second Chance" (MSS)

Volume 23: Typescript Articles
              Folder 1 — "The Black Creek Stopping House"
              Folder 2 — "All We Like Sheep . . ."
              Folder 3 — Miscellaneous Articles, undated
              Folder 4 — Miscellaneous Articles, undated
              Folder 5 — Miscellaneous Articles, undated
              Folder 6 — Miscellaneous Articles, undated

Volume 24:   Folders 1 to 4 — Typescript Articles

Volume 25:   Folder 1 — Notes on Speeches
              Folder 2 — Miscellaneous Notes on Speeches
              Folder 3 — Notes on Speeches
              Folder 4 — Speeches as an M.L.A.
              Folder 5 — Radio Talks
              Folder 6 — Speeches

Volume 26:   Notebooks and Diaries

4. Newspaper Clippings

Volumes 13-18:   Housed in grey boxes; various dates
Volumes 27-54:   Housed in individual scrapbooks, described below:
Volume 27:   Miscellaneous Clippings, 1895-1905
Volume 28:   Newspaper Clippings, various dates in the period 1910-1945
Volume 29:   Newspaper Clippings, 1908-1910
Volume 30:   Newspaper Clippings, 1909-1911
Volume 31:   Newspaper Clippings, 1909-1910
Volume 32:   Photographs and Clippings, c. 1912
Volume 33:   Newspaper Clippings, 1912-1913
Volume 34:   Newspaper Clippings, 1913-1915
Volume 35:   Newspaper Clippings, 1914 (The Election)

Volume 36:	Newspaper Clippings, 1915
Volume 37:	ewspaper Clippings, 1916-1917
Volume 38:	Newspaper Clippings, 1917-1918
Volume 39:	Newspaper Clippings, 1932-1933
Volume 40:	Newspaper Clippings re "Clearing in the West," 1935-1936
Volume 41:	Scrapbook, presented Easter 1936
Volume 42:	Scrapbook, Newspaper Clippings re "Leaves from Lantern Lane," 1936-1937
Volume 43:	Newspaper Clippings, 1937
Volume 44:	Newspaper Clippings, 1937-1938
Volume 45:	Newspaper Articles, 1938-1939
Volume 46:	Newspaper Articles, 1939-1940
Volume 47:	Newspaper Articles, 1939-1940
Volume 48:	Newspaper Clippings, 1939-1940
Volume 49:	Newspaper Clippings, 1940-1945 (approx.)
Volume 50:	Newspaper (and other) Articles, 1940-1941
Volume 51:	Newspaper Clippings and Miscellaneous, 1941
Volume 52:	Newspaper Clippings, 1941-1942
Volume 53:	Newspaper Articles, 1942; "The Stream Runs Fast" Book Reviews, 1945-1946
Volume 54:	Newspaper Clippings, 1947
Volume 55,56:	Two Scrapbooks containing greeting cards, messages, congratulations, telegrams, etc. of the McClungs' Golden Wedding Anniversary in 1946.
Volume 57:	"Handy Guide" containing newspaper clippings and photographs

5. Journal (Bound)

Volume 58:	Daily Journal, 1908

6. Typescripts (Bound)

Volume 59:	"Painted Fires"
Volume 60:	Cop. 1 & cop. 2 — "Clearing in the West"
Volume 61:	"The Black Creek Stopping House"
Volume 62:	"In The Land Of The Gopher"

Appendix B

Advertisements

The Proper Way to Eat Pie !

Don't Worry It With A Fork.   Point the sharp
end toward the mouth, and   then   push   it   in   with
gentle pressure.

This is the bright side of eating pie.   There is a
dark side—an Afterwards.   It is called

DYSPEPSIA

It makes unhappy homes, or rather it did until
Nyal's Dyspepsia Tablets were discovered.

Nyal's Dyspepsia Tablets.   50c Box

——SOLD AT——

McClung's Drug Store.

WORRY KILLS!

But STRYCHNINE does a neater job on Gophers.
Do you remember how your young Cabbage plants
disappeared about the second week in June,
last year? and how the fat and "Sassy" young
Gophers swaggered up and down the garden
paths, wishing you would set out some more?
One bottle of STRYCHNINE will upset all their
plans for the summer.

STRYCHNINE, the kind that kills, all ready for use,

For Sale at

McClung's Drug Store

Reproduced with the permission of the British Columbia Archives and Records Service,
H-5899.

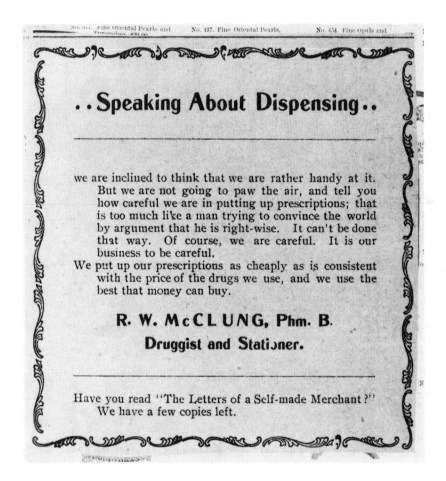

The Farmer's Wife . . .

Her hours are from 4 a. m. to 4 a. m. and she is tired of baking bread and of washing dishes. Her back aches and her nerves are shattered, and she has no comfort in the eight thousand bushels of wheat she has helped to raise, for it is all a weariness of the flesh to her. Less than two bushels of it will buy her a bottle of

Beef, Iron, & Wine

and Beef, Iron, and Wine will help to give her a rosier view of life. It will give her an appetite, and bring back her strength, and stimulate her when she feels faint. It is the Best Tonic on the market.

The Best cost $1 a bottle

all over the world. For sale by

R. W. McCLUNG.

Appendix C
Personal Correspondence

1965 Hamilton Street,
Regina, Sask.,
February 22, 1931

Dear Mrs. McClung: —

I have just finished reading "Be good to yourself" and must tell you how much I enjoyed this particular part: "Any one who has picked wild strawberries will know how I felt when I saw my hostess opening a jar of them . . . she said, like you, that wild strawberries are a test of friendship. . . ."

I know something about picking wild strawberries and could go with my eyes shut to a place in Ontario near a tall old stump wherein a highholder always had a nest and where a song sparrow always held forth in a nearby willow tree. Lots of berries right there.

A few years ago I visited in this province an old friend and during my short stay she not only opened a jar of wild strawberries, but she gave me one to take home with me. Can you beat that? The dear, kind soul has gone forward now and in a life piled high with sorrows I think she never har bored an unkind thought. Perhaps it was because she had spent so many peaceful, quiet hours under God's blue sky picking wild strawberries.

Here's to you Nellie McClung. You have refreshed me many times and these words about the wild strawberries simply renewed my youth.

Sincerely yours,
(Mrs. James Quigley)   Mabel Quigley

Box 213
Calmar Alta
March 5th

Dear Chatelaine

I am writing to let you know How much I enjoyed hearing part of Mrs Nellie McClungs Book. Unfortunately I did not hear the first part of it, until a Friend told me about it. I have never *enjoyed a Book so much*, since coming to Canada. My home was in England before. But I have been in Canada 41 years. I just cannot tell you how I drank in every word of it. & how I laughed over the very things & names, & styles of dresses etc, especialy the "Scarlet Bloomers" It brought back so many memories of my girl hoods days. The *warnings* our darling little Mothers use to give us I am wonder if it would be too much trouble for you to let me know where I could purchase the Book. & what price it would be, for I just want to *read it all* & more than once, Im sure. Thanking you in Advance I remain

Sincerely yours
Mrs Fred Wyss
Box 213 / Calmar / Alta

Grosmont, Alberta
February 28, 1936

Dear Mrs. McLung,

For the many happy hours spent listening to your story "Clearing in the West" please accept my sincere thanks.

This afternoon "The Chatelaine" will read the last chapter of your book. I only wish there were many more chapters.

I am alone all day in a one room cottage, twenty-one miles north-west of Athabaska. In the afternoons on which your story was read, I filled the stove with wood pulled my chair to the fire and with my fancy work in hand I was ready to travel to Manitoba through the medium of your very interesting book.

I have been a teacher for six years, but this year I was unable to secure a school. Many of your problems of early teaching days were mine also.

Again I thank you for the pleasure which the reading of your book gave me on so many lonely afternoons.

I am,
Yours sincerely,
Marguerite Meiklejohn.

10973-129 St.
Edmonton Feb. 26

Mrs. Nellie L. McClung
c/o C.F.R.N.

Dear "Nellie L.": —

Kindly forgive the freedom but that is how I always think of you since our first meeting about 1914 in Macleod.

This is just to express my greatest pleasure in your book "Trailing in the West" which is being read by C.F.R.N.'s Chatelaine of the Air.

I realize that we lived in very similar times and many of your references to styles in dress making, to experiences in teaching, to evangelistic meetings, Epworth League, and leading your first League meeting, etc, etc, might have been out of my own diary . . . if I were clever enough to describe them. I was born Mar. 17th and went to Michigan from Ont when small. Lived there until a young woman and then came to Stettler Alta.

Allow me again to thank you for your book.

Would also congratulate you on Mark's appointment as Rhodes scholar.

Wishing you all health and happiness and trust we will have more of your splendid literary compositions.

Sincerely
Nellie L. Richard

(Mrs. A.D.)

Torlea, Alberta
February 27, 1936

Susan Egar, Chatelaine of the Air
Radio Station CFRN; C.P.R. Bldg.,
Edmonton, Alberta.

Dear Susan Egar,

I should first of all like to say that I think it is a splendid idea for a radio program to feature the reading of a book and have often wondered why it has not been done before—at least I have never heard any book for adults being read over the air until I heard you—in place of some of the utterly horrid so-called music which is constantly presented for radio listeners. It is a wonderful thing for we busy housewives, who are really bookworms at heart but have not the time to indulge in the pleasure, to be able to sit and carry on with some work while listening to a reader giving us the contents of a delightful book.

I can truthfully say that of the many radio programs yours is the one to which I look forward with the keenest anticipation and I try to plan my work so that I am doing something at the time which permits me to give my attention to your reading of such a delightful book.

I do not know of any book which would have been more interesting than the one which you chose, "Clearing in the West," by Mrs. Nellie McClung and your natural and charming manner of reading makes me often feel that it is Nellie McClung herself telling us her experiences of early days.

I have enjoyed every word of the book as I have many others of Mrs. McClung's books since my early school years when I first became acquainted with one of her books, "Sowing Seeds in Danny." It was read to us by our teacher and I remember how we enjoyed it. Of all the books read to me by my teachers at school that one seemed to have made the most impression on my memory and many years later I chose that same book to read to my pupils who also enjoyed it very much.

As I have had some teaching experience myself I can appreciate that much more the part of Mrs. McClung's book dealing with her school life and teaching experiences. But that is the quality of her books — they have such a human appeal in their true-to-life element so that one can really live her stories with her. I have read many of her books and articles as I never pass any up if I have the opportuni ty to read them.

I realize that no words of mine can adequately describe her writings so that the best tribute which I can give to Mrs. Nellie McClung is that there are very few books which I can read a second time and thoroughly enjoy but some of hers I have re-read many times always with the same appreciation and I trust she may long continue to pass on to us the pleasure of her writing.

Yours sincerely,
Helen Piscia
(Mrs. Marion Piscia)

Meanook. Alta.
Feb 21 1936

Dear Mrs Mc Clung

I wish to tell you how very much I have enjoyed the radio half hour with your lovely book "Clearing in the West." Today I shed a few tears over the death of your Father, but I have laughed with the children so many times at quaint things you did in the first chapters. My two little children love to listen and every afternoon about three "little Dorothy" my baby asks "is Mrs McClung on the air today." I have missed quite a bit of it as we have only one battery for our radio and it had to be charged twice since Miss Agar started to read your book so I missed one part at the first that I was terribly interested in. . . . I was born near Chatsworth forty three years ago "near a stone school on the Garafraxa road Sydenham and Derby school" and was so anxious to know if you were born North of Chatsworth too, as I know a good many of the farms between Chatsworth and Owen Sound. I came West thirty years ago and married very young, and had a very large family, and your book brought me back to the years when I was a child in the East and I have loved every bit of it.

I saw you once in Edmonton sixteen years ago when you addressed a mass of soldiers wives at a convention. Mrs. Murphy was there too, and she was a dear old Irish Lady. I had a talk with her and she promised if we got in any difficulties while in the city she would be very lenient if "we came before her."

We read your articles in the Free Press and I have promised to show my little boy of nine, who has not been well all winter so does not walk the three miles to school, your picture but have no back issues and your picture has not appeared since he has become so interested in your book, but hope we have another article by you soon. I had read a good many of your books years ago and enjoyed them very much and hope you will be very happy in your home in Vancouver and write many more books as there is something so human and understanding about them all.

Yours very sincerely
Ruby Macintyre

Mrs. S.M. Crickmore,
Clarkson, Ont,
Feb. 16th, 1936
2 a.m.

Dear Mrs. McClung: —

With two children in the ups and downs of a bad case of whooping-cough, I should have enough sense to go to bed when they do.

But though I'm bug-eyed with lack of sleep and my face feels as if it were hanging in festoons like a bloodhound's, I've been too firmly rooted in "Clearing in the West" to even consider sleep.

I've torn myself away several times to dash from one to the other with a basin and a kind word, but back I've come, either beside the big stove in your big room down-stairs or by that fine Inspector who said that with feeling and imagination you'd get a lot out of life. They do help.

I've had a great time getting acquainted with your family and I've loved your father. I'm filled with admiration for your Mother. What a splendid manager! How I wish I had as firm a control over my three.

I smiled over Jack's dislike of the "love stuff" It reminds me of my fourteen year old son (now away) who during a love scene in "Captain Blood" during the Christmas holidays amused several round us by saying "Nerts" in tone of deep scorn.

It has been a great joy to go with you on your journey from Ontario to the west, and to have shared with you your young experiences. I almost wept over "Lady's" death and was so relieved you saved "Nap." I filled up when the clergyman came and helped save Lizzie.

I'm too sleepy now to say more than "thank you." O yes and this. I hope you have several grand children — how they will love your stories!

If I wait to write a tidier and better letter I probably wont get it off at all.

Sincerely and sleepily yours
Evelyn Hawkes Crickmore

P.S. My father Arthur Hawkes was an admirer of yours too — E.C.

Appendix D

"Letter on Militant Hysteria" by Sir Almroth Wright*

* Reproduced from Sir Almroth E. Wright, *The Unexpurgated Case against Woman Suffrage* (New York: Paul B. Hoeber, 1913).

TO THE EDITOR OF THE TIMES

SIR,—For man the physiological psychology of woman is full of difficulties.

He is not a little mystified when he encounters in her periodically recurring phases of hypersensitiveness, unreasonableness, and loss of the sense of proportion.

He is frankly perplexed when confronted with a complete alteration of character in a woman who is child-bearing.

When he is a witness of the "tendency of woman to morally warp when nervously ill," and of the terrible physical havoc which the pangs of a disappointed love may work, he is appalled.

And it leaves on his mind an eerie feeling when he sees serious and long-continued mental disorders developing in connexion with the

167

168   THE CASE AGAINST WOMAN SUFFRAGE

approaching extinction of a woman's reproductive faculty.

No man can close his eyes to these things; but he does not feel at liberty to speak of them.

For the woman that God gave him is not his to give away.

As for woman herself, she makes very light of any of these mental upsettings.

She perhaps smiles a little at them. . . .[1]

None the less, these upsettings of her mental equilibrium are the things that a woman has most cause to fear; and no doctor can ever lose sight of the fact that the mind of woman is always threatened with danger from the reverberations of her physiological emergencies.

It is with such thoughts that the doctor lets his eyes rest upon the militant suffragist. He cannot shut them to the fact that there is

[1] In the interests of those who feel that female dignity is compromised by it, I have here omitted a woman's flippant overestimate of the number of women in London society who suffer from nervous disorders at the climacteric.

mixed up with the woman's movement much mental disorder; and he cannot conceal from himself the physiological emergencies which lie behind.

The recruiting field for the militant suffragists is the million of our excess female population—that million which had better long ago have gone out to mate with its complement of men beyond the sea.

Among them there are the following different types of women:—(a) First—let us put them first—come a class of women who hold, with minds otherwise unwarped, that they may, whenever it is to their advantage, lawfully resort to physical violence.

The programme, as distinguished from the methods, of these women is not very different from that of the ordinary suffragist woman.

(b) There file past next a class of women who have all their life-long been strangers to joy, women in whom instincts long suppressed have in the end broken into flame. These are the sexually embittered women in whom every-

thing has turned into gall and bitterness of heart, and hatred of men.

Their legislative programme is license for themselves, or else restrictions for man.

(c) Next there file past the incomplete. One side of their nature has undergone atrophy, with the result that they have lost touch with their living fellow men and women.

Their programme is to convert the whole world into an epicene institution—an epicene institution in which man and woman shall everywhere work side by side at the selfsame tasks and for the selfsame pay.

These wishes can never by any possibility be realised. Even in animals—I say *even*, because in these at least one of the sexes has periods of complete quiescence—male and female cannot be safely worked side by side, except when they are incomplete.

While in the human species safety can be obtained, it can be obtained only at the price of continual constraint.

MILITANT HYSTERIA   171

And even then woman, though she protests that she does not require it, and that she does not receive it, practically always does receive differential treatment at the hands of man.

It would be well, I often think, that every woman should be clearly told—and the woman of the world will immediately understand—that when man sets his face against the proposal to bring in an epicene world, he does so because he can do his best work only in surroundings where he is perfectly free from suggestion and from restraint, and from the onus which all differential treatment imposes.

And I may add in connexion with my own profession that when a medical man asks that he should not be the yoke-fellow of a medical woman he does so also because he would wish to keep up as between men and women—even when they are doctors—some of the modesties and reticences upon which our civilisation has been built up.

Now the medical woman is of course never

172   THE CASE AGAINST WOMAN SUFFRAGE

on the side of modesty,[1] or in favour of any reticences. Her desire for knowledge does not allow of these.

(d) Inextricably mixed up with the types which we have been discussing is the type of woman whom Dr. Leonard Williams's recent letter brought so distinctly before our eyes—the woman who is poisoned by her misplaced self-esteem; and who flies out at every man who does not pay homage to her intellect.

She is the woman who is affronted when a man avers that for him the glory of woman lies in her power of attraction, in her capacity for motherhood, and in unswerving allegiance to the ethics which are special to her sex.

I have heard such an intellectually embittered woman say, though she had been self-denyingly taken to wife, that "never in the whole course of her life had a man ever as much as done her a kindness."

[1] To those who have out of inadvertence and as laymen and women misunderstood, it may be explained that the issue here discussed is the second in order of the three which are set out on p. 139 (supra).

The programme of this type of woman is, as a preliminary, to compel man to admit her claim to be his intellectual equal; and, that done, to compel him to divide up everything with her to the last farthing, and so make her also his financial equal.

And her journals exhibit to us the kind of parliamentary representative she desiderates. He humbly, hat in hand, asks for his orders from a knot of washerwomen standing arms a-kimbo.[2]

(e) Following in the wake of these embittered human beings come troops of girls just grown up.

All these will assure you, these young girls —and what is seething in their minds is stirring also in the minds in the girls in the colleges and schools which are staffed by unmarried suffragists—that woman has suffered all manner of indignity and injustice at the hands of man.

[2] I give, in response to a request, the reference: Votes for Woman, March 18, 1910, p. 381.

And these young girls have been told about the intellectual, and moral, and financial value of woman—such tales as it never entered into the heart of man to conceive.

The programme of these young women is to be married upon their own terms. Man shall —so runs their scheme—work for their support—to that end giving up his freedom, and putting himself under orders, for many hours of the day; but they themselves must not be asked to give up any of their liberty to him, or to subordinate themselves to his interests, or to obey him in anything.

To obey a *man* would be to commit the unpardonable sin.

It is not necessary, in connexion with a movement which proceeds on the lines set out above, any further to labour the point that there is in it an element of mental disorder. It is plain that it is there.

There is also a quite fatuous element in the programmes of the militant suffragist. We have this element, for instance, in the doctrine

MILITANT HYSTERIA   175

that, notwithstanding the fact that the conditions of the labour market deny it to her, woman ought to receive the same wage as a man for the same work.

This doctrine is fatuous, because it leaves out of sight that, even if woman succeeds in doing the same work as man, he has behind him a much larger reserve of physical strength. As soon as a time of strain comes, a reserve of strength and freedom from periodic indisposition is worth paying extra for.

Fatuous also is the dogma that woman ought to have the same pay for the same work —fatuous because it leaves out of sight that woman's commercial value in many of the best fields of work is subject to a very heavy discount by reason of the fact that she cannot, like a male employee, work cheek by jowl with a male employer; nor work among men as a man with his fellow employees.

So much for the woman suffragist's protest that she can conceive of no reason for a differential rate of pay for man.

176   THE CASE AGAINST WOMAN SUFFRAGE

Quite as fatuous are the marriage projects of the militant suffragist. Every woman of the world could tell her—whispering it into her private ear—that if a sufficient number of men should come to the conclusion that it was not worth their while to marry except on the terms of fair give-and-take, the suffragist woman's demands would have to come down.

It is not at all certain that the institution of matrimony—which, after all, is the great instrument in the levelling up of the financial situation of woman—can endure apart from some willing subordination on the part of the wife.

It will have been observed that there is in these programmes, in addition to the element of mental disorder and to the element of the fatuous, which have been animadverted upon, also a very ugly element of dishonesty. In reality the very kernel of the militant suffrage movement is the element of immorality.

There is here not only immorality in the

ends which are in view, but also in the methods adopted for the attainment of those ends.

We may restrict ourselves to indicating wherein lies the immorality of the methods.

There is no one who does not discern that woman in her relations to physical force stands in quite a different position to man.

Out of that different relation there must of necessity shape itself a special code of ethics for woman. And to violate that code must be for woman immorality.

So far as I have seen, no one in this controversy has laid his finger upon the essential point in the relations of woman to physical violence.

It has been stated—and in the main quite truly stated—that woman in the mass cannot, like man, back up her vote by bringing physical force into play.

But the woman suffragist here counters by insisting that she as an individual may have more physical force than an individual man.

And it is quite certain—and it did not need suffragist raids and window-breaking riots to demonstrate it—that woman in the mass can bring a certain amount of physical force to bear.

The true inwardness of the relation in which woman stands to physical force lies not in the question of her having it at command, but in the fact that she cannot put it forth without placing herself within the jurisdiction of an ethical law.

The law against which she offends when she resorts to physical violence is not an ordinance of man; it is not written in the statutes of any State; it has not been enunciated by any human law-giver. It belongs to those unwritten, and unassailable, and irreversible commandments of religion, ἄγραπτα κἀσφαλῆ θεῶν νόμιμα, which we suddenly and mysteriously become aware of when we see them violated.

The law which the militant suffragist has violated is among the ordinances of that code which forbade us even to think of employing our native Indian troops against the Boers; which brands it as an ignominy when a man leaves his fellow in the lurch and saves his own life; and which makes it an outrage for a man to do violence to a woman.

To violate any ordinance of that code is more dishonourable than to transgress every statutory law.

We see acknowledgment of it in the fact that even the uneducated man in the street resents it as an outrage to civilisation when he sees a man strike a blow at a woman.

But to the man who is committing the outrage it is a thing simply unaccountable that any one should fly out at him.

In just such a case is the militant suffragist. She cannot understand why any one should think civilisation is outraged when she scuffles in the street mud with a policeman.

If she asks for an explanation, it perhaps behoves a man to supply it.

Up to the present in the whole civilised world there has ruled a truce of God as between man

and woman. That truce is based upon the solemn covenant that within the frontiers of civilisation (outside them of course the rule lapses) the weapon of physical force may not be applied by man against woman; nor by woman against man.

Under this covenant, the reign of force which prevails in the world without comes to an end when a man enters his household.

Under this covenant that half of the human race which most needs protection is raised up above the waves of violence.

Within the terms of this compact everything that woman has received from man, and everything man receives from woman, is given as a free gift.

Again, under this covenant a full half of the programme of Christianity has been realised; and a foundation has been laid upon which it may be possible to build higher; and perhaps finally in the ideal future to achieve the abolition of physical violence and war.

And it is this solemn covenant, the covenant

MILITANT HYSTERIA 181

so faithfully kept by man, which has been violated by the militant suffragist in the interest of her morbid, stupid, ugly, and dishonest programmes.

Is it wonder if men feel that they have had enough of the militant suffragist, and that the State would be well rid of her if she were crushed under the soldiers' shields like the traitor woman at the Tarpeian rock?

We may turn now to that section of woman suffragists—one is almost inclined to doubt whether it any longer exists—which is opposed to all violent measures, though it numbers in its ranks women who are stung to the quick by the thought that man, who will concede the vote to the lowest and most degraded of his own sex, withholds it from "even the noblest woman in England."

When that excited and somewhat pathetic appeal is addressed to us, we have only to consider what a vote really gives.

The parliamentary vote is an instrument—and a quite astonishingly disappointing instru-

182 THE CASE AGAINST WOMAN SUFFRAGE

ment it is—for obtaining legislation; that is, for directing that the agents of the State shall in certain defined circumstances bring into application the weapon of physical compulsion.

Further, the vote is an instrument by which we give to this or that group of statesmen authority to supervise and keep in motion the whole machinery of compulsion.

To take examples. A vote cast in favour of a Bill for the prohibition of alcohol—if we could find opportunity for giving a vote on such a question—would be a formal expression of our desire to apply, through the agency of the paid servants of the State, that same physical compulsion which Mrs. Carrie Nation put into application in her "bar-smashing" crusades.

And a vote which puts a Government into office in a country where murder is punishable by death is a vote which, by agency of the hangman, puts the noose round the neck of every convicted murderer.

So that the difference between voting and

direct resort to force is simply the difference between exerting physical violence in person, and exerting it through the intermediary of an agent of the State.

The thing, therefore, that is withheld from "the noblest woman in England," while it is conceded to the man who is lacking in nobility of character, is in the end only an instrument by which she might bring into application physical force.

When one realises that that same noblest woman of England would shrink from any personal exercise of violence, one would have thought that it would have come home to her that it is not precisely her job to commission a man forcibly to shut up a public-house, or to hang a murderer.

One cannot help asking oneself whether, if she understood what a vote really means, the noblest woman in England would still go on complaining of the bitter insult which is done to her in withholding the vote.

But the opportunist—the practical politi-

cian, as he calls himself—will perhaps here intervene, holding some such language as this:—"Granting all you say, granting, for the sake of argument, that the principle of giving votes to woman is unsound, and that evil must ultimately come of it, how can you get over the fact that no very conspicuous harm has resulted from woman suffrage in the countries which have adopted it? And can any firm reasons be rendered for the belief that the giving of votes to women in England would be any whit more harmful than in the Colonies?"

A very few words will supply the answer.

The evils of woman suffrage lie, *first*, in the fact that to give the vote to women is to give it to voters who as a class are quite incompetent to adjudicate upon political issues; *secondly*, in the fact that women are a class of voters who cannot effectively back up their votes by force; and, *thirdly*, in the fact that it may seriously embroil man and woman.

The first two aspects of the question have

MILITANT HYSTERIA 185

already in this controversy been adequately dealt with. There remains the last issue.

From the point of view of this issue the conditions which we have to deal with in this country are the absolute antithesis of those ruling in any of the countries and States which have adopted woman suffrage.

When woman suffrage was adopted in these countries it was adopted in some for one reason, in others for another. In some it was adopted because it appealed to the *doctrinaire* politician as the proper logical outcome of a democratic and Socialistic policy. In others it was adopted because opportunist politicians saw in it an instrument by which they might gain electioneering advantages. So much was this the case that it sometimes happened that the woman's vote was sprung upon a community which was quite unprepared and indifferent to it.

The cause of woman suffrage was thus in the countries of which we speak neither in its inception nor in its realisation a question of

186 THE CASE AGAINST WOMAN SUFFRAGE

revolt of woman against the oppression of man. It had, and has, no relation to the programmes of the militant suffragists as set out at the outset of this letter.

By virtue of this, all the evils which spring from the embroiling of man and woman have in the countries in question been conspicuously absent.

Instead of seeing himself confronted by a section of embittered and hostile women voters which might at any time outvote him and help to turn an election, man there sees his women folk voting practically everywhere in accordance with his directions, and lending him a hand to outvote his political opponent.

Whether or no such voting is for the good of the common weal is beside our present question. But it is clearly an arrangement which leads to amity and peace between a man and his womenkind, and through these to good-will towards all women.

In England everything is different.

If woman suffrage comes in here, it will

MILITANT HYSTERIA   187

have come as a surrender to a very violent feminist agitation—an agitation which we have traced back to our excess female population and the associated abnormal physiological conditions.

If ever Parliament concedes the vote to woman in England, it will be accepted by the militant suffragist, not as an eirenicon, but as a victory which she will value only for the better carrying on of her fight à outrance against the oppression and injustice of man.

A conciliation with hysterical revolt is neither an act of peace; nor will it bring peace.

Nor would the conferring of the vote upon women carry with it any advantages from the point of view of finding a way out of the material entanglements in which woman is enmeshed, and thus ending the war between man and woman.

One has only to ask oneself whether or not it would help the legislator in remodelling the divorce or the bastardy laws if he had con-

188   THE CASE AGAINST WOMAN SUFFRAGE

joined with him an unmarried militant suffragist as assessor.

Peace will come again. It will come when woman ceases to believe and to teach all manner of evil of man despitefully. It will come when she ceases to impute to him as a crime her own natural disabilities, when she ceases to resent the fact that man cannot and does not wish to work side by side with her. And peace will return when every woman for whom there is no room in England seeks "rest" beyond the sea, "each one in the house of her husband," and when the woman who remains in England comes to recognise that she can, without sacrifice of dignity, give a willing subordination to the husband or father, who, when all is said and done, earns and lays up money for her.

A. E. WRIGHT.

March 27, 1912.

Bibliography

1. Primary Bibliography: McClung

McClung Papers, Provincial Archives of British Columbia, Victoria, B.C. See Appendix A for full listing of holdings.

Works by Nellie L. McClung (in chronological order)

Sowing Seeds in Danny. 1908; rpt. Toronto: Thomas Allen, 1965.

The Second Chance. Toronto: William Briggs, 1910.

The Black Creek Stopping House. Toronto: William Briggs, 1912.

In Times Like These. 1915; rpt. Toronto: University of Toronto Press, 1972.

"Speaking of Women." *Maclean's,* 29 (May 1916), 25-6, 96-7.

The Next of Kin. Toronto: Thomas Allen, 1917.

Three Times and Out: A Canadian Boy's Experience in Germany. Boston: Houghton Mifflin, 1918.

"The Awakening of Women." Address to the Fifth Ecumenical Methodist Conference. *Proceedings, Fifth Ecumenical Methodist Conference, London, England, September 6-16, 1921.* Toronto: Methodist Book and Publishing House, n.d., 257-60.

Purple Springs. Toronto: Thomas Allen, 1921.

When Christmas Crossed "The Peace." Toronto: Thomas Allen, 1923.

Painted Fires. Toronto: Thomas Allen, 1925.

"Can a Woman Raise a Family and Have a Career?" *Maclean's* (15 February 1928), 20, 70-1, 75.

All We Like Sheep. Toronto: Thomas Allen, 1930.

Be Good to Yourself. Toronto: Thomas Allen, 1930.

Flowers for the Living. Toronto: Thomas Allen, 1931.

Clearing in the West: My Own Story. Toronto: Thomas Allen, 1935.

"Outdoor Religion." *Edmonton Bulletin,* 18 July 1936.

Leaves from Lantern Lane. Toronto: Thomas Allen, 1936.

More Leaves from Lantern Lane. Toronto: Thomas Allen, 1937.

"The World of Tomorrow." *Winnipeg Free Press* (Magazine Section), 2 August 1941.

The Stream Runs Fast: My Own Story. Toronto: Thomas Allen, 1945.

2. Secondary Bibliography

Allen, Richard. *The Social Passion: Religion and Reform in Canada, 1914-28.* Toronto: University of Toronto Press, 1973.

Alper, Joseph, *et al.* "Sociobiology is a Political Issue." In *The Sociobiology Debate.* Ed. Arthur A. Kaplan. New York: Harper and Row, 1978, 476-88.

Atwood, Margaret. "Writing the Male Character." *This Magazine*, 16, 4 (September 1982), 4-10.

Bacchi, Carol Lee. *Liberation Deferred? Ideas of the English-Canadian Suffragists, 1877-1918*. Toronto: University of Toronto Press, 1983.

Birney, Earle. *Spreading Time*. Montreal: Vehicle Press, 1980.

Black, Claudia. *It Will Never Happen to Me*. Denver: M.A.C. Printing, 1981.

Braude, Ann D. "Spirits Defend the Rights of Women: Spiritualism and Changing Sex Roles in Nineteenth-Century America." In *Women, Religion and Social Change*. Ed. Yvonne Yazbeck Haddad and Ellison Banks Findly. Albany: SUNY Press, 1985, 419-31.

Brown, Karen McCarthy. "Heretics and Pagans: Women in the Academic World." In *Private and Public Ethics: Tensions between Conscience and Institutional Responsibility*. Ed. David G. Jones. New York: Edwin Mellen Press, 1978, 266-88.

Cleverdon, Catherine L. *The Woman Suffrage Movement in Canada*. Toronto: University of Toronto Press, 1974.

Clifton, Lloyd M. "Nellie McClung: A Representative of the Canadian Social Gospel Movement." Unpublished M.Th. thesis, Toronto, 1979.

Cline, Sally, and Dale Spender. *Reflecting Men at Twice Their Natural Size*. London: André Deutsch, 1987.

Cole, Susan G. Book review of *Women against Censorship*, ed. Varda Burstyn (Vancouver: Douglas and McIntyre, 1985). *Canadian Journal of Women and the Law*, 1, 1 (1985), 226-39.

Cook, Ramsay. *The Regenerators: Social Criticism in Late Victorian English Canada*. Toronto: University of Toronto Press, 1985.

DuBois, Ellen. "The Radicalism of the Woman Suffrage Movement: Notes toward the Reconstruction of Nineteenth-Century Feminism." *Feminist Studies*, 3, 1/2 (Fall 1985), 63-71.

Ehrenreich, Barbara. *The Hearts of Men: American Dreams and the Flight from Commitment*. Garden City, N.Y.: Anchor, 1983.

Fishburn, Janet Forsythe. *The Fatherhood of God and the Victorian Family: The Social Gospel in America*. Philadelphia: Fortress Press, 1981.

Geertz, Clifford. "Religion as a Cultural System." In his *The Interpretation of Cultures*. New York: Basic Books, 1973, 87-125.

————. "Thick Description: Toward an Interpretive Theory of Culture." In his *The Interpretation of Cultures*. New York: Basic Books, 1973, 3-30.

Gilligan, Carol. *In a Different Voice: Psychological Theory and Women's Development*. Cambridge: Harvard University Press, 1982.

Gilman, Charlotte Perkins. *Herland* (1915). Intro. Ann J. Lane. New York: Pantheon, 1979.

————. *His Religion and Hers: A Study of the Faith of Our Fathers and the Work of Our Mothers*. New York: Century, 1923.

————. *The Home: Its Work and Influence*. New York: McClure, Phillips, 1903.

_____. *The Man-Made World; or, Our Androcentric Culture*. 1911; rpt. New York: Source Book Press, 1970.

_____. *Women and Economics: A Study of the Economic Relation between Men and Women as a Factor in Social Evolution* (1898). Intro. and ed. Carl Degler. New York: Harper and Row, 1966.

Goldstein, Valerie Saiving. "The Human Situation: A Feminine View." *Journal of Religion*, 40 (April 1960), 100-12.

Gray, Stan. "Sharing the Shop Floor." In *Beyond Patriarchy: Essays by Men on Pleasure, Power, and Change*. Ed. Michael Kaufman. Toronto: University of Toronto Press, 1987, 216-34.

Hallett, Mary. "Nellie McClung and the Fight for the Ordination of Women in The United Church of Canada." *Atlantis*, 4, 2 (Spring 1979), 2-16.

Hancock, Carol. *No Small Legacy*. Winfield, B.C.: Wood Lake Books, 1986.

Harrison, Beverly. *Making the Connections*. Boston: Beacon Press, 1985.

Hayden, Dolores. *The Grand Domestic Revolution: A History of Feminist Designs for American Homes, Neighborhoods, and Cities*. Cambridge: M.I.T. Press, 1987.

Hedenstrom, Joanne. "Puzzled Patriarchs and Free Women: Patterns in the Canadian Novel." *Atlantis*, 4, 1 (Autumn 1978), 2-9.

Huff, Ronald P. "Social Christian Clergymen and Feminism during the Progressive Era, 1890-1920." Unpublished Ph.D. diss., Union Theological Seminary, 1987.

Jaggar, Alison. "Political Philosophies of Women's Liberation." In *Feminism and Philosophy*. Ed. M. Veterling-Braggin, *et al*. Totowa: Littlefield, Adams, 1977,

Jeffreys, Sheila. *The Spinster and Her Enemies: Feminism and Sexuality, 1880-1920*. London: Pandora Press, 1985.

Kidd, Bruce. "Sports and Masculinity." In *Beyond Patriarchy: Essays by Men on Pleasure, Power, and Change*. Ed. Michael Kaufman. Toronto: University of Toronto Press, 1987, 250-65.

Kuhn, Thomas. *The Structure of Scientific Revolutions*. 2nd ed., enlarged. Chicago: University of Chicago Press, 1970.

Leacock, Stephen. *Essays and Literary Studies*. Toronto: Gundy, 1916.

_____. *Further Foolishness: Sketches and Satires of the Follies of the Day*. New York: John Lane, 1917.

_____. *The Garden of Folly*. New York: Dodd, Mead, 1924.

_____. *The Leacock Roundabout*. New York: Dodd, Mead, 1965.

_____. *The Social Criticism of Stephen Leacock*. Intro. and ed. Alan Bowker. Toronto: University of Toronto Press, 1973.

_____. *Winnowed Wisdom*. Toronto: Macmillan, 1926.

Lindbeck, George. *The Nature of Doctrine: Religion and Theology in a Postliberal Age*. Philadelphia: Westminster Press, 1984.

Lindley, Susan. "Woman and the Social Gospel Novel." *American Society of Church History* (March 1985), 56-73.

McClung, Mark. "Portrait of My Mother." Transcript of a 20-page speech given 27 September 1975 at the Nellie McClung Conference, University of Guelph, Guelph, Ontario.

Miles, Angela R. "Ideological Hegemony in Political Discourse: Women's Specificity and Equality." In *Feminism in Canada: From Pressure to Politics.* Montreal: Black Rose Books, 1982, 213-27.

Morgan, Kathryn. "Women and Moral Madness." Unpublished paper given at the Toronto Area Women's Research Colloquium, 14 November 1986.

Nicholl, Grier. "The Christian Social Novel and Social Gospel Evangelism." *Religion in Life*, 34 (1965).

Pacey, Desmond. "The Novel in Canada." In *Canadian Novelists and the Novel.* Ed. D. Daymond and L. Monkman. Ottawa: Borealis Press, 1981, 160-65.

Penner, Carol L. "The Theology of Nellie L. McClung." Unpublished M.A. thesis, Toronto, 1986.

Plaskow, Judith. *Sex, Sin and Grace: Women's Experience and the Theologies of Reinhold Niebuhr and Paul Tillich.* Washington: University Press of America, 1980.

"Premier Roblin Says Home Will Be Ruined by Votes for Women." *Manitoba Free Press*, 20 January 1914.

Roberts, Wayne. " 'Rocking the Cradle for the World': The New Woman and Maternal Feminism, Toronto, 1877-1914." In *A Not Unreasonable Claim: Women and Reform in Canada, 1880's-1920's.* Ed. Linda Kealey. Toronto: Women's Press, 1979, 15-45.

Roper, Gordon. "New Forces: New Fiction (1880-1920)." In *Literary History of Canada.* Ed. Carl Klinck. Toronto: University of Toronto Press, 1965, 260-83.

Rose, Phyllis. *Parallel Lives: Five Victorian Marriages.* New York: Vintage Books, 1983.

Ruether, Rosemary Radford. *New Woman/New Earth: Sexist Ideologies and Human Liberation.* New York: Seabury Press, 1975.

————. "Radical Victorians: The Quest for an Alternative Culture." In *Women and Religion in America: A Documentary History.* Vol. 3: *1900-1968.* Ed. Rosemary Radford Ruether and Rosemary Skinner Keller. San Francisco: Harper and Row, 1986, 1-10.

Savage, Candace. *Our Nell: A Scrapbook Biography of Nellie L. McClung.* Saskatoon: Western Producer Prairie Books, 1979.

Sayers, Dorothy L. *Are Women Human?* (1947) Grand Rapids: William B. Eerdmans, 1971.

Schieder, Elsa. "She Came to the Rescue: The Life and Writings of Nellie L. McCLung, Feminist." Unpublished M.A. thesis (English), Concordia (Montreal), 1982.

Socknat, Thomas P. *Witness against War: Pacifism in Canada, 1900-1945*. Toronto: University of Toronto Press, 1985.

Strong-Boag, Veronica. "Ever a Crusader: Nellie McClung, First-Wave Feminist." In *Rethinking Canada: The Promise of Women's History*. Ed. Veronica Strong-Boag and Anita Clair Fellman. Toronto: Copp Clark Pitman, 1986, 178-90.

_____. Introduction to Nellie L. McClung, *In Times Like These*. Toronto: University of Toronto Press, 1972, vii-xxii.

Stubbs, Patricia. *Women and Fiction: Feminism and the Novel, 1880-1920*. London: Methuen, 1979.

Verkruysse, Patricia Louise. "Small Legacy of Truth: The Novels of Nellie McClung." Unpublished M.A. thesis (English), New Brunswick, 1975.

Vipond, M. "Blessed Are the Peacemakers: The Labour Question in Canadian Social Gospel Fiction." *Journal of Canadian Studies*, 10 (1975), 32-43.

Warne, R.R. Book review of Ramsay Cook's *The Regenerators* (*q.v.*), *Toronto Journal of Theology*, 3, 1 (Spring 1987), 163-5.

Wilson, Edward O. *Sociobiology: The New Synthesis*. Cambridge, Mass.: Belknap Press of Harvard University, 1975.

"Women Score in Drama and Debate." *Manitoba Free Press*, 29 January 1914.

Woodsworth, J.S. *Strangers within Our Gates*. Intro. J.W. Sparling. Toronto: The Missionary Society of the Methodist Church, Canada, 1909.

Wright, Sir Almroth. *Alethotropic Logic*. London: William Heinemann, 1953.

_____. *The Unexpurgated Case against Woman Suffrage*. New York: Paul B. Hoeber, 1913.